MW00399626

Prelude to
GREATNESS

Sooner Football in the 1990s

By **JAY SMITH**

With **JIM WILLIS**

Foreword by **DAVID L. BOREN**

UNIVERSITY OF OKLAHOMA PRESS : NORMAN

Library of Congress Cataloging-in-Publication Data

Smith, Jay, 1975–
     Prelude to greatness: Sooner football in the 1990s /
by Jay Smith with Jim Willis; foreword by David L.
Boren.
          p.   cm.
     Includes bibliographical references and index.
     ISBN 0–8061–3520–4 (hard: alk. paper)
     1. Oklahoma Sooners (Football team).   2. University
of Oklahoma—Football.   I. Willis, William James,
1946–   II. Title.

GV958.O4 S65 2003
796.33263'0976637—dc21

                                                2002035815

1   2   3   4   5   6   7   8   9   10

CONTENTS

ILLUSTRATIONS

Foreword

DAVID L. BOREN

President, The University of Oklahoma

At the University of Oklahoma, we take pride in tradition. Those familiar with our university are aware of its reputation for excellence in academics. They know of our Honors College and our national leadership in the enrollment of National Merit Scholars. They know of the special sense of family and community on our campus and the commitment of our faculty to mentorship. The Templeton Foundation has honored these values by designating OU as one of the most outstanding character-building public universities in the nation.

Similarly, those acquainted with the University of Oklahoma likely know about our winning athletic tradition. With 162 conference championships, 20 national championships, and more than 700 All-Americans, OU athletics has built a lasting reputation for excellence in the university community and beyond. Tradition at OU—both on the field and off—is defined by a positive attitude, a diligent work ethic, a dogged determination, and perseverance.

The excitement that embodies OU football dates back to the university's early years. In 1895, five years after the founding of the University of Oklahoma, football was introduced on campus. One of the earliest coaches was Vernon Louis Parrington, who actually came to Norman to organize the new university's English Department. Parrington achieved not only one of the highest winning percentages among OU coaches, he also went on to win the Pulitzer Prize in History, proving early on that academics and athletics can work in tandem to shape winners whether they be individuals, teams, or institutions.

Oklahoma's sixth coach, Bennie Owen, led the Sooners for twenty-two seasons, longer than anyone else in school history. By 1928, his vision and fundraising resulted in the original construction of the stadium with thirty thousand seats, as well as the fieldhouse. In 1950, Owen was elected to football's first National Hall of Fame, and today his name graces the field on which the "Crimson and Cream" play in Norman.

Respected Hall-of-Famer Bud Wilkinson kicked off the winning tradition of the modern era in 1947. From 1953 to 1957, Wilkinson's teams won an impressive forty-seven straight. Forty-six years later, Wilkinson's achievement is still an NCAA Division I record for most consecutive wins.

Later, coaching greats Jim Mackenzie, Chuck Fairbanks, and Barry Switzer all brought their own brand of achievement to OU football, gaining national recognition and membership in the upper echelons of college football. Coach Switzer led the Sooners to three national championships and established one of the most successful records for a college coach in U.S. history.

Today, at the beginning of the twenty-first century, the university community is proud of the integrity of our athletic department, under director Joe Castiglione, and its commitment to continuing the winning tradition at OU. Our recent "Great Expectations: The Campaign for Sooner Sports" surpassed its $100 million goal, raising $102 million in less than two years. With a 10,000-seat addition to the Gaylord Family–Oklahoma Memorial Stadium, a new weight-training facility and state-of-the-art indoor practice arena, the football team is not alone in reaping the benefits of the athletic department's efforts and the generosity of donors. Basketball, track-and-field, gymnastics, cheerleading, tennis, and soccer now or soon will also enjoy renovated and expanded facilities. Housing and dining areas have also been improved.

Emphasizing the importance of academic excellence, the athletic department donated $165,000 to launch a $1 million endowment fund for the university library system. A special ticket surcharge will also raise $1 million this year to support academic programs. No university in America has a stronger partnership between athletics and academics.

However, success has not come without its challenges. In past years, beleaguered by coaching changes and tough losses to our rivals, our teams stood out in their persistence and desire to sustain OU's high-achieving traditions. The year I became President—1994— our football program was in a foreign place: near the bottom. The head coach had resigned and our team was yearning for direction. That same year, Texas blue-chip offensive lineman Jay Smith signed with OU. Along with the administration of the athletic department and the players themselves, Jay was eager to help the team get back on track and winning again. The road was not always smooth, but the foundation built by Jay and members of the 1990s teams paved the way for the successes of teams that followed. Since the time author Jay Smith played at OU, the football program under its nationally acclaimed new head coach Bob Stoops has won a national championship in the Orange Bowl in 2000, a top 10 ranking in 2001, and the Rose Bowl trophy culminating the 2002 season. Back at the top again, OU will not easily forget how it got there.

Jay Smith's *Prelude to Greatness: Sooner Football in the 1990s* is a testament to a young man determined to do his part. Working his way up the ranks under each of his four head coaches, Jay exemplifies the importance of poise, faith, and, most important, hard work. Overcoming injuries, devastating losses, and grueling two-a-day practices, Jay and many other young players learned many lessons from college football. Jay Smith's story is engrossing. It offers an exceptional glimpse of the selflessness, the resolve, and the mental and physical exertion required to be a college football player and the pride it takes to be a Sooner.

Jay Smith, OU Football, and the Crucible

In the long and rich history of football at the University of Oklahoma (OU), many stellar linemen who have contributed mightily to the success of their team have come and gone. Jay Smith is one of those linemen, but this blue-chip Texas tackle came with a notebook and a desire to record history in the making.

Jay's story-telling impulse seems only natural when you consider the football tradition in his family. His great-grandfather played for the University of Minnesota exactly one hundred years before Jay entered his freshman year of football at the University of Oklahoma. Jay's father, Bruce Smith, was an NCAA Division II All-American when he played football for the University of North Dakota in the 1960s. And Jay's brother Allan, a year his senior, was a scholarship player at Angelo State University in San Angelo, Texas. So Jay comes from a family that cares deeply about the sport, a family that for a century has offered up its men to sacrifice their bodies for the love of the game. On many occasions Bruce Smith had lamented to Jay that he had now forgotten much of what happened during his five years of playing college football. Jay vowed to himself he would not make the same mistake, so when he showed up in Norman in the summer of 1994, he began a journal that would cover all of the six years he was with the program, counting a redshirt year and a medical redshirt year.

Jay was a starting lineman in three of his four playing seasons, and he lettered in all four seasons. What he didn't know when he started, of course, was that he would wind up his tenure at OU as the only Division I football player in the country who had played under four different head coaches at one school. ESPN picked up on that fact and made it an on-air trivia question in early fall of 1999. But for Jay, the experience was anything but trivial. These were the toughest six years of his young life, he was betting on a good outcome, and his own personal stakes were high. He was offering the university a level of talent and dedication that twenty-five of the other top football programs in the country had wanted and lost when Jay chose OU. In return he was expecting a chance to play for a high-profile, winning football team. And he was hoping that doing so would propel him into the ranks of professional football.

What he got from OU football was something radically different, and that is what this book is all about. It is about the personal impact all this had on Jay and how he and his family reacted to each passing year of dramatic change. And, in a larger vein, Jay's story offers insight to youths who dream about playing college football, especially in Division I-A. It takes them behind the scenes, behind the glory, and onto the field, where the coaches are tough and the expectations are, at times, impossible to meet.

In this book, Jay recalls the defeats and eventual victories of OU football during those seasons of 1994 through 1999: the years from Coach Gary Gibbs, through Howard Schnellenberger, John Blake, and finally to Bob Stoops. This was an extremely difficult and awkward time in OU football history, matched in modern times only by the years from 1963 to 1968, when the Sooners took to the field under four different head coaches: Charles "Bud" Wilkinson, Gomer Jones, Jim Mackenzie, and Chuck Fairbanks. But even this comparison is somewhat misleading: in the mid-1960s, OU was moving on after the retirement of coaching legend Bud Wilkinson, who left OU to run as the Republican nominee for the U.S. Senate, whereas in the early nineties the Sooners were reeling from the tumultuous departure of controversial coach Barry Switzer and were beginning a stinging three-year NCAA probation for sixteen rules violations and facing a national image of a "good-ol'-boy team gone bad."

When Switzer left OU, Assistant Coach Gary Gibbs was handed the head coaching job, and he guided the team through the probation years with limited success. By 1993, however, when Jay Smith was a high school senior looking at prospective college programs, it seemed that the OU program had turned the corner and was on its way back to national prominence. The team's favorable depth chart, plus the memories of former Sooner greats like Joe Washington in his patented silver shoes racing toward the end zone and Heisman Trophy winners Billy Vessels, Steve Owens, and Billy Sims working their magic, convinced him to give OU a try.

But instead of being filled with glory, the six years from 1994 through 1999 were crucible years for the Oklahoma football team, which endured hardship after hardship, change after change, and loss after loss. They finished the era with an average of only five wins per season, losing a total of thirty-eight games and tying one. At 30-38-1, this was the worst six-year record in the history of Oklahoma football, and it came at a time when the team and its fans were expecting a return to the greatness of OU's past. For Jay Smith, that disappointing record contrasted sharply with his Texas high school team's overall winning record of 30-6-1.

A coaching change can be hard on any team, but the kind of changes Jay Smith witnessed during six years with the OU football program were unprecedented. In this book, he recounts these changes. More importantly, he describes the impact this quick succession of coaches (as well as entirely new offensive and defensive schemes) had on the team. The hardships and losses continued to snowball, at times causing the team to simply give up in midseason. This was not what one might expect from a team that had won six national championships, three of them in the 1970s and 1980s under Switzer.

Oklahoma was extremely fortunate to succeed in recruiting Jay Smith. The team started to recruit him during his junior year at famed Arlington Lamar High School in Arlington, Texas. By the end of Jay's senior season in 1993, he was listed by virtually all of the recruiting services as an All-American. *Blue Chip Magazine* listed him on its Dream Team as the fourth best offensive lineman in the nation. He was the only Texas lineman mentioned by *USA Today* in an article listing the top high school players in the nation. In Texas, Jay was first team All-State, All-Area, All-District, and All-City.

In addition to his success in football, Jay was also a standout in the classroom. This combination of excellence in athletics and academics was recognized by the presentation of the prestigious Christa McCauliffe Leadership Award to Jay by the Arlington Independent School District. As a result, he was recruited by fifty different colleges, including almost all of the traditional top 25 college football schools identified by the Associated Press, and he received scholarship offers from thirteen schools, including Nebraska, Texas A&M, Arizona State, Alabama, and Miami. Clearly, Jay's talent runs far beyond the playing field. He understands the value of academics and is now a graduate student in the MBA program at the University of Oklahoma and working as a management specialist in Tulsa.

I met Jay in the fall of 2000 when he came into my office in the Gaylord College of Journalism and Mass Communication at OU and laid out his vision and his notes for this book. I was on leave from the University of Memphis to be the McMahon Centennial Professor of Journalism at OU. In search of writing and editing help, Jay had learned that I had written seven books on the news media and wondered if I could help. The uniqueness of his project was evident, and I jumped at the chance. It was clear to me that Jay's story went far beyond a focus on OU's football team. It is a story of modern-day college football and what it expects—no, demands—of the young men who play it. It also is a story of the personal impact this endeavor has on the lives of men like Jay Smith. And finally, it is the story of a young high school graduate who had every reason to dream for a great future in football and of how those dreams were altered dramatically in six years of the crucible of Oklahoma University football.

Getting to know Jay personally made me care all that much more about his story. In addition to all his talents, Jay is a real nice guy, plain and simple. If he is an example of what the teamwork and discipline of college football can turn out, then that may be the best value of this sport. So sit back and enjoy a unique view from the trenches as Jay Smith looks back on this severe, pivotal time in OU football history.

JIM WILLIS

ACKNOWLEDGMENTS

Jim Willis and I would like to thank the following people and sources that contributed to the production of this book: the *Daily Oklahoman* and especially Managing Editor Joe Hight and Sports Editor Berry Tramel; the *Tulsa World* sports staff; the sports information department at the University of Oklahoma and its football media guides; the Louisville *Courier-Journal*; the Associated Press; CBS.SportsLine.com; *Sports Illustrated*; the *Sports Illustrated Sports Almanac*; ESPN.com; the Fort Worth *Star-Telegram*; the *Detroit News*; authors Gary T. King *(An Autumn Remembered)*; Armen Keteyian *(Big Red Confidential)*; Charles Thompson and Allan Sonnenschein *(Down and Dirty: The Life and Crimes of Oklahoma Football)*, and Coach Barry Switzer and Bud Shrake *(Bootlegger's Boy)*. We would also like to express our thanks for the sound advice and counsel of Charles Rankin, editor-in-chief at the University of Oklahoma Press.

And a very personal note of thanks goes to the following: To Merv Johnson for always being there. To Bob and Mary Margaret Gann for their connection back to the days of Barry Switzer and the nights at The Mont after the games. To Coach Mangino for knowing how to build an O-line, for wearing his shorts backwards, and to the OU O-line for doing the same. To Greg and Terri Davis at the Sooner Schooner for their continued encouragement and the most awesome replica of the OU Schooner you have ever seen. To J. R. Conrad for being my role model of an O-tackle even when they let you park your Harley in the weight room. To Barry Switzer for pulling me over one afternoon just to let me know I was part of the Sooner family. To Joe Corolla for showing me how to work through a serious injury. To Dr. Don McGinnis for his skill as a surgeon and for giving me the most valuable gift of two more years of playing time at OU. To Eddy Peach and Elvin Jones, my football coaches at Arlington Lamar High School, who taught me to be an excellent Texas high school football player. To Coach Danny Hope, who taught me how to be an O-lineman. To Tim Macias, my roommate for the first two years, who suffered many of the same frustrations but finished his career with an awesome game against Texas Tech. To Coach Kent Stephenson of the Pittsburgh Steelers for giving me the connection back to my father's playing days at North Dakota. To my brother Allan for always pushing me to be the best at OU, while at the same time setting an example by excelling at Angelo State. To Coach Bob Stoops for bringing the winning tradition back to Oklahoma. To my mom and dad, Ann and Bruce Smith, for their unconditional love and support. And to the fans of OU football. Without all of you, none of this would have been possible.

JAY SMITH

PRELUDE TO *Greatness*

CHAPTER 1

The Sooners Bottom Out

I fell into a burning ring of fire. I went down, down, down, and the flames went higher.

JOHNNY CASH

On November 11, 1995, the legendary University of Oklahoma (OU) football program hit rock bottom.

We Sooners had just lost to archrival Oklahoma State University (OSU), 12–0, in Norman. Adding insult to injury, the next week Nebraska would bury us, 37–0, and we would finish the season at 5–5–1 under first-year coach Howard Schnellenberger. We won only two games in the Big Eight Conference, over then-conference doormats Iowa State and Missouri.

And that was the season we were supposed to win the national championship.

The OSU loss was especially stinging. In Oklahoma some things seem certain, year after year. There will be long periods of frying-pan heat and drought in the summer, a season that can stretch into late October. There will be tornadoes in the spring, and Oklahoma thunderstorms will be accompanied by the patented Oklahoma streak lightning that often sends the uninitiated streaking to cover. And OU will beat the OSU Cowboys in football.

The Bedlam Series between the two rivals began in 1904, when the Sooners trounced the Cowboys, 75–0, and since then OU has won seventy-three of the games, while OSU has won only sixteen. Oklahoma State didn't even score a touchdown until the ninth game of the series and has won back-to-back games against the Sooners only three times. In a normal year, seeing the Sooners lose to the Cowboys on the gridiron is akin to watching the sun come up in the west.

But 1995 was not a normal year, and we were losing the game everyone expected us to win. The sun was taking up residence in the wrong side of the sky.

The day started with Coach Schnellenberger's delivery of a curiously incoherent radio interview, and it ended with a locker room fight between players and coaches who had expected more of one another on this day. One fight actually took place in the hallway outside the locker room. The handful of reporters who witnessed the event described the tussle as an argument, but it was really a fistfight between linebacker Broderick Simpson and offensive coordinator Gary Nord.

Simpson had taken exception to Nord's play calling, which included four passes, all incomplete, from the shotgun formation at first-and-goal on OSU's four-yard line. With the game on the line and with a senior-laden offensive line of J. R. Conrad, Joe Carolla, Chuck Langston, Milt Overton, and Harry Stamps along with running backs Gerald "Thunder" Moore and James "Lightning" Allen, I will never know why we didn't run the ball instead of backing off into the shotgun. I guess you could say that I took exception to Nord's calls as well. I was also surprised that the press releases the next day covered up the fact that it was a fight by describing it as a "verbal altercation."

In between Coach Schnellenberger's inability to speak on air in complete sentences and those postgame "altercations," the veteran-heavy Sooner defense made enough mistakes to last a season and the offense was unable to score, even given that first-and-goal from the OSU four-yard line.

This was near the end of my second year with the Sooners; 1994 had been my "redshirt" year, when I had practiced but not played in order to extend my eligibility. My parents had driven to Norman from Arlington, Texas, to watch the game, and I had hoped the Sooners would score enough to get me in to play. My folks had made reservations at a local motel and were planning to spend the weekend in Norman.

But after the game, I was in shock. When I came out of the locker room, I asked them if we could get as far away from Norman as possible. So my parents canceled their reservation and we drove the three hours back to Arlington.

During the long drive home I just stared out the window and kept asking myself, "What happened?" The University of Oklahoma was supposed to have been the embodiment of my dreams, not of my nightmares. Norman was supposed to be the place where all my hard years of high school football success finally paid off. Instead, we had just been shut out of any kind of bowl contention at all in the year we were supposed to have won it all. As we drove south over the Red River, I leaned back and let my mind wander back to Arlington Lamar High School.

DREAMING ABOUT THE SOONER MAGIC

As a junior in high school, I had been one of the most highly recruited offensive linemen in the country, sought by some fifty college football programs. I had picked Oklahoma over the twenty-five other schools I was considering because it was in the Big Eight Conference, which carried more prestige than the Southwest Conference, and its football program was returning to power. Merv Johnson was highly regarded as an offensive line coach, and Oklahoma was returning to natural grass in Owen Field. I had turned down offers from other programs like the University of Miami, Arizona State, Nebraska, and Texas A&M, to name a few, because OU had seemed like a good bet. It was 1993, and the Sooners appeared to have turned the corner from their three-year probation. Under Coach Gary Gibbs, the Sooners claimed the prize as "Texas State Champs" by beating all four big Texas football teams: the University of Texas (UT), Texas A&M, Texas Tech, and Texas Christian University (TCU). The future looked bright, and based on the talent of the Oklahoma players, I saw no reason why the team couldn't live up to the rich tradition of Oklahoma football.

And the OU tradition was in large part about winning football games. The tradition was built on the backs of superstars like Heisman Trophy winners Billy Vessels, Steve Owens, and Billy Sims. The tradition was an amalgam of some of the most memorable college games in football history. Among the many such games was the Orange Bowl matchup against Florida State University (FSU) following the 1980 season. Fourth-ranked OU played the Seminoles in that bowl for the second time in two years. The Seminoles had given up only one fourth-quarter touchdown all year, and that was to the Sooners with 1:27 on the clock. Oklahoma was down, 17–10. The touchdown came on an eleven-yard pass from senior J. C. Watts to Steve Rhodes at the end of a seventy-eight-yard come-from-behind drive, mostly in the air. The Sooners needed the two-point conversion, and they got it when Watts ran a play-action pass and hit Forrest Valora in a deep corner of the end zone. The Sooners won, 18–17. The frustrating irony for FSU, as Coach Bobby Bowden pointed out after the game, was that OU was a wishbone team, but they had won by throwing the ball.

Perhaps some of the most memorable games, however, were against perennial conference contender Nebraska. In fact, the name "Sooner Magic" was born in the 1974 Oklahoma-Nebraska game when the Sooners emerged from a 14–7 deficit and won, 28–14. Then in the 1976 game, the term really gained popular momentum. OU was fielding an inexperienced team that year against a veteran Nebraska squad. The game was played in Lincoln on a cold November afternoon, and the Huskers had led by as many as ten points. With three minutes left in the game, Nebraska was still ahead by four, and OU was starting from its own sixteen-yard line. At that point, Woodie Shepard threw a surprise fifty-yard halfback pass to freshman Steve Rhodes, who made a circus catch. Two plays later, quarterback Dean Blevins found Rhodes again on a hook-and-lateral play. Rhodes pitched it to Elvis Peacock, who was knocked out of bounds at the three-yard line with just over thirty seconds left. The Sooners scored to win the game, 20–17, becoming the third member of a three-way tie for the Big Eight Conference Championship.[2]

That kind of excitement is what Oklahoma football has been about for as long as I can remember. It even predates the legendary Charles "Bud" Wilkinson, who took over from Jim Tatum as head coach of the Sooners in 1947. Going back a few more years was another winning era spearheaded by Coach Bennie Owen, who led the Sooners from 1905 to 1926 with a record of 122–54–16. In recognition of Owen's contribution to the school, OU named the new Oklahoma Memorial Stadium at Owen Field for the legendary coach, who in 1925 led the Sooners in their first game in the stadium, which then seated sixteen thousand.

But the modern-day era of OU winning would not arrive until the year after World War II ended. It began with the long and happy Bud Wilkinson era, when the Sooners reeled off a record forty-seven-game winning streak from 1953 to 1957. That streak still stands as the longest winning streak by any Division I-A football team, and I doubt seriously it will ever be broken. As Gary King wrote in *An Autumn Remembered*, the high point of that winning era was the famed 1956 Sooner season. Of that season, he wrote:

> These men, particularly these seniors, who returned to the University of Oklahoma in 1956, played the game of college football better than it has ever been played before or since. This senior class was all-victorious during its years of college eligibility. They played thirty-one games, winning all thirty-one. This is a record without equal in modern football history. . . . The '56 Sooners are to college football what the '27 Yankees are to baseball. The Sooners fashioned their own

version of "Murderer's Row" with victories of 45–0 over Texas, 40–0 over Notre Dame, 53–0 over (then) Oklahoma A&M, 54–6 over Nebraska, and 67–14 over Missouri. The Sooners also established a new collegiate record of 391 rushing yards per game. They set the record for the most first downs (222) in a single season. The team also led the nation in scoring with 466 points. The Sooners scored 51 touchdowns by running (a record for ten-game seasons). In only one game did they fail to score more than four touchdowns. They led the nation in total offense that year. And they were second nationally in total defense. They recorded six shutouts and allowed only 51 points to be scored against them all year.[3]

Making it happen were players like center Jerry Tubbs, who in 1956 won the Walter Camp Memorial Trophy given by *Collier's* magazine to the outstanding player in the United States. That same year, halfback Tommy McDonald won the Robert W. Maxwell Trophy given to the outstanding player in the United States. Also, McDonald and fellow halfback Clendon Thomas finished in the top four in individual scoring nationally. In sum, eleven members of this team went on to play a total of almost sixty years in the National Football League (NFL), and five members of this team were consensus All-Americans: Tubbs and McDonald in 1956, Thomas and guard Bill Krisher in 1957, and center Bob Harrison in 1958. In addition, both Coach Wilkinson and McDonald have been inducted into the College Football Hall of Fame.[4]

So Saturday afternoons were party time for OU fans, as the Sooners steamrolled their opponents without fail. Owen Field became known as the Snake Pit, into which unwitting and outmatched opponents were cast to be bitten again and again.

Sooner fortunes would take a three-year turn for the worse when Wilkinson retired from coaching at the end of the 1963 season. Gomer Jones, who took over as head coach in 1964, had the unenviable task of following a living coaching legend. After two years Jones would win only nine games, and the eleven losses included the first of back-to-back one-point losses to OSU, in 1965 and 1966. Jones stepped down after his second season.

To fill his shoes, OU chose a winner in Coach Jim Mackenzie, who turned two seasons of losing into a 6–4 season in 1966. Mackenzie would not live to see greater glory with the Sooners, however, because he died of heart failure after his first season at OU.

Stepping in as the third head coach in just over three years was Chuck Fairbanks, who survived a "Chuck Chuck" campaign by angry fans and turned the 1967 edition Sooners into Big Eight Conference winners.[5] Oklahoma took on Tennessee in the 1967 Orange Bowl and won, 26–24. There would be many more wins under Coach Fairbanks over the next five years, as he led the Sooners to a record of 49–18–1 before leaving college coaching for the NFL and a stint as head coach with the New England Patriots and later with the University of Colorado.

It was Fairbanks who introduced the successful wishbone offense, a veer-oriented ground game that returned the Sooners to a consistent level of winning. With that option-studded attack, the Sooners roared back into the winning column, taking that Orange Bowl. It was the beginning of another golden era for Oklahoma football. That momentum continued and blossomed in the Barry Switzer era, which began in 1973 after Fairbanks left.

Under Coach Switzer, the OU football team reveled in Sooner Magic.[6] Year after year, the team destroyed opponents, winning a trio of national championships in 1974, 1975, and 1985 and coming close several other years. Overall, Switzer's teams went 157–29–4, making Switzer the all-time winningest head coach in OU football history. During his tenure, the Sooners were bowl regulars and won the Orange Bowl no fewer than five times.

Under Switzer, wonderful players like Joe Washington matured into university superstars. Washington was the back who would paint his shoes silver before each game. Switzer would call them "Joe's silver wheels," and in them Joe would race down the sidelines for almost four thousand yards during his years with the team.

Legendary University of Texas Coach Darrell Royal once called "Little Joe" the purest runner he'd ever seen, describing him as "smoke through a keyhole." Washington would help lead the Sooners to back-to-back national championships in 1974 and 1975, which ironically were two years in which the National Collegiate Athletic Association (NCAA) prohibited OU from appearing in televised football games because of an earlier rules violation. Barry Switzer said of Washington, "Every time Joe tucked the football under his arm there was a sense of anticipation, like you were about to witness something that you had never seen before. If you couldn't see him you couldn't touch him, and if you couldn't touch him you couldn't tackle him." At five feet, eight inches tall and 169 pounds, he was the smallest player in NFL history. The San Diego Chargers picked him in the fourth round, and he played in the pros for an entire decade.

In 1974 the Sooners led the nation in three major offensive categories, had a total offensive average of 570 yards per game, and finished with a rushing average of 438 yards per game. That year would bring the first of three national championships under Switzer, although the victory was not quite complete: the Associated Press (AP) named OU first in the nation, but United Press International (UPI), the coaches' poll, refused to acknowledge the Sooners at all because of their NCAA probation.

Then the Sooners came right back the next year with a second championship and a chance to go bowling, playing the University of Michigan in the Orange Bowl and winning, 14–6. This time, both AP and UPI put Oklahoma at the top of the national rankings.

BUT WHAT ABOUT THE PROBATION?

All that Sooner glory ended in turmoil as the 1980s closed. On February 25, 1988, the NCAA issued an official letter of inquiry charging the University of Oklahoma football program with violating sixteen different NCAA rules. Some of the alleged violations dated back to 1983; they included unauthorized gifts and monetary payments to OU athletes and recruits and promises of extra benefits to recruits. In the end, the NCAA ruled that OU was sufficiently guilty to merit a three-year suspension on the program, which prevented it from appearing on television or going to bowl games. In addition, the NCAA cut drastically the number of scholarships OU could award for football during these probationary years. At this point, Gary Gibbs took over to clean up the program.

When I became serious about attending OU, I started to read as much as I could find about the history of the university and the football program. This led me to Coach Switzer's book, *Bootlegger's Boy.* As you might expect, it provided an entirely different perspective of the Sooner program than had been portrayed by the Texas media. Certainly the offenses were serious and the punishments were warranted, but similar events were happening at other places during the same period. I felt that if these events hadn't occurred in such rapid succession in 1989, the penalties might have been less severe. On the positive side, when I was invited to campus I could clearly see the changes that were made to prevent these problems from reoccurring. For example, the first floor of Bud Wilkinson House was now enclosed in a glass-and-brick entry and secured by computerized door locks.

Most of the freshmen in my recruiting class knew about the drugs and shooting that had gotten the Sooners into trouble in 1989. But, like most eighteen-year-olds, we felt that four years ago was ancient history. We would tease each other about our room assignments: "You got the room (311) where defensive back Zarak Peters was shot." Some of the freshmen that year were assigned to rooms where a visiting Oklahoma City woman was raped and where a drug bust took place. But beyond the bantering, the program's past troubles didn't really matter to us. We could see that the university and the athletic department had taken the steps necessary to prevent anything like that from happening again, and that was good enough for us. In fact, by the time I was a senior at OU, a recruit might never know the violations had ever happened if he hadn't read Coach Switzer's book. Remember, the recruits who were eighteen during my last season at OU were only seven years old in 1989, when the events Coach Switzer called "the nightmare on Jenkins Street" took place.

As I watched the Sooners tear up the Texas competition in 1993, I detected the winds of positive change. Surely OU was back, I thought, and I was willing to stake my college football career on it as I signed with the Sooners for 1994. But looking back, I realize the weeds that choked the OU program and produced the 12–0 loss to OSU in 1995 actually had very deep roots.

LIVING THE SOONER MAGIC?

The 1995 season was my inauguration to regular game action on Saturday afternoons on Owen Field. I was now playing in an offensive line that many experts believed would lead the Sooners to a national championship. This was near the end of my second year with the team, and my first year of playing. Coach Gibbs had been fired at the end of 1994 after going 6–5.

Enter Coach Howard Schnellenberger. Our hopes were high, and we believed the hype about national championship possibilities that year. From the onset of the season, Coach Schnellenberger boasted that he could take the team to the top. Surprisingly, we were well on our way until we played Colorado in the fourth game of the season. This game was marked by a series of poor coaching decisions, a condition that would get increasingly worse and more obvious to even the most casual observer as the season wore on.

Aside from poor coaching, several other factors contributed to the downfall of the Sooners that year. During the summer, *Sports Illustrated* had run an article comparing Coach Schnellenberger's "boot camp" at OU to Coach Rick Neuheisel's summer camp at Colorado. After the article was published, the only way Coach

Schnellenberger could sell the boot camp mentality to the players was to hint it would lead the Sooners to the national championship.

Then ESPN's Lee Corso got on the Schnellenberger bandwagon, hyping the Sooners as the best bet for the national championship. This virtually locked in the notion that the exhausting workouts were justified because they would lead to the national title.

As a result, the fourth game of the season in mid-October against Colorado became the pivotal point in the season. When OU lost the game to the "summer campers" from Colorado, our national championship hopes went down the drain. At the same time, we "boot campers" from OU began to question the purpose of the seemingly endless practices. The rest of the season was simply an agonizing matter of watching us crash and flame out at 5–5–1.

A hoped-for 12–0 season ended with the 12–0 loss to OSU and the 37–0 loss to Nebraska. It was not what anyone had expected, certainly not me. Had I made a huge mistake in choosing the Sooners?

So as I drove home with my parents to Arlington after the loss to OSU on November 11, I replayed the events of the past two seasons. I was mystified over what had happened and why. I would eventually realize that our dreams of Sooner victory were based on shaky grounds. Personally, I had expected great things of my college football career, but with the end of the 1995 season, I began to wake up to the painful truth.

CHAPTER 2

That's Why
They Call Them Dreams

Dream, dream, baby. How long must I dream?

CINDY WALKER

I had brought many dreams to OU in 1994, and by the end of 1995, most of them had been shattered. When I got home to Arlington after that terrible game against OSU in November 1995, I started recounting the dreams I had nurtured as a senior in high school, starting with my dream of playing under Coach Gibbs, who left OU after the 1994 season. I didn't know it then, but his departure was a big sign of bad things to come.

Part of my dream was the expectation that I would fit like a glove with a program that now had it together. Before joining the team, I had visions of a team unified in purpose, dedicated to the mission, and led by a coach who seemed the right fit for the team. Obviously, I had no idea that nothing could be further from the truth. I couldn't have predicted the revolving door that would spin head coaches in and out of the OU program faster than I could dry the sweat from my body.

When I signed on with Oklahoma, I had also imagined that the

OU football program had cleared the hurdles of the past and was on the road to a conference championship, and maybe even a national championship. How impossible could that be for a team with the tradition of winning like OU had? Very impossible, as I was sadly discovering.

Another dream was that I could shine at Oklahoma as I had at Arlington Lamar High School, and that by my junior year I would be at the top of my game and attracting the attention of many NFL scouts. But I had not predicted the two injuries that almost sacked my collegiate football career and ruined my chances of a future in the NFL.

I had also dreamed about the sheer enjoyment I would have of being a student at the University of Oklahoma. Although I knew a big part of my average day would be devoted to football, I hoped to pledge a fraternity and get involved in campus life like everyone else. There had to be free time left over after practice, right?

Wrong. Until my junior year and my season-ending injuries, I could only dream about being a "regular" college student; I was not able to experience anything like college life beyond trying to cram my classes around a year-round football regime.

Although I hadn't known it in 1994, I was about to enter the crucible years of OU football. All my expectations of winning, all my hopes for glory, all the fruits of my labor on the high school football field were about to descend into a meat grinder in Norman, Oklahoma. Cranking the handle would be four different head coaches, six different offensive coordinators, hordes of Sooner football fans used to seeing their team win, and the prying eyes of an expectant news media. For those of us who joined the Sooner football team in 1994, things were about to go from wonderful boyhood dreams to awful nightmares, and we would not wake up to a brighter day for six long seasons. And for me, the harsh reality would be especially difficult: the Sooner Magic would not return until the year *after* I graduated. Then, in 2000, the Sooners would go undefeated and the team would win its seventh national championship. But during my own years of pain and sacrifice on the team, Owen Field would remain just a field of dreams.

FAMILY: THE WORLD'S BEST BOOSTERS

Two things would center me and keep me going through the long dark period of my first few years at OU. First was the support and love of my parents and my older brother Allan, and second was the confidence I had in my own abilities as a football player. I had paid my dues in hard work, and I had learned a lot from my high school coaches, my dad, and Allan.

My father, Bruce Smith, has been a major influence on my life and football career. From 1965 to 1969 he played offensive center at the University of North Dakota, where he was an NCAA Division II All-American. Like me, he had dreamed of playing professional football and did, in fact, receive a letter from the Dallas Cowboys inviting him to try out for their team. But that was at the height of the Vietnam era, and the military had its own designs on Dad. He joined the U.S. Air Force and became a pilot and flight instructor before going on to receive his master's degree at Arizona State University and his doctorate in education at Florida State University. Blending his knowledge of education and flying, he became a training and development director for the F-117A Stealth Fighter and B-2 Stealth Bomber programs, and today he is dean of the John D. Odebard School of Aerospace Sciences at the University of North Dakota, where a lot of eager college students learn to fly.

Dad and my mother, Ann, have always been my most ardent supporters. They have spent much of their time encouraging my brother Allan and me and being a part of our athletic endeavors over the years. My father's career in aerospace took us many places. Born in Mesa, Arizona, I lived in five states before we moved to Arlington, Texas, where I spent my high school years. I spent my junior high years in Endicott, New York, where my dad was assigned to the B-2 Stealth Bomber program. Endicott had an excellent football program, and at the end of my ninth grade year, our school finished seventeenth in the *USA Today* national rankings. Living in New York also allowed me to play two sports that didn't exist in the south at that time—ice hockey and lacrosse—and in my mind, no other sports provide better off-season training for football. It goes without saying that the football coaches at Endicott High School were disappointed when our family moved to Arlington, but the skills and experience I gained in football, as well as hockey and lacrosse, would be invaluable to me when I arrived in Texas.

My brother Allan, who is a year older than I, began his college football career at Angelo State University in San Angelo, Texas. For several years, we played on the same Saturday at different schools and in different states, and Mom and Dad always found a way to be at one game or the other, always going together and never splitting up.

How reassuring it was for Allan and me to know that, no matter what troubles we had on our respective teams, our parents were always there for us. They kept telling us how gifted we both were, assuring us that if we just played the way we could and had self-confidence, we'd see a lot of playing time on the field. Overall, Dad and Mom were overjoyed that they had two sons who were turning out well and who were both playing college football. Like me, my parents were frustrated at all the coaching changes I endured at OU, and they were a comfort to me when my injuries occurred, always letting me know I'd rebound. I talked with them every day while I was at OU and discussed everything with them.

As for Allan and me, no two brothers could have been closer. Allan was happy at Angelo State, and he was also happy I had the chance to play at OU. There was no sibling jealousy at all, and he seemed excited to tell his friends that his brother played for the Sooners. He had a picture of me on his fridge, and he even displayed one of my OU helmets in his home.

And I was very proud of Allan. He really worked hard to develop as an excellent offensive lineman. As the left side, or "quick" tackle, he started twenty-four games during his last three seasons at Angelo

State. The team won eighteen of those games and was ranked as high as No. 3 in the Division II national ratings. I don't recall that Allan ever gave up a sack during his whole career.

Without my family's love and support, things at OU would have been much rougher for me. The second thing that kept me going during those six long years was confidence in my own skill as a player, which had been built over many years of playing the game.

LAUNCHING MY FOOTBALL CAREER

The path I took to college football wasn't so different from that of many other entering freshmen recruits, I suppose, with one possible exception: I didn't play Pee Wee football. Many parents believe that a child has to start playing football at an early age to be successful in high school and college, and so they start their kids in Pee Wee football as young as four years old. My experience dispelled that myth because I didn't play Pee Wee football at all. At the time, I was more interested in other sports, and, frankly, I was too big to qualify for the Pee Wee League, anyway. When I started third grade as an eight-year-old, I already stood five feet, four inches, and weighed 145 pounds. That's pretty hefty for a kid that age, and I guess they were worried I'd crush my opponents. So instead I focused on other sports that actually contributed more to my overall athleticism than football alone could have. Early on I played golf and soccer, and baseball to a lesser degree. Later on I played ice hockey and lacrosse. Football was not a major factor in my life until I entered the eighth grade.

Junior high football came complete with smelly pads and zany coaches. The seventh- and eighth-graders were combined into one team at my junior high school in Endicott, New York, and the ninth- and tenth-graders were combined to make up the high school's junior varsity (JV). While on the junior high team, I started and played on both the offensive and defensive lines, usually at tackle.

My JV year was very exciting. Allan and I played at the ends of the offensive line, and people called us the "twin towers." Our offensive line coach was suitably impressed: it was the first time he'd coached linemen at this age who were taller than he was.

That year the JV team went undefeated, and at the end of the season, both Allan and I were called up to the varsity squad. This gave us the chance to suit-up for the last varsity home game of the season and travel to the regional championship game. I didn't get to play, but it was a great experience to travel with the varsity team as a ninth grader. The varsity team was undefeated that year, finishing seventeenth in the nation in the *USA Today* poll of high schools.

Later that season, I watched on ESPN the Texas 5A High School State Football Championship game in the Houston Astrodome between Houston MacArthur and Arlington Lamar High Schools. I had absolutely no idea that in less than eight months I would be standing on the football field at Lamar High School in Arlington, Texas, ready to start fall football practice.

Leaving Endicott was not a hard decision for my family in the spring of 1991. The company my father worked for was starting to downsize, so he jumped at a chance to relocate to the Dallas–Fort Worth area. Before we left, he received a call from the varsity head coach in Endicott, who asked if there was anything he could say to make us stay. I understood his concern because in Allan and myself he was losing 40 percent of his offensive line. But there was no way I wanted my dad to reverse his decision. Pushing it a little hard, the coach asked us to read the 1990 book by H. G. Bissinger, *Friday Night Lights*, which documents the pressures of Texas 5A high school football by focusing on the team at Odessa Permian High School, where studies were described as a "sidelight." In describing a moment in one player's life, the author writes:

> After the pep rally he went to class, but it was impossible to concentrate. He sat there in a daze, the messages of algebra and biology and English lost to him. Like most of his other teammates on game day, he couldn't be bothered with classes.

THAT'S WHY THEY CALL THEM DREAMS

They were irrelevant, a sidelight to the true purpose of going to Permian High School: to play football for the Panthers. Only one thought crossed his mind as he sat in those antiseptic, whitewashed classrooms until the middle of the afternoon, and it didn't have anything to do with schoolwork. He desperately wanted to perform well against Midland Lee, to break tackle after tackle, to be Boobie once again.[1]

We read the book, but the coach's strategy backfired. Moving to the higher level of play and commitment that Bissinger described was what I wanted. The book documented the Texas "no pass, no play rule," but I wasn't afraid of not passing because I have always been a good student.

My father arrived in Arlington five months before our family moved from New York in the spring of 1991. During that time he checked out all the local high schools. He visited the schools, talked to parents, talked to the football coaches, attended spring practices to check out coaching styles and see who needed linemen, met with the high school principals, and asked everyone which high school was the best. As a former collegiate football player himself, my dad knew the importance of playing for a good high school team, and I'll always appreciate his going to this much trouble for Allan and me.

The unanimous choice was Lamar High School in Arlington, one of the large suburbs in the Dallas–Fort Worth metroplex. Lamar had a good ethnic balance, a principal who believed in discipline, an academic program that was ranked in the top forty nationally, and a significant lead over the city's other four high schools in merit scholars and SAT averages. It didn't hurt that it also had one of the finest high school football programs in the nation.

One of the things that impressed Dad about Lamar's football team was the size of the athletes. Other high school teams had some big players and some tall players, but Lamar was the only team with players who were both big *and* tall. Not surprisingly, my dad decided to settle in Arlington, and Allan and I went to Lamar. I was a sophomore and Allan was a junior.

For one-half of my first season at Lamar, I played what was called "Saturday morning football." Football is a wonderful sport if you are a starter, but it can be very cruel if you are not. Lamar and the other schools in the district tried to solve this problem with a second level of teams. The schools had enough players on their rosters so that they could each outfit a second, complete team of guys who didn't play in the Friday night varsity games. These players gained experience by playing on Saturday morning.

As a concept, it made sense. But in reality, Saturday morning football was agonizing for everyone involved. It was almost like Pee Wee football, only with much bigger players. There was little or no support for the teams, as only a handful of parents showed up.

Then there were the injuries. Just because they weren't playing on varsity didn't mean these players were immune from getting hurt. At one Saturday game, for instance, a player who had torn up his knee just sat unattended on the opposite sideline until the end of the game, when the bus could take him back to school. To make matters worse, some coaches were reluctant to substitute players at the end of the Friday night blowouts because they needed enough players for Saturday. So you could just sit there, watching your chance at getting varsity experience pass by.

Saturday morning football was very painful and downright humiliating. How far it is from Saturday morning football in high school to Saturday afternoon football in college! Fortunately, by mid-season, I was starting under Friday night lights.

My first start in the fall of 1991 was against the archrival Colts from Arlington High School. Very early in the game an Arlington receiver dropped a perfectly thrown pass. I remember thinking at the time that the players from Arlington looked like they were afraid of us. I may have been right, because we won, 52–7. It was my first exposure to the major role that intimidation can play in football, especially in high school. I later found it also plays a role in college football. I was the only non-senior starter on offense; we ran a single back set behind an offensive line with an average player weight of 250 pounds. We were undefeated through the regular season and easily won the first two rounds of the Texas 5A playoffs. This set up the regional final against the Odessa Permian Panthers at Ratliff Stadium in Odessa.

At about this time, my mother began prodding my father to write a book about high school football in Texas. His response was always the same: "It has already been written, and it's called *Friday Night Lights*." After reading the Bissinger book I can say that the events portrayed in the book were accurate; I can recall incidents at Lamar that paralleled every event described in the book. However, I believe the author overstated the significance of some of these events. If you believe the book, you might think you'd need an armed escort just to survive the pregame warm-up. I found the exact opposite to be true. Make no mistake, the people of Odessa are committed fans of their football teams, but they are a very gracious group of people.

Heading into that game at Ratliff Stadium, with twenty thousand people (that's right) in attendance, Lamar High School was 12–0 and ranked by *USA Today* as the third-best high school football team in the nation.[2] The only non-senior starter on offense, I would be one of four high school All-Americans on Lamar's roster that day. But it wouldn't be good enough.

The weather was awful at game time, with a gusting north wind and a wind chill of twenty-five degrees. We were unable to get untracked and play like we should, partly because of the weather and partly because the officials seemed unable to call any holding penalties. The Panthers had a unique technique—they would roll block while they grabbed your ankles and held on for dear life. We lost, and our great season came to an abrupt end.

The following year, I was a junior, and lucky to have a great season. To start with, I broke my collarbone on the first day of summer workouts in 1992. More correctly, I had it broken for me. One of my teammates, who was a hyperactive linebacker to begin with, had a special burst of energy and decided to attack me from behind. He wrapped his arms around my upper body, and so I couldn't break the fall with my arms, breaking it with my shoulder instead. Something had to give, and it was my collarbone. This set me back at least three months, as I lost the entire summer. The good news was that I was cleared to play the week of the opening game of the season.

We lost the season opener, 3–0, when our last drive in the fourth quarter was stopped on the one-yard line by an interception. After that loss, we returned to form by winning the remaining nine regular-season games. Our 1991 team had included plenty of seniors, now graduated, so this team was less experienced and less overpowering and had fewer star players. But it was just as determined to win. Ironically, the seniors from this team who went on to success in college football were, for the most part, the ones who were unheralded in high school. This included my brother Allan, who went on to have a great college football career on scholarship at Angelo State University in San Angelo, Texas, and Scott McGarrahan, who went on to play in the NFL for the Packers.

The most important distinction for this team was that it continued Lamar's five-year winning streak and surpassed the Texas state record for consecutive district wins. The 1992 season ended in a heartbreaking 24–23 loss to a the Dallas Carter team led by future OU quarterback Eric Moore, who would soon be my teammate in Norman. That loss came in the opening round of the playoffs, played in the Cotton Bowl in Dallas.

My collarbone healed well, and at the end of the year I was listed as First Team All-District, All-Area, and All-City. Over the summer I was named to the First Team 5A All-State Texas Team by the AP and First Team All-State in the preseason publication of Dave Campbell's *Texas Football Magazine*. The national recruiting services listed me consistently among the top fifteen offensive linemen in the nation,[3] and one recruiting magazine had me listed as the best lineman, offensive or defensive, in Texas. The recruiting letters were starting to fill up our mailbox at home.

Despite a couple of dark clouds, my senior year at Lamar can only be described as a dream season, making my first couple years at OU seem even more nightmarish. 1993 was a fun year: I was gaining a lot of national recognition, a lot of interest from college teams. It started in the spring of my junior year, when the scouts from the major colleges started to appear at Lamar's spring football practices. It was an advantage for me to play for a school like Lamar because of the high level of overall talent. The scouts were always around because there were several Lamar players who were destined for NCAA Division I-A. I had a dominating spring of 1992, right up to the last scheduled practice before the spring game, when a defensive tackle rolled over my knee. It caused a minor strain, and the coaches kept me out of the spring game as a precaution. If it had been a regular season game I would have played easily, but the spring game wasn't worth the risk. The only disappointed coach/ recruiter was Doug Cosby, the former Dallas Cowboys tight end, who had flown in from Stanford to see me play the game.

In the fall of 1993 Lamar's team was again loaded with talent, with seven players going on to Division I programs on scholarship—six on offense and one on defense. Several others found homes in other college programs as walk-ons. Although this team was talented enough to go undefeated and deep into the playoffs, it finished 9–3 and lost in the second playoff round to Dallas Lake Highlands, a team we had beaten in our regular season opener. As good as that record was, it turned out to be the worst record of any Lamar team in the decade from 1988 to 1999, in large part because this talented group of individuals played more like individuals than a team.

We lost two district games that year to our archrivals Arlington High and Sam Houston High. The Arlington game got away from us after the offense lost two fumbles inside our own seven-yard line and another on the Arlington one-foot line. We lost the Sam Houston game when one of our linebackers hit a Sam Houston running back out of bounds on a desperation fourth-down play late in the fourth quarter. This was the same linebacker, by the way, who had

Kneeling, Tackle Delanso Edwards; *left to right:* guard Chris Sign, tackle Brandon Cumby, and guard Jay Smith, Lamar High School, Arlington, Texas, spring 1993.

This picture was taken right after the four of us completed our last practice of spring ball for Head Coach Eddy Peach of Lamar. Lamar was preseason No. 1 in the state in 1993, and the four of us were the major part of the offensive line. We were the biggest offensive line in the state that year. (Photograph by Bruce Smith)

broken my collarbone the year before. We were clinging to a lead at the time, and Sam Houston was out of time-outs. The change of possession would have iced the game for us, but instead, the fifteen-yard penalty against us gave Sam Houston a first down and they went on to score the winning touchdown.

During my high school career, I had three good starting years at Lamar, and our teams finished 30-6-1. That is a very good record, especially given the high-powered teams we played year after year in

Texas. The end of my high school career came in the fall of 1993, when our defense collapsed against Lake Highlands in the playoffs. Although we would score on four long, sustained drives, our defense gave up fifty-two points. Most of them were on quick, easy touchdowns scored either by kickoff returns or long runs by the Highlands quarterback off the option. After the game I walked out to the star in the center of the field at Texas Stadium and made a vow that I would return to that same spot some day as a pro.

THE RECRUITING PROCESS

After the season ended in 1993, I was listed by virtually all of the recruiting services as an All-American. *Blue Chip Magazine* listed me on its Dream Team as the fourth best offensive lineman in the nation, and I was the only lineman from Texas mentioned in *USA Today*. In Texas I was First Team All-State, All-Area, All-District, and All-City. I was looking forward to the college recruiting season, which was starting now in earnest.

When I started my senior year in 1993, I had a pretty good general idea of how the recruiting process worked. So I took steps along the way to minimize the stress and confusion that accompanies it. I read a book written by a former TCU player detailing the entire recruiting process, which helped a great deal. I prepared further by talking to the parents of a former Lamar All-American, Jim Brady, who had gone through the same process two years before. I needed all this help: I was contacted by more than fifty NCAA Division I-A schools and I received more than thirty media guides and countless letters that, in the end, filled three large cardboard boxes. I tried to read all the letters, but since there were so many, I focused only on those that contained personal comments from the coaches. I made several informal visits during my senior year and took three of the five allotted formal visits to campuses. I used the informal visits to determine which five schools were best for the formal visits. In the end, I had scholarship offers from twenty-five major college football programs, most of which were included in the traditional Top 25 in the nation.

Recruiting letters began to arrive at an average rate of five to six per day. Rarely a day went by that I didn't get at least one, and some days there were as many as ten letters. The media guides that arrived were interesting because they contained a complete description, both past and present, of the school's football history. The University of Minnesota's media guide even listed my great-grandfather and great-great-uncle as former letter winners. Had I chosen to attend Minnesota I would have played exactly one hundred years after my great-grandfather played there.

The media guides were particularly valuable because they contained depth charts and biographies of the coaches and current players. This gave me a good idea of the team makeup and provided a way to analyze how long it might take for me to move into a starting position. Early in the recruiting process, the guides were particularly helpful. If a school didn't care enough to send a media guide, I dropped them from consideration very quickly. This really hurt Texas A&M. During my junior year I had been very interested in A&M, and I even attended their bonfire prior to the Texas game that year. But I lost interest during the recruiting season of my senior year because they didn't send me a media guide.

It is interesting how even some of the most innocuous material had an effect on me. For example, Nebraska's media guide has a map of the United States depicting Lincoln as the center of the country, including mileage to the nearest major cities. When I saw the map I realized that Lincoln was closer to Minneapolis than to Dallas, which turned out to be a deterrent. Other things deterred me as well. For one thing, the depth charts for the offensive lines at both Nebraska and Alabama showed players standing five deep in each position, which meant I could get a lot of pine time, waiting for my chance to play.

One of my early top choices was Florida State, where my father went to graduate school. Since we moved around to all different parts of the country when I was growing up, FSU was really the only school to which I felt connected. I attended their football camp during the summer before my senior year in high school. Overall it was a good experience because it gave me a firsthand view of a premier football program, and it gave me some exposure to the FSU coaching staff. The good news was that the FSU coaches later said they wouldn't have recruited me if I hadn't come to their camp. The bad news was they saw some things at camp that reduced my chances of getting a scholarship at FSU.

When I went to the Florida State camp I was completely over the knee strain that had kept me out of the spring game in 1993, but I hadn't worked out much because I wanted to rest my knee. In addition to being in less than top running condition, my weight was 270 and my electronically measured time for the forty-yard dash had slipped from 4.8 seconds in the spring to 5.0 in the camp.[4] In an age of 300-pounders, you don't want to appear smaller or slower. I was selected as one of four group leaders in camp and made a very favorable impression on Brad Scott, the FSU offensive line coach. But Coach Scott left the next season to become head coach at South Carolina.

After camp I didn't get much attention from FSU, which for all intents and purposes stopped recruiting in Texas. They found it more effective to recruit in the same areas as the University of Florida and Miami because when they sign a top prospect it counts double—giving them a good player and taking one away from their archrivals at the same time. In the end I was recruited by FSU for their B-list and never really had a chance to move up to their A-list.

My parents were very supportive throughout the recruiting process, emphasizing that the final decision would be mine and not theirs. During the time between the end of my junior season and signing day, I tried to visit as many programs as I could. After it became apparent that I would receive offers from several schools, the only restriction my parents made was that I wouldn't accept a formal trip to a school without receiving a scholarship offer up front. The logic for this restriction was they didn't want me to visit a school and decide it was my first choice, only to have the school fail to offer me a scholarship. They also didn't want me to visit one school, with no offer, and then pass up another school that was committed to me and that I might like. This restriction caused some heartburn at Notre Dame and Iowa, but it opened up a trip to Arizona State, which turned out to be my second choice behind Oklahoma.

Recruiting began with the letters in the spring and summer before my senior year. Phone calls from the coaches started August 15. There were so many phone calls that my mother kept a computer spreadsheet by the phone to keep track of the calls from the coaches and recruiters. Informal visits usually took place on Saturdays during the season, and I got to see some great games during these visits. The formal visits usually took place on weekends after the end of the high school football season and continued until letter-of-intent signing day during the first week of February.

Over fifty teams contacted me throughout the recruiting process. I was recruited by all of the teams in the Southwest Conference, seven teams from the Big Ten, eight teams from the Pac Ten, more than half of the Southeast Conference, most of the teams in the Big East, and Notre Dame as an independent. Because so many schools were contacting me, it would be confusing to cover the whole recruiting experience on a day-by-day basis. Instead, I'll cover the more interesting stories on a school-by-school basis, to highlight the teams that were most interested in me and those that were unusual in their recruiting.

The Oklahoma Sooners

I start with Oklahoma because that is where I decided to go to school and play football. It is no coincidence that Oklahoma also did the best job of recruiting. Arizona State was only an eyelash behind Oklahoma in the quality of recruiting, however, and if Tempe had been closer to Dallas, I might have been a Sun Devil. But more on that later.

Oklahoma helped me out with respect to the whole recruiting process by offering me a scholarship before the start of the football season my senior year. It was really a surprise to open their envelope expecting another typical form letter and to find instead a personal letter and an offer of a full scholarship. This relieved much of the pressure of recruiting; if Oklahoma is the worst you can do, then you are in pretty good shape. In addition, it provided a benchmark with which to compare all of the other schools, and it allowed me to focus on the teams with the storied football traditions. It also allowed me to cross the northern schools off of my list. For example, if Minnesota is the only Division I school that offers you a scholarship, you are going to be a Gopher, but if you are a top recruit from Texas and Minnesota and Oklahoma both offer, you are most likely going to be a Sooner. A winning tradition and conference make-up are important, but the weather is also a major factor. My parents later asked the Oklahoma coaches if they offered early as a standard recruiting ploy, and they said, "very seldom," explaining that they recognized "from the onset that I was the kind of special athlete we wanted in our program." Thank you, OU!

At the time I signed a National Letter of Intent to play at Oklahoma, in February 1994, it was clearly the right choice. It seemed that the Sooners' head coach, Gary Gibbs, had turned the corner—OU had swept the Texas teams in 1993. Oklahoma was close to home and had just switched from artificial turf to natural grass. The most important factor, however, was the depth chart. At the start of the 1994 season there would be five junior offensive linemen at OU, with no one coming up behind them. I knew that if I was redshirted in my first year, which was likely, I would have the opportunity to be a three-year starter with very little pine time on the bench. During the turmoil that followed, this factor became part of the glue that held the whole picture together for me because no matter how many times OU changed coaches, I knew we would have a void in the offensive line that I could fill.

The Texas A&M Aggies

My first taste of college recruiting came at the end of my junior football season in 1992. Lamar's early departure from the play-offs gave me the opportunity to visit a former Lamar All-American, Jim Brady, who had signed with Texas A&M the previous year. During the week before the A&M–University of Texas football game, I visited the school and went to the A&M pep rally and bonfire.

I was a little awestruck by the experience. Everything was like Arlington Lamar High School except on a much bigger scale. The sheer size of the place was impressive, and when you add to that the school spirit, the cohesiveness of the student body, and the biggest bonfire I'd ever seen, you get a remarkable college experience centered on the football team. It was just the kind of place I had dreamed about.

By the time I returned home, A&M was ahead in the recruiting race. The Aggies may have won out in the end had it not been for an apparent oversight during football season the next year.

The recruiting coordinator for Texas A&M, Tim Cassady, called me on August 15, one of the first coaches to call. His calls continued through the start of the high school football season, when they mysteriously stopped. I thought the school had lost interest for some reason, an impression only reinforced by the fact that the letters that had come on a regular basis also stopped and we didn't get a media guide. Six weeks into the season, still with no word from A&M, Jim Brady "inadvertently" stopped by the Lamar training room. When he asked why I had lost interest in A&M, I explained that they had stopped recruiting me. That night I got a phone call and an apology from Coach Cassady, and later that week the media guide came in the mail. I took another informal trip and a formal visit to A&M, but it was never the same after that six-week lapse.

The formal visit was memorable, as it was the Thanksgiving holiday weekend and northern Texas was covered with ice. It took us five hours in our four-wheel drive to cover a trip that normally takes three hours. My dad said it was the coldest he had been at a football game since he left North Dakota. We met in the field house–weight room complex before the game. It was so cold that the Aggies did their pregame warm up inside. Texas, of course, had to warm up outside. Tim Cassady did an excellent job of finding a room for us to stay in overnight so we wouldn't have to return to Arlington that night in the ice. He also found wool stocking hats for us to wear at the game. We paid for the room, of course, and we returned the stocking hats per NCAA rules.

Because I had chosen the Aggies for a formal visit, the head coach, R. C. Slocum, and the defensive line coach, Ron Johnson, who was also the recruiter for the Dallas–Fort Worth area, made a personal visit to my home in Arlington. Coach Slocum was very charming and articulate, but all he talked about was himself. His emphatic description of the A&M football program as a family was hard to buy entirely, as we knew that there was an amazingly high turnover rate among his assistant coaches.

The oddest part of this visit resulted from the NCAA rule that only allows two coaches to visit a prospective player's home. Tim Cassady also came on the trip, but they made him sit outside in the car during the whole two-hour visit. The next year, my next-door neighbor, Shea Holder, who was a First Team All-State tight end and a year behind me at Lamar, was recruited by A&M. We tried to find out when they were going to visit the Holders so my dad could invite Tim over to our house for a beer instead of waiting in the car. As it turned out, only two coaches came to Arlington to visit Shea, so my dad missed the opportunity. It would have been interesting to get an "after the recruiting" update from Tim.

The last word on Texas A&M recruiting comes from Shea's father, Randy Holder. Shea did sign up to play for the Aggies. When Coach Slocum visited the Holders, he pledged that their son would be a tight end at A&M as long as he wanted to be a tight end at A&M. When Shea went to practice the first day of his freshman year the next fall, they issued him number 79, the number for an interior offensive lineman. So much for the promise of being a tight end. Shea's dad was unhappy about this, first because of the deception and later because of the difficulty Shea experienced in learning to be an offensive lineman.

The Florida State Seminoles

During the middle of the 1993 football season, my dad had a business meeting in Tallahassee, Florida, and he used this opportunity to set up a visit with the coaches at Florida State. As I mentioned earlier, this is when he found out that attending FSU's football camp had helped me from a recruiting standpoint. But from the onset, I was disappointed in the way FSU handled recruiting.

The recruiting coordinator, Ronnie Cottrell, gave me his number and told me to call any time. However, every time I called that number I was connected to a voice message promising to call me back, which rarely happened. At the same time, my classmate Aaron Oliver, a wide receiver, and the other All-Americans from Lamar were also being recruited by FSU.

One day I asked Aaron if Coach Cottrell was returning his calls, and Aaron said that he never had to leave a message because Coach Cottrell always answered his phone. It turns out that Aaron had been given a different phone number. The next time I called, I used the number they had given Aaron, and Coach Cottrell answered the phone. He seemed surprised I had called him directly and even asked where I got the number. Do these coaches really think players from the same team aren't going to talk to each other?

There was always a hint of deception in the way FSU recruited. For example, my dad's visit happened to fall during the week the Seminoles (the 'Noles) were preparing for their "game of the century" with Notre Dame. Coach Cottrell told my father to tell me not to expect a call that week because Coach Bowden had placed a moratorium on recruiting so that his coaches could focus completely on preparations for the big game. He was right; I didn't get a call that week, but they were unfocused enough to call my teammate Aaron Oliver. Notre Dame must not have been as serious as FSU, as the Irish called me during that same week. Incidentally, Notre Dame won.

In retrospect, I see that I didn't fit the profile of the FSU recruit. Of the seventeen players in FSU's 1994 recruiting class, three were offensive linemen: One had limited playing experience, coming from a high school varsity program in Orlando that was only two years old. Another was a junior college transfer, and the third never made it to campus in the fall, having been arrested on drug charges over the summer. It seemed that FSU felt it needed recruits who were street tough enough to stand up to Miami and Florida. It was almost like they were saying, "You are too nice of a kid to play for FSU."

The Arizona State Sun Devils

Arizona State was a school that I really didn't consider at first, but my parents requested that I check it out. Both of them had received their master's degrees from ASU, and they asked me to consider it because they loved the school, the climate, and the surrounding area. And Arizona State did an outstanding job of recruiting. If Tempe were closer to Dallas, things might have turned out differently.

Arizona State shares a location with the NFL's Phoenix Cardinals, providing the Sun Devils with outstanding facilities, second only to those at Florida State. The main difference between FSU's facilities and ASU's was found in the athletic dorm. FSU had townhouse-like cabanas that opened onto private swimming pools, whereas ASU's football team lived in a twenty-five-year-old converted apartment complex on the north end of campus. Not surprisingly, I never got to see the athletic dorms at ASU, either during our informal visit to Tempe in the fall of 1993 and our formal visit in December of the same year.

This became a private joke for my parents because they knew the athletic dorms were a converted apartment complex formerly called the Lemon Terrace Court (LTC). During my dad's early military flying days across town at Williams Air Force Base, LTC had been home to many of his unmarried flying friends, and they thought it was heaven. These bachelor pilots lived adjacent to a large college campus with an abundance of good-looking women. At the same time, they had a tremendous advantage over their college counterparts because they could party all the time; they didn't have to attend classes, prepare for exams, or write papers. More importantly, they had money. In essence, they had what many young women at ASU were looking for, a young stud with a college degree, money, and a real career path. LTC, which was dubbed "Sin City" by my parents' contemporaries, is now the athletic dorm. No wonder they didn't give us a tour.

One thing that does set Arizona State apart from the rest of Division I is their training camp in the mountains in northern Arizona. The summer temperatures in Phoenix, called the Valley of the Sun, are too hot for practice during the day. So the football team packs up and heads for Camp Tontozona, located in the Tonto National Forest. Here the Sun Devils spend two isolated weeks in cabins and bunk houses, experiencing male bonding and preparing for the upcoming season. When the team members get up in the morning they have to chase the wild animals off the field before they can practice.

I spent the second day of my informal visit at Camp Tontozona, which is located in a beautiful setting. I really hadn't wanted to make the two-and-a-half-hour drive into the mountains to visit the camp, but my parents insisted. After seeing the camp we went to the vista at the top of the Mogillion Rim. I had no idea that Arizona had such beautiful mountains.

This informal visit came during ASU's homecoming weekend in the fall of 1993. From the onset, it was a special trip. Soon after I arrived on Saturday morning, I met one of the assistant coaches.

Unknown to me, he had just returned from Arlington, where he had watched me play the night before. On the second offensive play from scrimmage, I had pulled and matched the Arlington tailback stride for stride for sixty yards downfield, where I literally ran over the opposing safety on the ten-yard line, allowing the tailback to score. Some recruiters and college football scouts say you can tell if a player is a champion in three plays. That night it only took two plays. When the ASU coach told me he had only stayed for the first half, I asked him if he saw the second offensive play from scrimmage. When he said "Yes," I said, "That's all you needed to see."

Throughout my informal visit, the coaches kept me separated from the other recruits who were at ASU that weekend. Whenever we would cross paths with the group, you could overhear comments about the "All-American from Texas." I was the only recruit they allowed into the locker room after Saturday's game, and the coaches made special arrangements to introduce my parents and me to the president of the university, the only college president we met during recruiting. The coaches did an excellent job of preparing the president for our visit, letting him know who I was and that my parents were ASU graduates. His comment to me was, "I hope you will be a second-generation graduate of Arizona State."

When Head Coach Bruce Snyder and Offensive Line Coach Dan Cozzetto visited Arlington, they were unlike any of the other coaches who visited. All of the other visiting coaches focused on the positive aspects of their programs and their universities, but Coach Snyder focused on me and where I would fit into ASU's plans. He drew a diagram of the depth chart of the offensive line and used it to explain what they expected to happen over the course of my career at ASU. He indicated that I would be a redshirt my freshman year, but added that I would travel in order to get used to the routine on the road. The second year they would play me at left guard behind Joe Cajic, who would then be a senior. Then in my third year, after Cajic graduated, the coach said he would move me up to be a starter at left guard. After that, he said, I should be ready to move out to left tackle to fill the vacancy when Juan Roque, their giant left tackle, graduated. Who knows if any of this would ever have happened, but Coach Snyder was a lot more credible than the coaches who said I would start right away.

My host coach at ASU was Hue Jackson. Coach Jackson had a connection to my father through his prior job as an assistant coach at Cal State Fullerton. At the time, the head coach at Fullerton was Gene Murphy, who had been one of my father's coaches back at North Dakota. Coach Jackson was a great guy and a great recruiter. I wish I had an opportunity to play for him.

The coaches at ASU were a little astonished at their luck that one of the best offensive line recruits in the nation was born in Arizona, had parents who were both graduates of ASU, and had grandparents who lived just up the road in Sun City. After I committed orally to Oklahoma, as a courtesy I called Coach Snyder so he would hear of my decision firsthand before the news hit the media and the recruiting services. It was the hardest call I have ever made in my life. Coach Snyder said he "felt like someone had just kicked him in the stomach." At that moment, I had exactly the same feeling. In closing, he said, "There will always be a place for you at Arizona State." I wonder if he knows that he came within an eyelash of fulfilling that promise the next year.

The Nebraska Cornhuskers

There was no middle ground in my recruiting experience at the University of Nebraska. For every extremely positive factor in Nebraska's presentation, there was another factor that was prohibitively negative. Nebraska was known for producing the best offensive linemen in the country, but these same linemen had difficulty going on to the next level. They had the potential of being national champions (and they were for the next two years), but their depth chart was intimidating for a freshman recruit. They had some of the most respected coaches in the nation but some of the least respected players. Their football facility was outstanding, but the area surrounding their campus was old and depressing and the weather was terrible. Nebraska was the only team, other than Arizona State, that didn't show us their athletic dorms. In fact, the Nebraska coaches kept me sequestered in their football facilities during the whole visit and didn't show me their campus either.

I was recruited by Nebraska's offensive coordinator, Turner Gill. Like Head Coach Tom Osborne and Offensive Line Coach Milt Tenapur, Coach Gill was a true gentleman, and I consider it an honor that he thought enough of me as a person and a player to recruit me. (I think that Coach Osborne and Coach Joe Paterno from Penn State are the only two head coaches in Division I who hold doctorates.) When I arrived in Lincoln on a Friday afternoon, the Huskers were preparing for their Orange Bowl game against Florida State. I spent Friday evening at a team banquet celebrating the Husker's Big Eight championship, and on Saturday I toured the football facilities. On Saturday night my parents were invited to Coach Osborne's home, and I went out with a couple of players and other recruits.

That evening, my escort got drunk and I had to drive him home, but first I had to step in and break up a fight between a player and another recruit. This sort of thing worried my parents, who were also concerned about the constant rumor of the use of growth hormones and steroids. There seemed to be a "win at any cost" and a "don't ask, don't tell" attitude among the coaches. My dad was particularly upset about some of Nebraska's other recruiting techniques.

Nebraska was the only school that tried to administer a psychological assessment during my recruiting. One night I answered a phone call from a University of Nebraska graduate student, who asked if she could ask me some questions about my personal preferences for things like dorm life and classes. I consented, but by the time I finished it had become clear from the questions (such as "Would you play with an injury?") that the questioner's interest went far beyond student life. This experience really presented me with a dilemma: I didn't want to challenge Nebraska because I wanted them to continue to recruit me. After all, they had a solid reputation and a winning tradition, and they were on the verge of a national championship. Yet my father, who holds a doctorate and knows about research, felt that the questionnaire was inappropriate and improperly administered and suspected that the results would be invalid. I didn't want Nebraska to turn me down because of the results of an inappropriate and invalid questionnaire. My dad resolved the issue with a call to the recruiting coordinator at Nebraska, requesting that the answers be destroyed without applying any scoring algorithms or analysis to my responses.

My father had called the recruiting coordinator in order to resolve the conflict at the lowest level possible; the graduate student I had spoken with worked for the recruiting coordinator, and Dad figured that if they tossed the raw data away before they did any scoring or analysis, that would be the end of the story. Not quite: after he spoke with the recruiting coordinator about our concerns, my dad received immediate return calls from Coach Gill and Coach Osborne. He repeated his concerns, and they said they would comply with the request to destroy the data. I will always wonder whether they analyzed it anyway, just to see if it was really different.

According to the recruiting services, you can tell how badly a team wants a recruit by the number of times and when the head coach telephones the recruit. If this is true, then Nebraska really wanted me. Coach Osborne called me more often than any other head coach. He even called from the Orange Bowl on the eve of their national championship game against Florida State. At one point my parents thought I might commit to the Cornhuskers. Turner Gill kept asking me when Coach Osborne could visit us in Arlington. I wanted to wait until I decided where I wanted to go. If I opted for Nebraska, I wanted to tell Coach Osborne in person. I decided to commit to Oklahoma, so the visit never took place.

It is interesting to recall that I really didn't know who I would pick until two weeks before signing day. I had narrowed it down to Nebraska, Arizona State, and Oklahoma, with a glimmer of hope kept alive for Florida State. I was comfortably assured that I couldn't go wrong with any of the schools on this list.

The Alabama Crimson Tide

The University of Alabama started out as one of my top five choices. This made sense for a number of reasons, including their football tradition and the fact that in the late 1970s, when I was very young, we lived in Enterprise, Alabama, for a short time. In fact, we were living in Alabama when I was first redshirted in kindergarten. I liked Alabama enough to schedule a formal visit, but it never took place. I canceled the visit after a series of interesting events that led up to my visit. I will probably never know the whole story, but here are some pieces of the puzzle.

I felt strongly enough about the University of Alabama to commit to a formal visit before the end of the football season in my senior year, which was somewhat early in the recruiting process. At the time the Alabama assistant coaches who were recruiting me seemed to be very excited that I had picked Alabama for a formal visit. In fact, one of the Florida State coaches told me that Alabama was teasing FSU that I was already "a lock" for them. And Alabama did have a really good shot at getting me, but right after I scheduled this visit, the whole thing rapidly unraveled.

The week after I scheduled my formal visit to Alabama, during the weekend of their game against Auburn, Chris Sign, a teammate of mine at Lamar who played at the opposite offensive line position (left guard), took an informal visit to Alabama. During that weekend, Alabama's head coach, Gene Stallings, offered Chris a scholarship, which Chris immediately accepted. Chris came back to school on Monday after his visit and announced he was going to Alabama. At this point, Alabama had not even given me a scholarship offer. I was excited for him because I felt Alabama was an excellent program. At the same time, I was disappointed because Alabama was one of my top choices and I knew I would no longer have a chance to visit.

Please don't misunderstand me—I like Chris and to this day we are still very good friends, but I wanted to set my own course away from him. After Chris committed to Alabama, I didn't have a choice but to cancel my visit.

The Texas Longhorns

When I was being recruited, the University of Texas (UT) had gone through some difficult years but was now showing some definite signs of recovery. For me, the only drawback of attending Texas was their team personality; the Longhorns were seen as a taunting, in-your-face team with a bad attitude. This was reinforced by their marquee players, wide receivers Mike Adams and Lovell Pinckney. I had a close-up view of Adams's career earlier in high school, when he played for our crosstown rival, Sam Houston High School.

I had an informal visit to Austin early in the season. Normally my parents went along on the informal visits, which made them virtually the same as the formal visits. But my brother Allan's Angelo State team was playing its first home game, and my parents went to San Angelo to watch. So I took the trip to Austin by myself. I went on a Saturday morning with a group of other Lamar recruits to watch Texas play Syracuse.

It was a hard trip because I had played the night before and had to get up very early to make the three-hour trip to Austin. Chris Sign's father took the bulk of the players in his Suburban, but there wasn't enough room for everyone, so I had to drive. The Texas-Syracuse game was a thrilling contest, ending in a tie, but I was so tired I left at halftime and went back to Arlington. UT just didn't feel right. It was too urban and unfriendly for me. I guess having the campus in the heart of the downtown area made it seem cold and uncomfortable.

Later in the season the Texas offensive line coach came to Arlington to watch me practice at Lamar. After practice he asked me if he could visit us at home that evening. At first I said no, but after I talked to the high school coaches and the head coach made a call to my parents, I relented and said it would be OK. After a short visit it was clear to my parents why I didn't want to play for this coach. It was a cordial visit, but I knew when he left that Texas was not going to be one of my final five choices.

The Iowa Hawkeyes and the Notre Dame Fighting Irish

Almost all of my recruiting experiences were very positive. The recruiting process gave me the opportunity to meet some wonderful coaches, and it gave me information about some terrific institutions. However, in two cases things weren't so pleasant.

After signing day I received a questionnaire from one of the recruiting services asking about our recruiting experience. One of the questions asked us to list the schools that did the best job of recruiting and the schools that did the poorest job of recruiting. Oklahoma and Arizona State were the best, the University of Iowa and Notre Dame were the worst.

Iowa was much like all the other schools until it came time to narrow down my selections to the final five for formal visits. Recruiters know that if a recruit doesn't make a formal visit to their school, they have virtually no chance of signing that player on signing day. Knowing that I was mostly interested in schools located in warm climates, Iowa's recruiting coordinator put a tremendous amount of pressure on me to commit to a formal trip in early December, before the heavy Iowa winter set in. I refused for two reasons. First, I was hoping that Lamar would go deep into the Texas state play-offs, which would take our season into the first two weeks of December, and second, the rest of December was already full, with my formal visit to Arizona State scheduled for the weekend of December 19th. This would have pushed a visit to Iowa into mid-January. You don't have to be a meteorologist to figure this one out.

One evening, the recruiting coordinator from Iowa called and asked if I would commit to a formal visit on December 19th. After

I turned him down, he continued to pressure me by saying that they had already made arrangements for me to spend that weekend with one of my former Lamar teammates, Billy Coats, who was a defensive back for the Hawkeyes. After I declined again, the recruiter finished the conversation by saying he would "pencil me in for the 19th" in case something fell through. At this point I hung up, thinking that this was the end of the matter.

The following Wednesday I received a very formal letter from the head coach of the University of Iowa stating how happy he was that I had committed to a formal visit to their school on December 19th. That part didn't bother me at all because I knew that a phone call to the recruiting coordinator would straighten it out. What did upset me was the tone of the rest of the letter, which was a veiled threat: I had no choice but to make the trip on the 19th because it would count as one of my five formal visits whether I went or not.

At that point my dad replied in writing to the head coach of the University of Iowa, stating "that under no circumstances" would I be visiting the University of Iowa on December 19th, "or on any other date for that matter, period. End of recruiting." After they received my dad's letter, I received a phone call from the recruiting coordinator apologizing for the misunderstanding, but it didn't matter at that point. What I was really wondering was how many recruits did they pull this scam on, and how many felt they actually had to live up to this "penciled-in" commitment, expending a valuable formal visit on Iowa?

If my experience with Iowa was bad, Notre Dame was worse. The coaches there pulled every trick you could imagine during recruiting, from using my classmates and teachers to pressure me in a "win one for the Gipper" kind of tactic to flat out lying. The assistant coach who recruited me lied on at least three different occasions. Interestingly, I knew when he was lying and challenged him, a response that Notre Dame coaches are not used to from recruits. The first lie came when the coach told me that I had to apply and be accepted at Notre Dame before they could offer me a scholarship and that they were the *only* school in the country to hold their admissions in such high regard as to have that requirement. At this time, I was being recruited by Stanford and Duke, who also had the same requirement.

The assistant coach also said that Notre Dame didn't offer scholarships up front. He explained the school's policy like this: the recruit first had to commit to a formal visit, which allowed Head Coach Lou Holtz to present the scholarship offer in person on the Sunday of the formal visit. My case presented a problem for Notre Dame because I wouldn't accept a formal visit without an up-front offer. I continued to insist on an up-front offer, and Notre Dame continued to insist that they didn't make up-front offers.

Their story started to come apart during the weekend of the Texas–Texas A&M game in 1993, when I made an informal visit to A&M. My parents and I traveled to College Station on the Friday after Thanksgiving, in the worst ice storm in a decade. During the pregame dinner, I had the opportunity to talk with the parents of a recruit from Houston Clear Lake High School, Steve McKinney. Steve had verbally committed to A&M, and his father was trying to influence me to commit to A&M as well. During the course of the conversation, Mr. McKinney mentioned that Steve was going on a formal visit to Notre Dame the next day, and that although Notre Dame had offered Steve a full ride, he was still going to A&M.

Believing what Notre Dame had told us about not offering up-front scholarships, I said, "Oh, this must be your second trip to Notre Dame."

"No, this is our initial visit."

"Oh. Then how did Steve get an offer for a scholarship?"

"They offered it up front."

"Oh, I thought they didn't do that."

"Yes, they do, and they said it was valid until signing day, otherwise we wouldn't be taking this trip."

Again, do these coaches think that recruits, not to mention parents of recruits, never talk to each other?

On the Monday after Thanksgiving, the coach from Notre Dame called again and asked if I would commit to a formal visit. Again, I asked if they would commit to a scholarship up front. When the coach reiterated that "Notre Dame does not offer up front," I asked him, "What about Steve McKinney?" At that point the coach became belligerent, demanding to know who I thought I was, questioning the "integrity of the Notre Dame football program." I answered this question by asking the same question again. At this point the coach broke down and admitted that he had to get me to visit, but he couldn't give me an offer up front. I replied that without an offer, I wouldn't go. This was the end of my experience with Notre Dame's recruiting. Two weeks later, that coach was fired. I believe it was, in part, because he didn't get his quota of athletes from Texas to visit.

The TCU Horned Frogs

Texas Christian University would have been a good place for my brother Allan, to go. Allan had the desire and work ethic to become a solid offensive lineman, and TCU could provide the developmental support he needed to make that happen. For my part, I had a great deal of respect for their head coach, Pat Sullivan, and I was impressed with their linebackers' coach, Reggie Herring, who had been a linebacker at Florida State at the same time my dad was there in graduate school. TCU did a very good job of recruiting me, but there was no attraction for me there. I wish they would have recruited Allan instead. If TCU had recruited and signed Allan, I most likely would not have signed anyway, but without Allan they didn't have a prayer of getting me.

During the summer of 1993, TCU invited me and a number of my Lamar teammates to visit. In the middle of the visit, Coach Sullivan pulled me away from the rest of the group and offered me a scholarship to TCU. It is really a good feeling when someone of that stature says he wants you to play for him.

I did make an informal visit to TCU in the fall to watch their season opener against Oklahoma, but I was there to see the Sooners more than to see the Horned Frogs. During the game I focused more on the coaches than on the game. Merv Johnson, the Oklahoma offensive line coach, was pretty stoic and during the heat of the battle remained more of a teacher and mentor than his TCU counterpart, who appeared like a screaming maniac; guess which style I prefer? I very much liked Reggie Herring, the TCU coach primarily responsible for recruiting me, but he had already left TCU to join Brad Scott at South Carolina. So I had very little interest in TCU at that point.

The Southern Methodist Mustangs

Southern Methodist University (SMU) in Dallas barely had a chance to recruit me. As with TCU, my brother Allan would have developed into a solid player for SMU, but when my dad sent them a video of Allan's highlights, SMU had returned it unopened. When they called to recruit me the next year, my dad took the call and asked if they remembered the videotape he sent them last season of Allan. When they said no, he said, "That's why you're not getting a chance to recruit Jay." End of recruiting.

The Baylor Bears

I made an informal trip to Baylor University in Waco, Texas, but I really wasn't impressed by anything I saw there. I kept up an interest in Baylor for a short period because of the close personal relationship built by Coach Ken Rucker, who recruited me. I was later disappointed when Baylor's search for a new head coach didn't include Ken Rucker, as he would have been an excellent choice.

Other than Coach Rucker, there wasn't much attraction for me at Baylor. Even that attraction went away after signing day, when Coach Rucker left Baylor for Texas A&M.

The Michigan Wolverines

During the summer of 1993, before my senior year, my dad had a business trip in Detroit, and so we used that trip as an opportunity to take an informal visit to the University of Michigan. Michigan was impressive. It was everything I pictured a Big Ten football school to be, including the mammoth stadium and sprawling campus.

My dad had come directly from a business meeting and was still wearing a suit. We waited for a short time outside Head Coach Gary Moeller's office before we met with him. When he opened the door it was apparent that he had changed into a coat and tie to match what my dad was wearing, which was a nice touch on his part. The first thing he did was to grab me and gave me the body density check. I honestly believe that all head coaches formerly worked as weight guessers at the carnival. They can grab a recruit and guess his weight to within a pound. Unfortunately, I failed the "press the flesh" test, being lighter than the average Big Ten behemoth.

Coach Moeller had a picture of the previous year's offensive line propped up against the front of his desk so he could point out how important the O-line was to Michigan football. Unfortunately, I could see stacks of pictures of the other positions leaning up against each other in the corner, so I could tell what the strategy was: if the recruit is an offensive lineman, the offensive line picture comes out; if he is a D-back, the D-back picture comes out, and so on. It was so obvious that it was a turn-off.

It is too bad Michigan couldn't see its way clear to recruiting me as a two-sport athlete. I was actually more impressed by the hockey arena than the football facilities. However, after the press-the-flesh test, I knew I wasn't big enough to play Big Ten football in the offensive line.

The Texas Tech Red Raiders and the Ohio State Buckeyes

Texas Tech didn't recruit me; they were more interested in a couple of other Lamar players. But I did have an indirect experience with their recruiting, through my dad. Late in the season of my senior year, the Texas Tech offensive coordinator came to watch Lamar play Irving High School at Irving Stadium. The day was bitterly cold and windy, so the few people who attended from Lamar were mostly the parents. We were all huddled up against the press box to try to stay out of the wind. Being sensible, the Tech recruiter was up there with the parents.

According to the NCAA rules, if recruiters talk directly to parents it counts as a contact with the player. So the recruiters typically stay away from the parents. When my mom and dad arrived at the game, someone introduced them to the Tech recruiter. Since Tech was not recruiting me, my dad mentioned that they were my parents. The Tech recruiter then asked how big I was; my dad replied, "six feet, four inches and 270 pounds," after which, the recruiter leaned back up against the press box and said, "I see where he got 270 pounds. Where did he get six feet, four inches?" It broke everybody up. Two years later this same Texas Tech recruiter, Dick Winder, would become my offensive coordinator at Oklahoma.

I would also work with the coach who recruited me from Ohio State University (OSU), Bill Young, who became the defensive coordinator for Oklahoma that same year. I met him at OU after one of the spring practices; he said he was glad I hadn't chosen Ohio State and that he was "very happy I was at Oklahoma." I was happy as well because I felt that Coach Young had been one of the best coaches I had met during recruiting. It also turned out that he was a good friend of my dad's college O-line coach, Kent Stephenson, now with the Pittsburgh Steelers.

One night my dad took a phone call for me because I was studying for a test. He had a very nice conversation from a coach who said he was from OSU. Later I asked who it was, and he said he missed his name but that he was from OSU. Unfortunately for the coach, at that time I was receiving calls from Oklahoma State, Ohio State, and Oregon State, so I had no idea which OSU had called.

During the first four weeks of the college football season in my senior year in high school, I made informal visits to TCU, Oklahoma, Texas, and Baylor. After the Baylor game, during which I nearly expired from the heat, I decided that I needed to focus on playing football on Friday night instead of watching it on Saturdays. So after Baylor, we stopped taking informal trips.

The one exception was when we went to San Angelo for Angelo State's homecoming in October. It was great to see Allan, and the visit gave me the rare opportunity to see his team play. After the game we waited in the parents' lounge in the field house while Allan dressed. One of the assistant coaches recognized us and came over to say hello. Later, Allan took me into the locker room to meet his friends and meet briefly with Allan's head coach, but for the most part I just stood around and waited. No coaches or recruiting coordinators were hovering around like they did at the "big" schools. Here I was, one of the top college recruits, standing in the middle of a college football locker room during the height of the recruiting season with everyone virtually ignoring me. It was really a good object lesson for me, because it brought recruiting back into its proper perspective.

THE END OF RECRUITING

After recruiting ended, I sent thank you notes to five coaches, those who had done the best, fairest, most honest job of representing their schools throughout the recruiting process. They were Hue Jackson from Arizona State, Ken Rucker from Baylor, Turner Gill from Nebraska, Merv Johnson from Oklahoma, and John Williams from Miami.[5] My dad also sent notes to the head coaches who had done the best job of recruiting: Bruce Snyder of Arizona State, Tom Osborne of Nebraska, Gary Gibbs of Oklahoma, and Pat Sullivan of TCU.

At the end of recruiting, there is a three-day "silent period" before signing day, during which no coaches are allowed to contact prospective players. After finally having some quiet time to sort through all of the offers, I sat down with my parents in the kitchen and told them I had decided on Oklahoma. They were excited because it was close to home and they felt comfortable with the coaches, the football program, and the university. We called OU's recruiting coordinator, Dick Foster, with the news, and he said that Coach Gibbs would be very happy I was joining the Sooner family.

I picked Oklahoma for all of the right reasons, and I was confident that I had made the correct choice. In spite of some considerable turmoil along the way, in the long run I still think it was the correct choice. Finally, the dream of playing Division I college football was becoming reality.

CHAPTER 3

Coach Gibbs

FROM HIGH EXPECTATIONS TO UNCERTAINTY

Only the good die young.   BILLY JOEL

The beginning of the end for Sooner Coach Gary Gibbs was marked by the last play of the 1994 Texas game in Dallas. Down 17–10 with the ball almost touching the Texas goal line, we ran the reverse and handed the ball to running back James Allen. Stoney Clark, the lumbering Longhorn middle guard, deciphered the fake, and he ended up in the middle of the play. It was a lucky break, and it was the only tackle Clark made all day. That tackle ended the Sooners' chances of tying—or even winning—that game.

As I look back on my first four months at Oklahoma, it's obvious that they didn't go exactly the way I had expected. We won the games we were supposed to win, but we lost games we couldn't afford to lose. The loss to Texas, coupled with a couple other key losses that season, set into motion the events that would throw the remainder of my college career into turmoil.

In 1994 I was redshirted; I watched the action from the sidelines, traveling with the team to all of the road games but not playing. Coach Gibbs was the first of my four head coaches at OU, although this was to be his sixth and final year. Although the Texas loss dropped us to just 3–2 on the season, it marked the fifth time in six years that

Gibbs's Sooners had lost to our perennial Red River rival. To Oklahoma fans, that was bad because Texas is matched only by Nebraska as the biggest game of the year for the Sooners.

Coach Gibbs had some sizable shoes to fill when he inherited the Sooner head coaching job from legendary Barry Switzer in 1989. Not that Switzer had endeared himself to everyone in Oklahoma by that time. His team was clearly out of hand: some players were in trouble with the law, and the team's recruiting violations had not gone unnoticed by the NCAA, which slapped OU with a three-year probation that sealed Switzer's departure after the 1988 season.

Still, in his sixteen years with OU, Switzer had led the Sooners to 157 victories and four ties in 190 games, had gone 12–5 against Nebraska, and had won three national championships. But with Switzer's departure and the NCAA probation came the loss of television revenue for three years and, more importantly to the team, the loss of fourteen scholarships out of a possible eighty-five. That is the equivalent of more than half the second string of players.

It was Gibbs's task to clean up a program that had taken a lot of heat from the national media for its "bad-boy" ways. Gibbs had been the defensive coordinator under Switzer, and he was a good one. He had owed part of his success to the powerful offensive machine the Sooners had developed under Switzer and the vaunted wishbone attack. As the 1980s came to a close, opposing teams had pretty well identified effective ways of shutting down the option-based running attack, and a new type of offense was needed. Head Coach Gibbs would provide that with the leadership of OU's new offensive coordinator, Watson Brown.

Under Brown, OU moved to the I-formation and split formation, both passing offenses, and relied on the golden arm of Midwest City quarterback Cale Gundy to make it pay off from 1990 to 1993. During those years, Gundy set all the passing records for Sooner quarterbacks. Brown ran the offense, Gibbs ran the defense, and the Sooners found ways to win during those troubled years, albeit not at the level that Switzer's teams had played.

My senior season at Arlington Lamar High School, 1993, would be the peak year for the Gundy-led Sooners, as they finished 9–3 with a victory over Texas Tech in the John Hancock Bowl in El Paso. But that was Cale's senior year, and when I showed up in Norman in 1994 the Sooners were led by a new quarterback, Garrick McGee, a junior transfer from Northeastern Oklahoma Junior College.

MY FIRST FALL CAMP

I became a part of the Sooners' fall camp in the summer of 1994, starting my football and college career as a freshman in Norman. I moved into the Bud Wilkinson dorm just across the street from Memorial Stadium on Jenkins Street, where all the freshmen footballers were housed. My roommate was Tim Macias, an offensive lineman from Putnam City, and we waited with high hopes for the first day of practice to arrive on August 5.

Fall camp is no picnic at OU. For one thing, freshmen are doing two practices a day (called "two-a-days") for more than two weeks during the hottest part of the Oklahoma summer. The temperatures that August hovered in the 95-degree range with some in the 105-degree range. Later, I would rate Coach Gibbs's fall camp as average in its toughness. It was tougher than John Blake's would be, but not as tough as Howard Schnellenberger's or even Bob Stoops's August camps. Our daily schedule kept us in practice or meetings from 8:30 A.M. to 9:00 P.M., with breaks for lunch and dinner. We worked hard, but the expectations were not as great as those under Schnellenberger and Stoops would be later. Of course, I didn't know that then. I was just a freshman with one goal in mind: to make the depth chart and get on the team's traveling squad.

To make the depth chart, you have to make it onto the first two strings. For me as an offensive lineman, that meant I would have to lay hold of one of the top four tackle slots. That was no easy task, given the contenders for the position and the junior starters already

Left to right: Jay (#61). OU Coach Gary Gibbs, and Jay's brother Allan Smith, at Media Day, August 1994.

At eighteen years old, I had just reported to Oklahoma to begin my college football career. Coach Gibbs was the head coach of the Sooners. The previous season the Sooners had been crowned the Texas State champions, beating Texas, TCU, Texas A&M, and Texas Tech, and the Sooners had just been given a preseason ranking as tenth in the nation. This was Coach Gibb's sixth season as the head coach of the Sooners. I was given the number 61 when I arrived at OU. After fall camp, I was given the option to switch to number 71, which I took. My brother was visiting for Media Day from San Angelo, Texas, where he was a member of the Angelo State Rams. Although he had to report to his own team for fall camp the next day, he did make it to Norman with my dad. Media Day is when the Sooners meet with the media, have pictures taken for media productions, family, and friends, and also sign autographs for the Sooners fans. (Photograph by Bruce Smith)

there. Still, that became my goal, and I was committed to realizing it in my freshman year. To do it, I had to beat out guys who were bigger than I; the average per-man weight on OU's offensive line that year was over 300 pounds, and I weighed in at only 270. Most offensive linemen were benching 450–500 pounds. I wasn't even close to that as the season began.

As a result, I spent fall camp and the first part of the season holding blocking dummies and becoming a scout team player. Being on the scout team means you run offense or defense for the first and second strings in practice. That's where most freshmen gain their experience, but it wasn't good enough for me. I proved myself and caught the coaches' attention during the one-on-one blocking drills. I ran three or four freshmen over, and the coaches seemed impressed. I even got into a fight with one of those players, David Campbell. David had been suffering from bruised ribs, and I would best him by hitting him in those sore ribs. His frustration got the best of him one day, and we squared off right there on the practice field.

So it was a hard-hitting camp, but no one was dropping from exhaustion or heat stroke, as they would be the next year in Coach Schnellenberger's camp. With Coach Gibbs, we hit hard and practiced hard, but he knew when to shut things down and send us to the showers.

Eventually my determination and hard work paid off, and I was elevated from the scout team to the travel team three weeks into that first season. Others on the team were not so lucky, however.

BAD LUCK FROM THE BEGINNING

Our new quarterback, Garrick McGee, seemed to have a promising arm, but unfortunately he didn't live up to expectations. That was not all his fault. Perhaps if luck had been with us during fall camp that year, Garrick's luck might have changed for the year and the team would have had the anticipated 10–2 record that the media expected of us. But luck was not with us, and we started the year off by losing a dozen players to injuries in fall camp. Several of these players held key starting positions as linemen, linebackers, and receivers. Among the losses were flanker Michael Thompson, who broke his leg running a route in practice, and offensive lineman Joe

Carolla, who broke his ankle. Both were starters, and these injuries really had an impact on other players, like Garrick, who either didn't have the receivers to throw to or the blockers to keep defensive tackles off his back.

You could also make the case that more motivation from the head coach was sorely needed on the team during these years. Solid and steady as defensive coordinator, Gibbs as head coach was quiet and conservative, rarely displaying emotions to players or to the media. He cared about his players but had a habit of taking all the blame for team losses. He told us that we had to be better prepared for games and play better, but he was often short on direction and certainly short on emotional outbursts. He avoided conflict with players and coaches, and he seldom put his foot down or stressed his points emotionally. So despite the best of intentions, all of these things came together to dash my hopes for a great freshman season.

A DISAPPOINTING PATTERN

Before we knew it, the season was upon us, and we opened on the road against the Orangemen of Syracuse University. I didn't make the trip because I was still on the scout team, having not made the depth chart yet. But the team started into its season ranked as high as tenth in the nation during preseason, slipping to sixteenth by the start of the regular season. So our expectations for the coming year were as high as the media's.

Syracuse is never an easy opponent, so we were elated when OU built a 24–0 lead on the Orangemen. Our joy was short-lived, however, because Syracuse came back late in the game with twenty-four unanswered points to tie the score, and we had to kick a late field goal to win. We moved up to eleventh in the polls on the strength of that win, but we knew how close we had come to blowing the game, and we knew we would have a lot of work to do for the rest of the season.

It soon became typical of the 1994 season that we would do well enough one week to win, then fall flat the next week and lose. That pattern began with our second straight road game, against Texas A&M. The Aggies had a ranked team that year, and they are always especially tough at home on Kyle Field, a stadium that holds as many fans as OU's Memorial Stadium. And are they ever loud fans! It didn't take long to see that we were outmatched on that Saturday. We capped things off by fumbling twice in the fourth quarter and wound up losing, 36–14.

The loss was sobering to us and to the Oklahoma media. For one thing, it ended the team's year-long run as "Texas State Champs." During the 1993 season, the Sooners had beaten every Texas team it faced, including Texas Tech in the John Hancock Bowl. This was a huge point of pride for the Sooners and their fans, but we had now tripped over our second opponent of the season, which just happened to be a Texas team. We dropped to twentieth in the national polls, and the Oklahoma media began calling for Coach Gibbs's head.

Next up was Texas Tech, and since it was our home opener it was my first chance to see what college football means to OU fans. A beautifully sunny Saturday greeted me when I walked out of Bud Wilkinson House early that morning, and I immediately found myself in the midst of a huge throng of home fans already circulating around the stadium. At home games, everyone gets to suit up, so this would be my first game in uniform for the Sooners. We began getting taped about 11:00 A.M. for the 2:00 P.M. kickoff. I'll never forget the feeling of jubilation as we charged out of the south end-zone tunnel and onto Owen Field before about sixty-five thousand screaming fans. I had never experienced anything even remotely similar to that.

The afternoon went well for us, although not as well as we had hoped. Texas Tech had a decent team, but OU had beaten them the year before and we weren't supposed to have any trouble handling the Red Raiders. As it turned out, we did have trouble, winning the game by only six points, 17–11. Still, at the end of the day we were over the .500 mark for the year, which indicates an equal number of wins and losses, and had settled in at 2–1 with Iowa State coming to Norman the following week.

During the week, I reached my goal of moving off the scout team and onto the travel squad; I had made it onto the depth chart as the fourth offensive tackle. To reach this point as a freshman meant a great deal with a team like Oklahoma. Most freshmen wind up being redshirted to give them four years of eligibility as upperclassmen. I didn't mind being redshirted, but I also wanted to travel with the team. The dilemmas was this: if I got any playing time at all because of the injuries among the starting tackles, I would lose that redshirt status, and this year would count as one of my four years of eligibility.

Still, I felt things were starting to go my way and the team's way as well. The next Saturday went well; we hosted the Iowa State Cyclones at Memorial Stadium. This was not supposed to be a tough task for us, and it wasn't. We managed to put together back-to-back wins for the first time that season and won handily, moving to 3–1 on the season with archrival Texas up next.

THE BIG GAME WITH UT

Oklahoma's rivalry with Texas has always been big, and it probably always will be.[1] The Texas confrontation, held every year at the "neutral" site of the Cotton Bowl in Dallas, has long been more than a game. It has been an interstate rivalry between the swagger of the giant Lone Star State and the often thinly masked inferiority complex of Oklahomans. It seems one of the few ways Sooners let themselves feel superior to their southern neighbor is to beat the University of Texas Longhorns in October.

The importance of this game is no scoop to anyone who has followed the Sooners over the decades. It's a big game, and unique for many reasons. For one thing, the game has been sold out at the

Cotton Bowl for fifty-seven consecutive seasons. For another, since 1941 the winner has been awarded the Golden Hat Trophy donated by the State Fair of Texas, which goes on outside the stadium as the game is played. The fair attracts millions of people each year, making it one of the ten largest annual fairs in the world. The OU-Texas game is its centerpiece.

Oklahoma and Texas met for the first time at Austin in 1900, with the Longhorns winning, 28–2. The two teams did not meet at the state fair until 1912; the Longhorns had played the Dallas game against other teams in earlier years. In 1920 the Sooners joined the Missouri Valley Conference, which banned member teams from playing at neutral sites. That same year, Oklahoma A&M (now Oklahoma State) replaced Texas as OU's main opponent. After OU joined the Big Six (now the Big Twelve), they resumed play with Texas at Dallas. By the early 1960s it had become the number one college football rivalry in the country.

Although Texas was not a conference opponent until 1996, the Texas game has always been pivotal for Oklahoma's season. In fact, winning or losing this game has often spelled success or failure for the remainder of Oklahoma's season. The team puts such emotion into preparing for and playing this game that if they lose, it is often difficult for them to muster up emotion for the next game. So if the Sooners lose the Texas game and then go on a low emotional note into the next game, they could lose it as well and wind up with two losses even before the conference season really gets going. But OU never *expects* to lose the game to Texas.

For more than fifty years, the game has been played the second week of October in the Cotton Bowl in Dallas. There is a holiday spirit on the OU campus leading into that weekend, and many professors cancel their classes on the Friday before the game, knowing that few students will show up for class that day anyway. Many OU students head out on Thursday or Friday on the three-hour road trip south to Dallas. There is a Mardi Gras spirit in Dallas during the OU-Texas Weekend, and thousands throng Commerce and other downtown Dallas streets for nonstop partying the night before the game.

The Sooners stay at the Marriott at Dallas–Forth Worth Airport, about fifteen minutes from downtown. Getting to the game on Saturday morning is a lot of fun for the team. They board buses at the hotel and are led by a police escort through the downtown crowds of Sooner and Longhorn fans. People are everywhere, screaming and cheering all the way to the Cotton Bowl. When the team members get off the buses, they are shoulder to shoulder with the fans, who are shouting out good wishes and patting them on the shoulder as they walk by, carrying their gear to the stadium. The fact that the Cotton Bowl is in the middle of the Texas State Fairgrounds and that the Texas State Fair is under way just adds to the day's festivities.

For me, playing in the Cotton Bowl was like coming home. My hometown of Arlington lies between Dallas and Fort Worth, and I had played in the Cotton Bowl during a high school playoff game in 1992, when Arlington Lamar played Dallas Carter. Having made the travel team for the Sooners, I was with the squad in Dallas and again experienced a first: running onto the field of the Cotton Bowl as eighty thousand screaming fans, half of them dressed in red and half in orange, rose to their feet in jubilation to greet the Sooners and the Longhorns. In close OU-Texas games, many of these fans hold that standing position throughout most of the game.

As the game began, it became clear it would be an uphill battle for us. No matter what their national rankings, Texas and Oklahoma have a tradition of giving each other a tough time in the Cotton Bowl. This would be a tough game. It was then that we began a troubling pattern of finding it hard to score points. As the fourth quarter neared its close, we had managed only ten points and were down, 17–10. Still we were hopeful as our offense worked the ball ever closer toward the Longhorn goal line, a drive that ended on the last play of the game and Clark's lucky tackle in our backfield.

It is an OU tradition that the Sooners are allowed to stay in Dallas after the game and return to campus on their own if they wish.

There are numerous opportunities for partying on Saturday night, and it's usually a fun time. I took this option and didn't drive back to Norman until Sunday. I will never forget that drive because it seemed that every overpass I passed under as I drove north on I-35 carried a hand-painted score of the game: UT 17, OU 10.

JUST NOT GOOD ENOUGH

The drumbeat by the Oklahoma press, blaming Coach Gibbs for the loss and a seemingly mediocre season, continued throughout the week as it would the rest of the season. Our inability to score points was a sore point with fans and media alike. Everyone wondered if the team would be able to pull itself together and contend for the Big Eight title as the conference season began in earnest. Although we were 3–2 overall, our victory over Iowa State two weeks before put us at 1–0 in the Big Eight.

But Colorado was next. The game was at Boulder, the Buffaloes were a ranked team, and they were tough. Because of the high elevation in Boulder, the air is thin. I failed to take that into account as I ran onto the field with the team and found myself gasping for breath by the time I got to our sideline. It was a night game, televised by ESPN, and Colorado began its onslaught right from the beginning. Things soon got messy, and before long we had fallen behind and were on our way to losing our third game of the season.

The most memorable moment of this game for me was when my freshman redshirt status was threatened by injuries to two OU tackles as we trailed, 40–7. The coach called for me to take the field, and I immediately recognized the dilemma: this was a losing effort for us, there was no chance of pulling the game out, and as much as I wanted to play I didn't want to lose my redshirt status over this. So I "misplaced" my helmet and in the time it took me to find it, the coach had inserted another player in my stead. My redshirt status remained intact and all that was left for me to do was to watch the Buffs score yet another touchdown as oranges rained down onto the field from the Colorado fans. Colorado's stadium was built with Coors Brewing money, and beer is sold to the fans during the game. I think it's the only college stadium in the country where that happens, and the fans do get drunk and rowdy there as a result. This night was no exception, as their beloved Buffs ran over us and walked away with a 45–7 win.

Reality was now setting in for our team, the fans, and the media, and we all just hoped that we would become bowl eligible by the end of the season. That meant we had to win a total of six regular-season games. We had already lost three, and we had only five left. Fortunately, lowly Kansas was next on our schedule. Even though it would be another road game, we were not expected to have much trouble with the Jayhawks. But the way this season was going, who really knew for sure?

The doubts were justified. In what should have been a pushover game for us, we won by only three points in a low-scoring matchup. Although our defense was strong enough to whip the hapless Jayhawks, once again we failed to prove we could mount a formidable offense. Once again our passing attack failed to materialize, and we were left with a one-dimensional running game for the most part because it is hard to run the ball when you don't have a passing threat. Once again, the injuries during fall camp hurt us, and quarterback Garrick McGee either couldn't hit his receivers or just flat didn't have time to. Everyone ahead of me in the tackle position stayed healthy, however, and I remained on the sidelines, my redshirt status intact for another week.

Now we were 4–3, and 2–1 in the Big Eight. Two more wins and we would be bowl eligible, but we still had Nebraska and Kansas State up ahead, both formidable powers, and cross-state rival Oklahoma State, who in a recent good year had proven they could beat OU. The press continued to call for Coach Gibbs to step down as we prepared for game eight against Kansas State.

The Wildcats were just beginning their surge to power. They had not yet reached the level of national recognition they would enjoy in the years just ahead, but they were fielding a much better team than they had in the years when they were the perennial doormat of the Big Eight Conference. It was a home game for us, but that didn't pull us through. Following our up-and-down pattern for the season, we dropped a close game to K-State, 17–14, playing well but obviously not well enough to win. We were now 4–4 overall and 2–2 in the conference. The future grew more ominous for Gary Gibbs.

My parents, who were sitting in the stands during that 1994 K-State game at Norman, recall the moment when the OU student section started booing Coach Gibbs. One of the students began leading a chant, "We want Howard!" He was referring to the Louisville coach rumored to be favored as a Gibbs successor. My dad said it felt like being in the middle of a bad dream. He wanted to tell the student he was making a big mistake if he thought Howard Schnellenberger would be the coach to lead Oklahoma back into national prominence. But given the student's state of inebriation, he decided not say anything.

The ninth game of the season pitted us at home again, this time against Missouri. Some of the Oklahoma-Missouri games between teams coached by Coach Wilkinson and storied Missouri Coach Dan Devine are among the more memorable clashes for supremacy in the Big Eight. But this season the Tigers were mired in a losing streak—a troubling trend for this once-proud power in the Big Eight. A combination of coaching problems, subpar recruiting, bad execution, and even worse luck had plummeted the Tigers into the second division of the Big Eight. Success breeds success, and Missouri wasn't having much of it lately. Since we had lost the week before, this of course was our week to win, and we did handily. We were now 5–4 and had two more chances to win the bowl-clinching game.

Several major college football programs would greet a 7–4 or even a 6–5 season and a bowl game with a smile, but Oklahoma is not one of them. Although it had been almost ten years since the Sooners had won their last national championship, in 1985, the expectations—or at least the hopes—for that kind of season continue to reign in Oklahoma year after year. Certainly anything less than a 9–2 regular season isn't met with much enthusiasm. So even with the Missouri win and our move back above .500 on the season, the critiques of Coach Gibbs didn't stop.

COACH GIBBS STEPS DOWN

Before the Oklahoma State game we had a game-free week, called a bye week, built into the schedule, so we had two weeks to prepare. This game presented, by far, our better chance at winning the sixth game we needed, because our last game was against mighty Nebraska. But our preparation was thrown off immediately by a story that appeared in the *Daily Oklahoman* the Monday after the Missouri game. The article claimed that Coach Gibbs had decided to resign. The story was premature, to say the least, and it caught us all off guard.

However, a short time later, without notifying either players or coaches, Coach Gibbs shocked us by announcing his resignation at his weekly media luncheon during the bye week.[2] Apparently the media and alumni pressure was too much, and Coach Gibbs decided to step down, effective after this season. We all wondered what this would mean for the future of the team and for each of us personally, but those questions had to wait because we still had two games to go on our season. We took on the OSU Cowboys at Lewis Field in Stillwater the next week. This was my first introduction to one of the few football fields in the country with an east-west orientation and, more significantly, to the intense bedlam rivalry between the orange-clad Cowboys of Oklahoma State and the Big Red of OU. In a normal year this on-field clash is not much of a contest, as the Sooners traditionally win rather handily. But this was not a normal year, and the Cowboys, or the Pokes, as they are also known, had a way of bringing a mediocre team onto the field and surprising everyone with a victory now and then. Somewhat legendary among Cowboy fans, for instance, are the back-to-back OSU wins against the Sooners back in 1965 and 1966, winning one year 17–16 and the next 15–14. Bill-boards along I-35 between the ninety-minute drive from Stillwater to Norman proclaimed the scores for weeks following those two games. And years later, in the year 2000, when the Sooners would be contending for the national championship, they narrowly escaped disaster in Stillwater with a 12–7 victory, just barely preserving their No. 1 status in the country.

So OSU is not a game the Sooners take for granted. On this day in 1994, however, the Cowboys didn't pose that much of a problem for us, and we buried them, 35–3, to claim that important sixth victory and become eligible for a bowl game in the postseason. But the thrill of that victory was tempered by our anxiety over losing our head coach and our worries about what that might mean for the team the next season.

Winning the final game and finishing the season 7–4 would have been a nice gift for us to present to Coach Gibbs. But it didn't help matters much that our last opponent was Nebraska. Under longtime Coach Dr. Tom Osborne, the Cornhuskers were continuing to roll as they had for so many years. But to those who really knew college football, Nebraska was something of an anomaly: although the team had in Osborne one of the most respected coaches in college football, it also had some of the most troublesome players, and its teams didn't exhibit much personal discipline away from the foot-ball field. I had recognized that during my high school recruiting trip to Lincoln a year before.

On the field, however, Nebraska's team was highly ranked and came together behind a huge and talented offensive line. We weren't given much of a chance at winning that day, even though we were playing them in Norman. Our defense was good enough to make it a low-scoring game, but in the end we came out on the short end of a close contest, finishing out the regular season at 6–5. We tried hard that day and did play well. We wanted to win a big one for Gary Gibbs, now the outgoing Sooner coach, but Nebraska was just too tough.

Still, the season wasn't over for us. We were selected to play in the Copper Bowl, out in Tucson, Arizona, pitted against the passing attack of Brigham Young University (BYU). We accepted the invitation, but the game wouldn't affect our national recognition that much, win or lose. We knew it would be nice to finish the season at 7–5 rather than 6–6, but neither record is really the mark of a sterling season, especially given that we had expected to go 10–2 or 9–3 back before the season began. Besides, we were losing not only our head coach but, most likely, the rest of the coaching staff we had worked with all season long. Add to that the fact that our quarterback, Garrick McGee, contracted spinal meningitis and almost died after the regular season ended, and the air was out of the Big Red balloon. We would be starting a receiver-turned-quarterback in the Copper Bowl, and things did not look promising. The result of all this was that in the four weeks of practice before the game, we pretty much just went through the motions.

THE COPPER BOWL AND A NEW COACH

During the 1940s and 1950s, the vote for the national championship was taken at the end of the regular season. This meant that bowls had no bearing on the final rankings and were a true reward for a successful season. Bowl trips were fun and included sightseeing, banquets, and parties. Usually the time between the end of the regular season and the bowl was spent in the classroom preparing for final exams, not on the practice fields.

Beginning in the 1960s, however, things changed. When the Minnesota Gophers went to the Rose Bowl after the 1960 season, they had a fun time, including a trip to Disneyland, but they lost the game. When they returned to the Rose Bowl the next year, they stayed in a monastery. It was like a minimum-security prison. They didn't have fun, but they won the game. From that point forward, going to a bowl game became more drudgery than reward. Now teams hold two-a-day practices in the weeks leading up to the bowl games. They even transport their weight rooms to the bowl sites so the players don't miss a lift. Besides all this, the players still have to go to class and take their final exams.

During the time between the Nebraska game and the Copper Bowl, OU Athletic Director Donnie Duncan announced that Howard Schnellenberger, head coach at the University of Louisville, would be our new head coach for the 1995 season. Chalk up another distraction from our bowl game! Coach Schnellenberger had a history of turning programs around at the University of Miami and even Louisville, and that excited us as we pondered what his coaching would mean for us. But we also knew a new head coach would mean new assistant coaches, and we knew that each of us would have to prove ourselves all over again for the new staff.

As the bowl trip approached, we had little motivation for winning and wound up doing more partying than actual preparation for the game in Tucson. Nevertheless, the Copper Bowl trip was a great experience for me. My grandparents spent the winter living in Sun City, outside of Phoenix, and the bowl game in Tucson gave the family the opportunity to spend Christmas in the desert. The team stayed at the Conquistador Resort Hotel in the mountains north of Tucson, and we split time between my grandparents' place in Sun City and the resort. It also gave my grandparents a chance to see me practice, although they didn't attend the game.

Players for BYU are often a couple years older than other college players because many take time off for their mission work. Families also get started early out in Utah. When the two teams met during a pregame banquet, I counted fifty-three BYU baby strollers. One news reporter described the Oklahoma hotel as "Mardi Gras" and the BYU hotel as "day care."[3]

BYU's head coach had used the two weeks prior to the bowl to revert back to the two-a-day practices of pre-fall training, while we had taken most of that time off. To make matters worse, Duncan gave Howard Schnellenberger the VIP treatment throughout the festivities, ignoring the outgoing coaches. We lost to BYU, 31–6, and looked sluggish in doing so, which only prompted Coach Schnellenberger to proclaim that the situation was worse than he thought, setting him off on his "weight reduction" tirade.

I met the new coach on a chance encounter in the lobby of the hotel before the game. I remember him as very focused on himself in the conversation. This seemed unusual, since all of the coaches I had met prior to that focused on the person to whom they were talking. Allan and my parents were with me, and we explained that Allan also played college football and that my parents split the time between the two of us. That my parents weren't completely committed to Oklahoma seemed to upset the coach.

The only reason I mention this encounter is that it sets the stage for describing our future meetings, which continued to fit the same pattern. The man continued to be an aloof, self-centered bully. If Howard Schnellenberger had been the coach at Oklahoma when I was finishing high school, I wouldn't have even opened the first recruiting letter.

As you might have guessed, my parents and I thought from the outset that choosing Howard Schnellenberger as head coach at Oklahoma was a bad decision. He was never a good coach, and worse, he did not seem like a very likeable person, at least at this time. His career had been tainted with rumors that he stretched the rules. The University of Miami's notoriety as an outlaw program started with Coach Schnellenberger's tenure there. And his reputation for being a disciplinarian was misconstrued; in realty, there is a very distinct line between discipline and abuse, and his behavior seemed abusive. Surely those who hired him at OU had heard the same stories about Howard Schnellenberger that my parents and I had heard. Initially, I understand, he turned OU down. But when OU Athletic Director Donnie Duncan stepped up his efforts to get him, Coach Schnellenberger said yes. My parents were sick at the news.

By now the media attention's was on Coach Schnellenberger and the next season's team. Coach Gibbs was a forgotten man as far as the press was concerned, and this season was about to be a bad memory. The BYU Cougars helped seal that fate by trouncing us.

So my first season with the Sooners was over. Given the choice of almost any program in the country, I had chosen Oklahoma, and things had gone downhill for the team in my first year. In 1993, the year before I committed to OU, it had seemed that the Sooners had turned the corner from the probation years and that the team would again become the national power it had once been.

What a difference a year makes. This was 1994, and losses to Colorado, Texas, and Nebraska left OU's head coach, Gary Gibbs, with a 2–15–1 record against the Big Three. Even though Oklahoma was invited to play in the Copper Bowl, Coach Gibbs still lost his job. The era of Coach Gary Gibbs was now history at OU. One head coach was now gone, and three more would come before I would bid goodbye to the team five years later.

During the summer following my first year at OU, I was invited to travel to Tempe, Arizona, to visit the parents of a girl I was dating at OU. I didn't know at the time that they lived down the street from the Arizona State offensive line coach, Dan Cozzetto. Given the football connection, Coach Cozzetto and I were both invited to a party on a Saturday night at my hosts' home, so I had a chance to talk with him. He said that it looked like I had been "run to death," but he also told me that ASU had a scholarship available for me if I wanted to transfer.

I opted to stay at Oklahoma. I was afraid I had gotten too small for Pac-10 football. My original goal was to be a three-year starter, and the OU depth chart made it clear that there I could stick to that goal. Also, I had chosen OU not only because of the coach but also because it was the school I would have attended even if I hadn't been on a football scholarship. When Coach Gibbs left, everything else I liked about Oklahoma remained intact. There was no reason to leave.

CHAPTER 4

Coach Schnellenberger
THE YEAR-LONG BOOT CAMP

They ran through the briars and they ran through the brambles...

JOHNNY HORTON

An unforgettable scene in the movie *Patton* depicts George C. Scott as the flamboyant, egomaniacal General George Patton standing in full military dress, right down to his shiny black riding boots and ivory-handled pistols, ordering his men to "make the other poor fools die for their country." That image always reminds me of Coach Howard Schnellenberger, the man from Louisville who was hired to rebuild our football program at OU in 1995.

From the outset Coach Schnellenberger, or "Howard," as everyone called him, brought a strict, dictatorial, military bearing to his job as our new head coach. He treated the off-season training program, training camps, and practices like Marine boot camps, and the players were his "grunts," whom he vowed to tear down and build up in his perfect image. Most of us had played football for many years—through middle school, high school, and college. Clearly we were all dedicated to the game or we wouldn't have been recruited by OU. Several of us were good enough to be called bluechippers. We had seen tough coaches before, but we had never seen anyone like Coach Howard Schnellenberger.

Coach Schnellenberger had the personal background for all this. An ex-Marine trainee and a U.S. Army man who had coached under hard-driving Coach Paul "Bear" Bryant of Alabama, he was the field general in more ways than one. Perhaps the difference between Schnellenberger and Patton, however, was Schnellenberger's apparent desire to see his own players drop in pursuit of victory. It seemed to be one of his goals to see as many players as possible wilt from exhaustion or dehydration during practice and to get them on IV solutions. The IV effect seemed to be an index for him that his players were really putting out maximum effort.

As *Houston Chronicle* writer Bill Sullivan wrote, "The new staff was prepared to see as many as 20 players quit."[1] Sullivan's prediction was well on its way to proving true even before the regular season began. Preferring the highway to Schnellenberger's way were players like Dusty Loveless—the first to leave—followed by Brian Andres (Brian had fought with a graduate assistant who had jerked his helmet off and hit him in the head with it), Terry Collier, Perry Collier, Tim Denton, and Jason Harmon. Meanwhile, Paul Oatts, Tyrell Peters, and others seriously considered it, and some of them left before the year was out.

In the end, Schnellenberger's brand of treatment was a big reason for the eventual doom that met the coach after his first and only season leading the Sooners. More about that later.

WHO IS HOWARD SCHNELLENBERGER?

So how did Howard Schnellenberger become the new Moses who would lead the Sooners to the Promised Land? When Coach Gibbs resigned the season before, speculation about his successor had been rife. The day after Gibbs resigned, columnist John Rohde of the *Daily Oklahoman* listed twenty-six "plausible" candidates for the job. Howard Schnellenberger's name was not among them. Notables on that list were Barry Alvarez (Wisconsin), Frank Beamer (Virginia Tech), John Blake (Dallas Cowboys defensive line coach), Mack Brown (North Carolina), Watson Brown (OU offensive coordinator), John Cooper (Ohio State), Merv Johnson (OU assistant head coach), Rick Neuheisel (Colorado QB coach), Lucious Selmon (OU outside linebackers coach), and Mike Shanahan (San Francisco 49ers offensive coordinator).

In another *Daily Oklahoman* article that same day, OU Athletic Director Donnie Duncan mentioned no possible candidates at all, simply setting December 15 as the deadline by which OU wanted to have a new head coach in place. Duncan said he had talked with new OU President David Boren (who had been on the job only five days), and they would be constructing a short list soon. Staff writer Bob Hersom wrote that the only hint Duncan gave was that none of OU's assistants would get the job.

Some of us had hoped that the new head coach might be Watson Brown, Merv Johnson, or Lucious Selmon, all currently with the OU program as assistants, but the Hersom story seemed to burst that bubble. We knew that Barry Switzer had been promoting John Blake to OU athletic officials that year. In an interview with Blake, the *Daily Oklahoman*'s Mike Baldwin said that the Dallas coach liked "his chances of becoming the next football coach at Oklahoma." Blake was only thirty-three at the time, but Terry Donahue had been younger than that when he was named head coach at UCLA. Blake had been a player and an assistant coach at OU, he was known as a standout recruiter, and he seemed like the favored candidate. Instead of a young coach with a strong connection with OU, however, OU would choose a sixty-year-old with absolutely no ties to the campus.

By all signs and accounts, Howard Schnellenberger was Duncan's personal choice. Something about the Louisville coach intrigued the athletic director enough to hire him. So Duncan announced that Schnellenberger was his choice, and the new coach signed with OU on December 16. He had a background both in the pros and in college coaching. He had been an assistant with the Los Angeles

Rams from 1966 to 1969. As a Miami Dolphins assistant, he was part of the 17–0 Super Bowl team of 1972. He then moved on to coach the Baltimore Colts, but he was let go in 1974, the middle of his second season.

As a college coach, Schnellenberger was seen as a rebuilder, having taken the University of Miami from the brink of dropping its football program to winning the national championship in 1983. He left Miami to coach the U.S. Football League franchise in Miami, but the team folded before playing a game. He then accepted the head coaching job in his hometown at the University of Louisville. It was a school with one of the worst football programs in the country, but before long he had the team winning more games than before. His lifetime college coaching record was 100–76–3. That's not great, but the fact he took the University of Miami Hurricanes to the national championship overshadowed his overall record.

Now Schnellenberger told the media he felt the time was right to leave Louisville, largely because he disagreed with the school's decision to join Conference USA. He said he didn't think this league would propel its teams into national recognition, and beating the likes of Cincinnati, Houston, Tulane, and Memphis wouldn't attract the kind of national exposure he sought for his team. Also, OU was a clear step up in football programs in every way, from its funding and facilities to its national reputation to the quality of its players.

Sportswriter Dave Sittler said the following about Schnellenberger's motivation in coming to OU: "The five-year, multi-million-dollar contract offered by OU got his attention. But money can't buy the one thing Schnellenberger wants most out of his life—immortality. The 60-year-old Schnellenberger has often said that when he dies, his fondest wish is to be remembered as the first coach to win a national championship at two schools."[2]

However he saw himself fitting into the OU tradition, Howard Schnellenberger was the opposite of Gary Gibbs, and certainly of Barry Switzer. For one thing, he was the oldest head coach the college had hired in a long, long time. The past three decades had produced a tradition of young coaches at OU, with Chuck Fair-banks, Barry Switzer, and Gary Gibbs. You'd have to go back to the Gomer Jones days in the 1960s to find a coach of Howard Schnel-lenberger's age.

But that was only one difference. Schnellenberger was only one of two head coaches OU had ever hired outside the Oklahoma "fam-ily" of assistant coaches since the Bud Wilkinson era, the other being Jim Mackenzie in 1966, who died after his first season. Also, whereas Gibbs had kept a low profile with both the team and the media, Coach Schnellenberger insisted on hogging the spotlight. He had to be the focus of most conversations.

Coach Schnellenberger admitted his egotism. When Sittler asked him why he didn't return to the NFL, he said it was because "the coach is not the MVP of the team. That doesn't excite me." He defi-nitely liked to focus attention on himself, and he did it in a number of ways. Sittler reported, for example, that Schnellenberger's Louis-ville home was no less than seven thousand square feet in size, and that he had sold it for $750,000.[3]

As Rick Bozich, sports columnist for the Louisville *Courier-Journal*, said about him, "He's obsessed with being in the spotlight. I think he got tired of not being in the spotlight (at Louisville)." And then Bozich added, ironically as it turns out, "He's total football, and I don't think he wants to ever retire. He'll be at OU as long as they let him."[4] In his short time at OU, he proclaimed us the "Sooner Nation" and named himself as supreme commander.

The new coach's seemingly huge ego and his old-school methods were matched by his extravagant style. In public he was always dressed in black slacks tucked military-style into big black combat boots. His military demeanor was satirized by one syndicated editor-ial cartoon that showed him in his riding boots, carrying a sword and barking to his players, "Gone are the days of earrings, bandannas, rainbow hairdos and girls in the dorm!" His pipe became his trade-mark, and he was always strutting about, puffing on it. He'd even smoke it in our weight room during lifting sessions. I remember thinking how much I valued clean air as I was gasping for breath while lifting weights. In would come the coach with his pipe lit, literally and figuratively blowing smoke, often accompanied by someone he was trying to impress.

Former associates listed some of Coach Schnellenberger's traits: He's a workaholic, an excellent coach who will push his players and the rules to the limit; he loves the media spotlight and has a huge ego.[5] In my mind, with the possible exception of the "excellent coach" moniker, these traits fit him to a tee. As for pushing the NCAA rules to the limit, he certainly did that, as I'll discuss later.

Another difference between Gibbs and Schnellenberger was that Coach Gibbs took the blame for poor team performance, whereas Schnellenberger usually deflected that blame to the players. It didn't help us as a team that we had capped the 1994 season with such a sluggish performance in the Copper Bowl against BYU. But that sluggishness was the result of low motivation, the pending loss of Coach Gibbs, and too much partying in Tucson. It was not typical of how we played on the field in the 1994 season. Still, that was the first game Coach Schnellenberger saw us play, as he was being wined and dined by OU officials after having just been announced as head coach for the next season.

He told the *Daily Oklahoman* after the game, "It was the most embarrassing thing that happened to an Oklahoma football team since the War." This comment from a man who had hardly set foot in the state up to this time.[6] Nevertheless, what he thought he saw was a slow, bloated team, and he vowed to get us into shape. Thus began Schnellenberger's infamous one-thousand-pound weight-loss program for the OU football team.

THE WEIGHT-LOSS PROJECT

For us, the Schnellenberger nightmare started in January 1995, right after we returned to campus from the Copper Bowl loss. Coach Schnellenberger immediately began his program to drop one thousand pounds off the linemen. Although some did need to get into better shape, I was not among them. Still, I was tossed into the mix and dropped quickly to 254 pounds, which was less than I had weighed during my sophomore year at Lamar High School. In addition, I tore an arch during sprints and missed some of the workouts leading up to spring practice. For Coach Schnellenberger, this was malingering. It got to the point where he even questioned the validity of my injury. So I continued to work out when the trainers said I should be on crutches.

The off-season training program was run by Joe Juraszek, our strength coach, who was one of four assistant coaches retained by Coach Schnellenberger as his regime began. Gary Nord was our new offensive coordinator, and Kurt Van Valkenburgh was the new defensive coordinator. Both were strong supporters of Coach Schnellenberger as the season began. Nord had been with him for eleven years, and Van Valkenburgh had been with him for four years.

Juraszek knew what Coach Schnellenberger wanted, and he engineered the training program to get the desired weight-loss results. The daily regimen began the second week of January, and it was grueling. Each morning at 6:00 we hit the indoor football training facility behind Bud Wilkinson House to work our way through eight boot-camp-style drills. On the infield of the indoor track, the coaches had set up a true military obstacle course complete with ropes, pegboard climbing wall, sandbags to haul over a designated course, a two-mile run—the works. The worst of the drills was a seventy-five-rung overhead monkey-bar structure that we had to traverse from a hanging position, hand over hand. I felt like I'd joined the Marines instead of a football team.

As far as the run was concerned, Coach Juraszek added a little twist to make it even harder. On every lap around the eight-mile track, whoever was running last was required to sprint up to take over first place, adding wind sprints to an already tiring distance run. We still had to find other times during the day to lift weights; this morning program was just part of Coach Schnellenberger's plan to lean up the team by one thousand pounds. This daily grind, which he named "the Breakfast Club," ran for eight weeks, right up to spring break, and it was brand new in the annals of OU off-season training programs. Beyond normal off-season weight training, earlier teams had not had a February-March program.

To make the morning program even more like a military boot camp, Coach Schnellenberger's assistants would verbally abuse the players, constantly yelling at us, tearing us down, and accusing us of dogging it. If they felt you were really subpar or if, God forbid, you missed one of these mornings, you had to show up at 5:00 the next morning and do an additional distance run—often in the snow or ice outside—before going through the normal 6:00 A.M. workout.

Based only on his assessment of the Copper Bowl performance, Coach Schnellenberger had clearly decided the team lacked discipline, and his response was to implement the boot camp mentality. His rules included no resting on a knee, no sunglasses for the coaches, and no water on the practice field. This severe treatment not only covered players and coaches but extended to the fans as well. During a spring scrimmage a young mother spread out a blanket so that her three little children could sit down, and Schnellenberger sent a student trainer over to tell her she had to stand up. The fans were not supposed to carry water or wear sunglasses either.

Boot camp mentality aside, having practice without an abundant supply of water was simple stupidity. My high school is a point for comparison: Arlington Lamar High School recently consolidated its team by bringing the ninth graders into the high school. As a result, 250 players tried out on the first day of pre-fall football practice in August. The head coach commented after the first practice that the team went through five hundred gallons of water. A more ordinary example is provided by my dad, who estimates that he drinks at least two to three quarts of water every time he mows the lawn in the summer. Considering this, I cannot imagine in my wildest dreams what Schnellenberger was thinking when he held practices without water. Some of us wondered if it was just part of an extremely harsh personality.

The new treatment caught the attention of the media on more than one occasion. After the season ended, on December 24, 1995, the *Oklahoman* wrote, "Purportedly the most serious issue for [President] Boren was Schnellenberger's treatment of his players and his relationship with them. Boren is believed to have become seriously concerned and upset about two players being treated for heat exhaustion in the summer."[7]

One of those players, Aaron Findley, quit the team to recover from his health problems. According to the *Oklahoman*, his mother, Aundra Anderson, said that Aaron had complained about feeling ill, but a trainer did not send him to a doctor. The other player mentioned by President Boren was freshman defensive tackle Bryan Ailey, who "apparently came close to death." That's how it appeared to those of us on the team, too. As I recall, Bryan spent a lot of time in the hospital. His mother, Marsha Higginbotham, told the newspaper that President Boren had called and spoke to her for forty-five minutes about Bryan. The *Oklahoman* reported that "Boren stepped in after getting calls from a hospital emergency room. Concerned about the health of players, Boren purportedly called Schnellenberger and asked him to moderate his practices."[8]

Figures from the University of North Carolina in 2001 showed that eighteen high school or college players had died of heat-related causes nationwide since 1995,[9] the year that Ailey almost succumbed under Coach Schnellenberger's regime. That his was not a unique case didn't make it any less serious. As OU Director of Football Operations Merv Johnson later said: "That [Ailey's experience] was probably the scariest situation I've been around. We didn't know for a couple of days whether he was going to make it."[10] For his part, however, Coach Schnellenberger told the AP in a September 21, 1995, report: "He was unconscious, as most heat stroke people are. [But] he was never close to dying. They never told me that."

Ailey wouldn't be the last Sooner to suffer from heat exhaustion, but he would be among the last players to practice where no water was available when they needed it. And other safety-related measures were in the offing as well. Later, in 2000 under Coach Bob Stoops, for example, the Sooners altered their two-a-day practice schedule because of the heat, starting morning practice at 8:00 A.M., with the second session beginning at 6:15 P.M.

As Stoops said in 2001: "It takes good communication between players and coaches and trainers. We need to know if they've had any dehydration, or any cramping or any vomiting the night before. We understand everyone wants to be on the field, but we need to know your condition before we're on the field. It is for your own health. We know you want to practice, but if you've had a situation where you've lost fluid, or if our trainers or doctors don't feel you have enough in your tank, we're not going to allow you to."[11]

Coach Schnellenberger's practices of limiting water might not have been unusual twenty or thirty years ago, but as Dan O'Kane noted in his story on the subject, they were in the 1990s and they continue to be today. Whereas in the past players may have been used to being outdoors more while growing up, today's players grew up inside, for the most part, and are less conditioned to the heat than their predecessors were. It could be that Schnellenberger just didn't understand that well enough.

In any case, because of the harsh treatment, team members were doing a lot of complaining. We would talk about it to each other much more than to the media, but sometimes players would speak out publicly. Senior quarterback Garrick McGee recalled the early rough treatment, both physical and verbal, but said he eventually noticed a change for the better. Possibly that improvement came after Boren's call to the coach or later in the year, when Coach Schnellenberger started distancing himself more from the team at practices. An anonymous senior player was quoted by the *Oklahoman* as saying that before Schnellenberger's era, he had not seen OU coaches act like that. He cited the verbal abuse and "them grabbing you by the face mask and jerking you" and concluded, "I've seen more verbal abuse this past year than I have previous years. He [Schnellenberger] said something like we weren't working hard enough because we didn't pass out."[12]

Throughout the nightmare I was in the worst possible position. I knew better than anyone what was happening, yet I couldn't blow the whistle for fear of NCAA sanctions against the whole team or retaliation by the coach. To understand my position one must remember that in football at any level, the coach determines who plays and who doesn't. Careers are made and destroyed by the actions of the coach. If he blackballs you, you are not going to play.

Many of us younger players on the team, with our futures hanging in the balance, were afraid to criticize Coach Schnellenberger to the media. Many of us also thought at first that our hard work would have good results on the playing field. What we didn't realize was that success on the playing field depends on the *nature* of your hard work. If you spend all your time on a military obstacle course instead of drilling on football fundamentals, you may not perform well at all in a game situation. If all you do is run physical drills that have nothing to do with developing football skills, then you may create a killer attitude but you don't develop the needed skills. We became great at hauling heavy bags, but how exactly does that develop your blocking or tackling or ball-carrying skills? Indeed, one of the hallmarks of the coming season would be Sooner losses because of fumbles, missed blocks, missed tackles, and penalties.

As time went on, some players pushed the envelope, rebelling against the program to see exactly what they could and could not get away with. Several found they could *not* disagree with Coach Schnellenberger on the nitpicky points, like his prohibition against wearing a hat inside a building, but they *could* get away with missing spring or fall practice sessions. Over time the coach lost control of the team and discipline waned.

Sportswriter Ray Buck wrote about this in his online SportsLine USA column on December 23, 1995, after Schnellenberger's departure: "Speaking of practice, players reportedly came and went as they pleased. As one reporter assigned to the team said, 'With Howard, you couldn't wear a hat inside the building, but you could decide whether you wanted to go to practice or not.'"[13]

This pattern became more prevalent as the 1995 regular season wore on, especially after we dropped our first game and the coach himself started wandering away from practices for an hour or more at a time. But the philosophy behind Schnellenberger's coaching approach, carried out mostly by his assistants, was straight out of old Marine training manuals. Maybe Coach Schnellenberger got it from his days as an assistant with Alabama's Coach Bryant, but wherever he got it, it didn't work for us.

As for his weight-loss program, it failed. Anytime an athlete who is already in good condition loses thirty pounds over a short period of time, there is a loss of muscle as well as fat. If you cause your players to lose muscle strength as well as weight, then your cure is worse than your problem. As for our "problem," we didn't think Schnellenberger had diagnosed it right, anyway. We were not a sluggish team, and weight had not been our problem during the 1994 season. The bowl game in which Schnellenberger saw us being ripped by BYU was indicative of nothing as far as we were concerned. We simply had no motivation to win that game after our coaching staff had quit.

My case illustrates the problem. I had less than 15 percent body fat during my freshman year, and I dropped to 9 percent body fat in the spring of Coach Schnellenberger's campaign to cut weight from the line. By the first scrimmage of the fall, I had worked my way back up through the upperclassmen to second on the depth chart, at tackle. But during a scrimmage I hyperextended my left elbow. This was an injury that I felt was directly attributed to the loss of strength and exhaustion from the endless, waterless, two-a-day practices. Unfortunately, that elbow was more than enough excuse for Coach Schnellenberger to keep me on the bench through much of the season.

The military-style physical training program was supplemented by a crash team diet that consisted of nothing but chicken, rice, and vegetables two times a day for those first eight weeks. The one exception was Wednesday night, which was steak night. It got to the point that many of us couldn't face chicken for some time after that. For me, the bottom line was a weight drop from 270 pounds to 240. That is incredibly light for an offensive lineman; more like the weight of a linebacker. I knew I played best at a weight closer to 285, and that if I stayed at that low weight, my chances at starting as lineman would be few; even if I did play, I'd probably be run over by opposing 300-pound linemen.

Weight loss, in and of itself, isn't necessarily bad as long as you understand the consequences, some of which are not good for athletes who need their strength, like football players. The two main drawbacks to the amount of weight loss Coach Schnellenberger was aiming for are first, the loss of muscle strength, and second, increased vulnerability to injuries. When the off-season program ended, the team had dropped a total of 748 pounds, and Coach Schnellenberger proclaimed that he had met his goal of making us leaner and faster. But we had also lost a lot of muscle strength, something he didn't announce.

SCHNELLENBERGER'S SPRING TRAINING

Looking back, I see that one of the major problems with the 1995 OU football season was that the coach was chasing two goals that clashed dramatically. The first goal was for his team to drop those one thousand pounds, which prevented us from reaching our second goal, winning the national championship. You don't send a lightweight team onto the field expecting them to do battle with giants and to win all their games.

Coach Schnellenberger had kept four assistant coaches from the Gibbs era: Clarence James, the receivers coach; Merv Johnson, the offensive line coach; Lucious Selmon, the defensive line coach, and

Juraszek, our strength coach. These four, like the new assistants, understood the main rule of working for Howard Schnellenberger: that you buy into his philosophy or you are gone. "Howard's way or the highway," it was called in camp. So to secure their positions, most of these coaches bought into his philosophy. But often the signals got mixed between coaches and players.

Again, my training is a good example of the confusion. I remember going to Coach Johnson after I'd dropped thirty pounds in a few weeks and telling him I feared I was way too light for my position. He agreed and said, "I never had a problem with your weight." That was news to me, because I was worked just as hard and endured the same chicken and rice diet as everyone else. No one told me I didn't need to lose weight. So that summer I added back twenty pounds during the month of June, to get myself up to 260 and have a fighting chance for playing time.

Fueling the coaching pressure behind this grueling off-season program was, of course, Coach Schnellenberger's pronouncement from the start that we were going to win the national championship our first season out. This was not a coach given to saying he was going to work toward that goal and achieve it within two or three years. No, we were going to win it during his very first season as head coach. The national championship theme became a constant mantra, delivered relentlessly for the media and fans. He even had the players believing it for awhile. The mantra reached the national level when *Sports Illustrated* showed up at one of our spring practice sessions and Coach Schnellenberger announced to its reporter we would win the championship in 1995. Somewhere in the midst of this off-season, it obviously occurred to all the OU coaches that they'd better produce or else they'd look rather foolish in the public eye. So they tightened the screws on us, and the pressure was shoved down to the player level.

In any event, spring break was a welcome relief that year. The daily morning obstacle course was over, and many of us thought spring training would be a breeze in comparison. We received a jolt, however, when the coaches told us that our rankings for position would be set up initially by seniority and not on the basis of where we finished after the 1994 season. Coach Schnellenberger had decided that he wouldn't rank us on the basis of our performance in 1994; in fact, he wouldn't even view game films from that season. If you were a senior, you were slotted ahead of a junior or sophomore, even if you were not as good in your position. As a result, as spring training began, I was dropped off the depth chart not only by the first four positions, but by six positions, from fourth to tenth. And that was after having worked so hard to get there in the first place. Along with others in the same boat, I would now have to prove myself all over again to make the depth chart. If we were going to reclaim our old positions, we'd have to do it during spring training. So much for breezing our way through.

Daily spring training began at 4:00 P.M. with ten fifty-yard wind sprints. Then we would practice for two and a half to three hours over the four-week period. Practices were intense, and Coach Schnellenberger's presence was right there in the middle of it all. Literally. As we scrimmaged, he would occupy the position of referee, standing in linebacker territory and barking out orders. It seemed he would erupt on every play; nothing was good enough, no one was really trying hard enough for him. So no one was sorry to see him get blasted when running back De'Mond Parker ran right over him because he got in the way.

When he wasn't in the defensive backfield, Coach Schnellenberger would be up on what we would call "Howard's Tower," yelling out orders from above like the Ten Commandments coming down from God. The tower was actually the camera lift from where team photographers would shoot the practices for review the next day. Coach Schnellenberger would often go up with the cameraman, sometimes thirty feet in the air, and fill that air with his diatribes to us below. As a player, you had no trouble hearing Coach Howard Schnellenberger. Or smelling him, thanks to his ever-present pipe.

One of the things football teams don't do is practice during lightning storms. But that is exactly what we did during one Saturday practice scrimmage. The few spectators—parents and close friends—were huddled under the upper deck on the stadium's west side. They were smarter than we were; they didn't want to get struck by the lightning that was registering on the sideline meters as too close for comfort. The threat of lightning was matched by a driving rainstorm, which was quickly filling the sideline areas with standing water as we practiced in thirty-five-degree March weather. Three or four guys actually developed hypothermia from sliding through the near-freezing water that day. I remember a couple offensive backs disappearing completely in the end zone as they slid under a few feet of standing water, only to surface spewing water out of their mouths.

Commenting on that scrimmage to Dan O'Kane of the *Tulsa World*, Coach Schnellenberger said: "It was very important for us to practice in the rain and cold. Your offensive style needs to be able to change. You have to have the experience of going through inclement weather like today." He told O'Kane that he had considered postponing the scrimmage because of the threatening weather and that he finally stopped it when "it ceased being productive."[14]

The workouts not only took their toll on me physically, but they also hurt me dearly in academics. When I came to Oklahoma, one of my goals was to be an Academic All-American. I had proven during my freshman year that this was possible by obtaining a 3.3 GPA in my first semester and a 3.1 overall in my first year. Over the winter I was awarded the Athletic Director's Award for Academic Achievement for the first semester. However, it took only one semester under Coach Schnellenberger's coaching regime to snuff out my academic dream. My grades plummeted, as did the grades of my teammates. My GPA dropped so much that no matter what I did the rest of my college career, my cumulative GPA would never again be high enough to make Academic All-American. I feel grateful that in my final two years of school I was able to elevate my GPA enough to get into OU's well-respected MBA program.

Through it all, day after day, it became obvious that talking with Coach Schnellenberger was almost impossible. Players were so intimidated by him that most stayed away and tried to talk to their position coaches instead. Sometimes even that communication was impossible when it came to subjects like individually targeted weight goals. As for Coach Schnellenberger, he seemed to prefer his own company, keeping aloof from the players. Indeed, he was doing well simply to remember our names, which he often didn't do. Reflecting on the season just passed, Ray Buck wrote the following about Schnellenberger in his December 19 SportsLine USA column: "Through it all, Schnellenberger remained aloof and arrogant. Players used to laugh among themselves at his lack of discipline and total loss of control. This clearly was a man whose best foot forward was four years ago in Louisville. Lately, he had lost his grip." Then Buck added this barb: "In fact, members of the media used to have bets on how many players Howie knew by name. Most felt he couldn't name all 22 starters—even if his next drink depended on it."

Ray Buck's reference to the coach's "next drink" brings up the controversy and stories surrounding Coach Schnellenberger's drinking habits. It's a fact that we players did smell alcohol on his breath, sometimes during practice. This happened a lot, and many of us cracked jokes about it when he wasn't around. Articles in the *Oklahoman* and the *Tulsa World* alluded to it several times. For example, on December 24, a few days after Coach Schnellenberger left OU, Bob Hersom of the *Oklahoman* wrote, "Then there were the reports of drinking. Officials are said to have been unsure what to make of reports from players, players' parents and athletic department personnel about smelling alcohol on the coach's breath. No such reports were heard when Schnellenberger was being recruited from his former coaching position at Louisville . . . and no one ever said they saw him falling down drunk." According to Hersom, Cleveland County law enforcement agencies had no reports indicating that Coach Schnellenberger had ever been pulled over for any violations, and his administrative assistant, Ron Steiner, dismissed the whole drinking issue in an interview with the *Oklahoman*.

Hersom wrote: "Drinking was just one of many reports, or rumors, that cannot be proven or which can be traced to humble and insignificant beginnings." But he later noted, "Still, persistent reports to OU officials of alleged drinking (according to a "well-placed source") made several officials wonder: If Schnellenberger were drinking, was it because of stress? Was alcohol behind some seemingly 'reckless' remarks he had made? Was it contributing to the lack of respect many players obviously had for him?"

The *Tulsa World* seemed more emphatic about the drinking issue. A couple of days before the *Oklahoman* article, on December 22, writer Dan O'Kane wrote:

> Two high-level sources, who have asked that their names not be revealed, confirmed OU compliance officer Larry Naifeh interviewed players and athletic department personnel seeking information about Schnellenberger's personal habits, including the consumption of alcohol on university property and while representing the school in official business. Naifeh reportedly spoke with a player who smelled alcohol on Schnellenberger's breath during a university-related function. That would constitute a violation of university policy and put him in violation of his contract.[15]

The story continued, stating that although Coach Schnellenberger had repeatedly denied reports of his drinking while on the job, "the prospects of the rumors becoming public would make the job of rebuilding the football program next to impossible." Neither Athletic Director Donnie Duncan nor Naifeh would comment publicly on the drinking issue or the specifics of Coach Schnellenberger's abrupt departure.

The coach himself has repeatedly denied the reports of his excessive drinking. Aside from the season with us at OU, there appears to be no mention of a drinking problem at the other universities where he worked. Perhaps the issue was unique to his year at OU. Perhaps the kind of pressure he heaped upon himself, and us, created an extraordinary environment for him personally. I don't know, but I don't think any of this was key to our bad season under Howard Schnellenberger. He was just a bad fit in many ways.

THE DOG DAYS OF SUMMER

For me, spring training ended well. Through persistence and effort, I had managed to climb from tenth position to third as offensive lineman. I was back on the depth chart, in a position ahead of my final 1994 standing. I would probably not start as the regular season opened the next fall, but I would definitely get playing time as the top back-up lineman.

With spring practice over, we were released to take our finals and head home for the rest of May and June. I used the time to regain most of the weight I had lost during the February and March military drills. But unlike previous years when the team didn't have to return until August for fall camp, this year Coach Schnellenberger summoned us back in July for six weeks of conditioning before fall camp began in mid-August. The crux of this program was a daily two-mile run, which we often called the "Deli Run" because we would run down to the deli on West Lindsey and back again to make the required distance. Depending on your position, you were required to make this run in anywhere from twelve to eighteen minutes. It was good exercise, but it did nothing for developing your agility as a football player.

As summer began, Coach Schnellenberger took to the skies and the open road for what he called the "Boomer Sooner Blitz," making seventy stops in thirty Oklahoma towns and driving home his point that OU would definitely win the national championship next time up. The blitz generated a lot of publicity, and before it was over, most of the state had heard—often more than once—that we would be national champs after his first year with us. Most of the state's towns ate it up. The Houston *Chronicle*'s Bill Sullivan reported in an August 21 article that the City of Idabel honored Schnellenberger with an official Coach Schnellenberger Day, and Altus commemorated his visit with flowery proclamations. Cities like Seminole, Clinton, Weatherford, and McAlester gave him keys to the city. Is OU football big in Oklahoma? You bet.

"In McAlester, Schnellenberger signed autographs for three hours. In Pauls Valley, when word spread that the coach had stopped in a pastry shop, 100 people turned out to meet him and get his signature. In Lindsay, a radio station broadcast live from the street as fans waved signs and cameras clicked away, capturing the moment for posterity," Sullivan wrote. The response from the towns was incredible, and Schnellenberger loved it. However, as the season progressed, this local acclaim would only add to the pressure, leaving us in a bit of a lurch after we lost our first game, four contests into the season. More about that later.

Like the winter off-season training, this July conditioning program was new for OU, although the tradition has continued and under Coach Bob Stoops, the team has had to come back in June. College football has definitely become a full-time job for players in major programs like Oklahoma's. The time spent in conditioning, lifting, practicing, and playing—in addition to the millions of dollars teams bring to their university through television contracts and bowl games—has fueled the rhetoric of those advocates who say college players should be paid.

As August practice began in earnest, we could tell there would be no letup in Coach Schnellenberger's relentless regimen. Two-a-days began, and with only two hours between morning and afternoon practices, most of us didn't even bother to change our sweat-soaked pants after the morning drills. We'd just leave the field, head for lunch, then crash in the locker room for an hour before having to start all over again in the afternoon heat. On one occasion, Coach Schnellenberger was so displeased with our performance that he instituted a three-a-day practice regimen. Whether you've got two practices a day or three is immaterial, however; in either case it is impossible to do your best work when you are working all day in wet pants.

Two-a-days lasted for five days, after which Coach Schnellenberger pronounced to the media, in effect, that most of us were wimps. He said he was disappointed in the way we wilted under the "dog days of summer," a phrase he used again and again as if he'd invented it. One of the toughest things to bear was his limits on water breaks.

Until President Boren intervened, we had no water on the field during practice, and dehydration continued to be a big problem. After one scorching practice, Coach Schnellenberger quipped that Bobby Bowden at Florida State had eleven players on IVs, while OU had only nine. The inference was that FSU was working harder than OU. In order to protect myself, I would carry a one-gallon milk container filled with water during taping and prepractice meetings so I could overhydrate prior to practice.

Several players dropped from the intense Oklahoma heat and lack of water, and in Bryan Ailey's case, the problem was serious. The *Tulsa World* reported on December 19 that Ailey had been dehydrated the night before his last practice because of the flu. But Ailey charged later that he did not have the flu, and that this was a false story planted by Coach Schnellenberger. Whatever the case, at that practice, only one day after he reported to fall practice, the freshman from Fairland, Oklahoma, sustained a heat stroke. He collapsed shortly after walking off the field. The *World* noted, "He reportedly was close to dying and was hospitalized for a week. He never did return to football."

The *World* added, "The players, however, indicated that the incident with Ailey wasn't isolated. 'During two-a-days, we had guys falling out all the time,' said a senior player who asked that his name not be used. 'You'd go in the training room and you'd have five people lying on the table with towels on them trying to keep them warm, having to keep fluids in them because their body is cramping up.'" As one of the players who practiced under these conditions and felt the same dehydration, I can attest to the truth of that player's remarks. Tough was tough, but this seemed crazy.

Bryan Ailey thought Coach Schnellenberger was so off base with his treatment that he filed two lawsuits against him and the OU Board of Regents. The first suit was filed August 9, 1996, in Cleveland County District Court against Coach Howard Schnellenberger, seven of his assistants, and Athletic Director Donnie Duncan. In that suit, Bryan cited incidents on or after August 11, 1995, ". . . wherein the Plaintiff sustained injuries caused by the negligent, willful, wanton and/or intentional actions of the defendants." It further stated,

> Defendants willfully ignored recognized safety precautions concerning prevention of heat-related illnesses to athletes, thereby causing severe injury to the Plaintiff. Plaintiff was practicing in conditions of extreme heat and humidity. Defendants repeatedly denied water to the Plaintiff. After Plaintiff suffered a heat stroke caused by Defendants' actions, and was hospitalized, Defendants verbally ridiculed and harassed Plaintiff about his injuries.

The allegations went even further, stating,

> Defendant Howard Schnellenberger made false and malicious statements to third parties concerning Plaintiff's physical condition prior to the incident, thereby slandering and defaming Plaintiff.
>
> As a result of Defendants' negligent, willful, wanton and slanderous and defamatory actions, Plaintiff Bryan C. Ailey suffered severe bodily injury, mental anguish and harm to his reputation. These injuries have caused Plaintiff to incur medical expenses, pain and suffering, loss of income, loss of scholarship, and other damages.

The suit asked to recover "from each Defendant, an amount in excess of $10,000, together with costs and such other relief as the Court deems proper."

That petition was amended the following April to include the OU Board of Regents as defendants in the suit. The amended suit notes that Ailey collapsed at the OU athletic department weight room on August 11, 1995, as a result of severe dehydration leading to exhaustional heat stroke. It also notes that immediately prior to his injury, Bryan had been practicing under the control of the coaches and that he was not only repeatedly denied water, but he was required to continue exercising until he collapsed. It repeats the complaint that after being released from the hospital for heat stroke, Bryan was—on several different occasions—verbally harassed by the coaches, who "ridiculed and harassed Plaintiff for not being able to return to practice. These incidents occurred while Plaintiff was still under medical orders not to return to football practice."

Finally, the suit alleged that Howard Schnellenberger made false statements about Bryan to others. It claims that "Defendant Schnellenberger told third parties that Plaintiff's collapse was due to the flu and/or the fact that Plaintiff was out of shape. Plaintiff was not suffering from the flu and was in good physical shape as a result of training all summer."[16]

Four months after Bryan Ailey's suit was amended, he requested that it be dismissed, which the court did on August 8, 1997. Interestingly, on that same day, Bryan filed a second suit naming the Board of Regents at OU and Coach Schnellenberger as defendants. The suit cited the same incidents described in the first one, but this one charged that Bryan's rights had been violated under the Fourteenth Amendment to the U.S. Constitution. It alleged that, "as a result of Defendants' willful, intentional and reckless conduct, Plaintiff was deprived of a property interest in his athletic scholarship and the opportunity to complete a college degree, all without due process of law, pursuant to 42 U.S.C. (1883) and the Fourteenth Amendment to the United States Constitution."[17]

Nineteen days later, OU requested that this suit be removed from Cleveland County District Court and transferred to the U.S. District Court for the Western District of Oklahoma. The request was granted, and the suit went to the federal court, where it was not adjudicated for another eighteen months. Finally, on January 8, 1999, the court ruled in favor of the defendants and against Bryan. Neither Ailey's attorney nor Schnellenberger would comment on this suit.

Shortly after the end of our five days of two-a-days in August, Coach Schnellenberger defended his conditioning and practice system to Bob Hersom of the Oklahoman. He said he knew it was tough and even bragged about how tough it was. But he believed it had to be, and he said that he was sorry the players hadn't been more exposed to these "dog days of summer" under previous coaches. "This is the first time they've had to go through what everybody else in football has to go through. Some of them handled it, but a lot of them didn't. This football team has never been through the dog days of summer, and that's a great concern, because that was part of the demise last year."[18] He said we'd get used to it. His players were expected to be tougher, stronger, and better conditioned. The latter two characteristics were hard for me to achieve when I was losing thirty pounds off a weight that was already light for an offensive lineman.

MORE SIGNS OF TROUBLE

Coach Schnellenberger's offensive scheme was different from the one Coach Gibbs had used, as Schnellenberger brought in the complicated split offense of Miami Dolphins coach Don Shula. This was not surprising since Coach Schnellenberger had been an assistant under Shula when the Dolphins went to the Super Bowl in 1972. As the season progressed, however, it became apparent we did not have a Dan Marino in the quarterback slot to run that offense. Redshirt freshman Eric Moore was to be our starting quarterback. He was not a terrific passer, but even if he had been, you don't get a national championship with a rookie quarterback. But Schnellenberger felt Eric was the best we had, so he went with him.

The offensive line had to learn new blocking patterns and assignments, and Coach Schnellenberger's playbook, although consistent throughout the season, was huge. He was trying to get a college team to run a very complicated pro-set offense. This kind of offense is difficult to learn and to put into action on the field because it requires a great deal of reading and reacting to what the defense does in real time. There are no fixed assignments, so you can be doing two different things in the same play. Basically, Coach Schnellenberger installed the Miami Dolphin's playbook, and it was too much for us to learn in too short a time. Unlike pro football players, we actually had to attend college classes between practices. Often, out of confusion, we linemen would not know just whom we were supposed to block, partly because there was little communication between position coaches and players. All in all, it was a recipe for trouble when the regular season began.

Much of this escaped the notice of sportswriters, who picked up mostly on Schnellenberger's bravado. One Fort Worth *Star-Telegram* writer noted in late August:

> The loss to BYU . . . ended the Sooners' season at 6–6. Since then, Schnellenberger has set out to rekindle the team's pride and find its past glory. He demanded the Sooners shape up, setting a team goal of losing 1,000 pounds. He scrapped the 5–2 "Oklahoma" defense for an attacking 4–3 alignment. After spring drills that resembled boot camp, he installed redshirt freshman Eric Moore of Dallas Carter as his quarterback. And, during a barnstorming tour of the state's booster clubs, he preached the positive.
>
> "Pressure comes from within, and no one is going to put more demand on winning than me," said Schnellenberger. For the past nine months, Schnellenberger has strived to forge a new spirit. "Everything that happened before the Copper Bowl will be considered Before the Copper Bowl—BCB," he said. "And everything that happens after that is going to be the new era of Oklahoma football, or After the Copper Bowl—ACB."[19]

Clearly, many sportswriters were taken in by Coach Schnellenberger's boasting and heavy-handed discipline. It was largely because

Coach Howard Schnellenberger sends quarterback Eric Moore back into battle.
This picture was taken during the 1995 football season; the Sooners were on
the road, wearing their white jerseys. Schnellenberger had added stripes to the
sleeves of the Sooner jersey in 1995. The stripes were then taken off the jersey after
he resigned following the 1995 season. (*Daily Oklahoman*)

of his bravado, in fact, that the AP ranked us eleventh nationally even before we played our first game of the 1995 campaign. Although many of us on the team were determined to do well, we were not as enamored with Schnellenberger's tactics as was the press.

So it was somewhat surprising to us that the regular season began with a bang. Although the opponents were schools with lesser football programs, we did look pretty awesome.

THE 1995 SEASON

Our first four games were at home, and Coach Schnellenberger had instituted a few new features for home games. To avoid the distractions on campus, the OU team had always stayed in downtown Oklahoma City at the Embassy Suites the Friday night before the game, but Coach Schnellenberger moved us to the nondescript Sooner Motel, on campus. This wasn't that conducive to a good night's rest, as there was a little too much noise on campus from Friday night partying. Then, on the morning of Game Day, he had us march in our jerseys from the hotel, down Jenkins Street, to the stadium. It gave the fans a chance to see us before the game and actually wasn't a bad idea. It was fun and probably helped get our adrenaline pumping even higher.

As the season began, the wire services had us ranked fourteenth, largely because of Coach Schnellenberger's preseason boasting. By the end of the third week, we were 3-0, with good wins against San Diego State, SMU, and North Texas State. We had moved up to tenth in the polls, and to us, the media, and the fans it seemed that the national championship goal just might be realizable. Maybe the insanity of the boot-camp program was paying off, after all.

As the season began, I was in third position on the depth chart as a tackle, right behind J. R. Conrad. I wouldn't start, at least not right away, but I would get my share of playing time as first reserve. However, there was another problem with Schnellenberger: He was notorious for his inability to groom younger players. I had heard rumors from his previous school, Louisville, that starters played the entire game to the bitter end, whether the game was out of reach or well in hand. Unfortunately, he carried this tradition to Oklahoma. During the waning minutes of the North Texas game, with OU ahead by more than three scores, the coach still had the first team in the game. My dad nearly walked out of the game, vowing that if Schnellenberger didn't play me on the next series he would boycott the next game against Colorado and go watch Angelo State for the rest of the season.

Fortunately, I did play in the next offensive series. In fact, I became a part of Oklahoma football history, making a key block on the second longest run from scrimmage, ninety-six yards. But Coach Schnellenberger, true to form, played me sparingly and only in a clean-up role for the rest of the season. Not getting to play really hurt me, and this trend later hurt Coach Schnellenberger's successor, John Blake, who inherited a very inexperienced football team.

Then came Colorado.

Because of the ESPN coverage schedule, OU's game against Colorado was to be a night game, and that was unique for the Sooners since Owen Field didn't have lights for evening play. Coach Schnellenberger brought in huge portable light units and treated the fans to night football. The Sooners had played their first night game at Memorial Stadium back in 1987 using portable lights, but this didn't happen often. It's amazing what quick adjustments a school can make, expensive as they may be, when television comes to town. Coach Schnellenberger improvised, and we played under the stars. Unfortunately, on this night, Colorado had us *seeing* stars.

The Buffaloes were ranked fourth or seventh in the nation, depending on which polls you believed. We were ranked tenth. It would be our first real test of the year, and a tough one at that. We played well during the first half and actually took a 17–14 lead into the locker room at halftime.

During halftime, however, Colorado Coach Rick Neuheisel changed the Buffs' offensive scheme and went predominantly to the short pass. It made sense; our defensive backs had been playing ten to fifteen yards off their receivers in the first half because Coach Schnellenberger was afraid of getting burned by long pass completions. That opened up the short pass, but our coaches made absolutely no adjustment in our defensive scheme in the second half. As a result, the Buffs exploded in the second half, scoring twenty-four unanswered points. We lost, 38–17. Disaster had collided head-on with Coach Schnellenberger's much-touted goal for the season.

After the game, Coach Schnellenberger told the media he now regretted a comment he had made before the game. As I recall, he had been assessing the absence of injured starting Buffs quarterback, Koy Detmer, before the game when he said that even if we won it, there would be an "asterisk" beside the "W" because Detmer wasn't starting for Colorado. To that comment, Colorado Coach Rick Neuheisel had responded, "We'll kick their asterisk."

However, one newspaper reported a completely different comment. According to the *Oklahoman*, Coach Schnellenberger had bragged that the Sooners would kick the Buffs' "ass."[20] The paper continued to quote him as saying, "I shouldn't have called it an ass. I should have called it a mule. If that [quote] had anything to do with the game, then I'll have to come up with something better next time." In any event, the irony was that the replacement for the highly touted Detmer was John Hessler, who wound up breaking a Colorado record by throwing five touchdown passes.

Coach Schnellenberger also had to deal that night with another prediction that he had made to the media: that the Sooners would not lose a game that season but that the clock might run out on them. Asked after the game about that comment, he replied, "This is not what I call a game where we were behind when the clock ran out and the gun went off. We were beaten tonight and that's hard for me and my staff and for all of us to handle."[21]

As for the team, we expected a locker-room tirade from the coach. But he just clenched his teeth, entered the locker room, said we played a lousy game, and ordered us to show up for a Sunday practice. Worse still, however, we weren't sure if Coach Schnellen-berger's—and thus our—season goal was still the same. But Howard quickly answered that question in the affirmative: we'd simply have to win the national title with one loss. It had been done before, and we could do it again. He vowed to the media, "We shall return," and said that we weren't ready to "jump off a bridge."

At 3–1, we weren't quite as cocksure as before, and it seemed that Coach Schnellenberger himself was deflated after the loss. His ten-dency to leave for an hour or so in the middle of practice seemed to increase. In some ways, he began losing control of the team, as some players began to skip practice, feeling he wouldn't know if they were there or not since he wasn't around that much himself. Some weren't even sure if their coach knew who they were. Why? Because the sportswriters were right: Coach Schnellenberger would sometimes forget our names. Even more bizarre, he would sometimes mistake players for the players on his 1985 University of Miami national championship team. On some days it felt like Rod Serling's *Twilight Zone.*

Adding to an already troublesome situation, Coach Schnellen-berger had his assistants running practices beyond the twenty-hour weekly limit imposed by the NCAA. This is a very important rule, designed to leave at least some time for players to attend to their course work. But the coach routinely ran practices past the twenty-hour limit, and in that year, I think the entire team's GPA dropped a full point.

The NCAA checks the time sheets the players fill out and sign. The problem was that the coaches were giving us incorrect or even blank time sheets to sign, filling them in later to make them conform to the twenty-hour rule even though we were practicing longer than that each week. When we asked the coaches about the blank time sheets, they said not to worry, they'd be filled in later and this was simply a matter of expediency. Later, on December 16, the *Tulsa World* ran a story about all this after talking with more than ten players—most of whom wanted to remain anonymous. The article concluded that during the season, OU had exceeded the four-hour daily limit routinely, especially on Tuesday and Wednesday, when a work day could run up to six hours long.[22]

Coach Schnellenberger told the *World* that if the team had violated the rule, it was unintentional and that the discrepancies had amounted to "minutes rather than halves of hours." But that's not how I and a lot of other players remember it. When you add it all together (practice, meetings, and weight lifting), some work days did last six hours. On Tuesdays and Wednesdays we would meet at 2:30 P.M. for team meetings, which would last until 3:05, when we would meet as a team with Coach Schnellenberger. We hit the field fifteen minutes later. Practices would sometimes go until 6:30 P.M. or later. That's four hours. Then we'd break for dinner and return for meetings from 7:30 to 8:30 P.M. That's another hour. For those of us who lifted weights, the work days ran at least an hour longer. Officially, the weight lifting program required us to lift two times a week for about an hour each session. When we lifted was up to us, but most of us lifted on Tuesdays and Wednesdays.

Coach Schnellenberger responded to Dan O'Kane of the *Tulsa World*: "This is the first time I've ever been around a group of kids who kept a watch on how long we practiced. I understand that it can't be in excess of four hours a day. If it was in excess, it was a very short time. I'm not saying it was. I'm not saying we did."[23]

We caught a breather the fifth week of the season with our game against Iowa State. It was our first road game, but the Cyclones were unranked and not a contender for the Big Eight title. We played before a crowd of forty-five thousand in Ames and won the game, 39–26. The win buoyed us as a team; afterwards we were up to 4–1 on the year and ranked thirteenth nationally.

The first week in October, we took our annual bus ride down I-35 to Dallas to play in the Red River Rivalry against the Texas Longhorns. Texas was off to a decent start, ranked eighteenth in the nation, and at the half we were shocked to find ourselves down, 24–0. From there things seemed to go from bad to worse.

We knew we might be able to win the national title with one loss, but we certainly couldn't do it with two. So we resolved at halftime to do better, and we came out gunning in the second half. Before we knew it, our defense had stopped Texas cold while our offense mounted twenty-one points on the board. But toward the game's end, the best we could do was to put up three more points on a late field goal by Jeremy Alexander to tie the game. It was better than a loss, especially since it was Texas, but it left our season record even more scuffed up at 4–1–1.

Ironically, had one event in that game gone differently, the whole chain of events that led to Coach Schnellenberger's departure might not have happened at all and he and Donnie Duncan might have survived at OU. That event was a missed field goal at the end of the game. Jeremy Alexander, my roommate at the time and an excellent kicker, missed that kick. A forty-two-yarder into the wind in the closing seconds of the game, it was a tough kick, but I thought it was good. The referee, however, said it sailed just wide of the upright, and the game with UT finished in the 24–24 tie. If the ball had been a few inches to the right, the Sooners would have won the game. More important, this win would have given Oklahoma the six victories needed to qualify for a bowl game, assuming the rest of the season turned out as it did. We didn't know it then of course, but we would win only one more of our five remaining games that season. Most likely we'd have gone to the Aloha Bowl in Hawaii. Beating Texas and going to a bowl probably would have saved Coach Schnellenberger's job.

I missed not getting to go to Hawaii, but believe me, it was worth missing. I later said to Jeremy, "I know you feel bad, but thanks for missing that kick against Texas, because it spelled the end for Coach Schnellenberger." The next year Jeremy didn't miss the kick, and OU beat Texas in overtime in what was my most thrilling college football game ever.

After Texas, we were in a quandary. We dropped only two notches in the polls, to fifteenth, but what was our new goal now that it appeared the national title was a lost cause? The coach was slow in coming up with one, but we did know that we had to try for the Big Eight Conference title and grab the best bowl we could, even though we were 1–1 in the league at that time. Coach Schnellenberger became more distant from the team at practice, returning only at the end of the sessions to yell at us. He continued to lose more control with each passing week, and the players were doing a lot of grumbling behind his back. Obviously, the media and fans weren't all that happy either.

Our national title hopes disappeared completely the following week, when seventh-ranked Kansas came to Norman and we lost big-time, 38–17, before a sellout crowd. That loss was followed by a narrow 13–9 win over unranked Missouri the next week. Then we lost big to ninth-ranked Kansas State at Manhattan, 49–10. We dropped out of the national rankings for good after that loss, sitting at 5–3–1.

Now our much-anticipated dream season had turned into yet another nightmare. After starting off 3–0, we had gone 2–3–1 over the next six games. Our fast-fading bowl hopes evaporated completely in the tenth game, against our archrival Oklahoma State. Going into that home game we needed only one more win to become bowl eligible. OSU was definitely our better shot, since the final game was against Nebraska. The Cowboys weren't having a banner year themselves and we felt fairly confident, especially since we were playing at Owen Field. That confidence proved to be misplaced. After falling behind, we could do absolutely nothing to score points, let alone catch up. When you have a first and goal on the four-yard line and can't score, something is definitely wrong. We lost the game, 12–0.

As if losing the game by a shutout wasn't enough, that was the day that erupted in locker-room shouting matches between players and coaches and at least one fight, involving linebacker Broderick Simpson and Offensive Coordinator Gary Nord. Coach Nord didn't like players disagreeing with him about his play-calling, and that's just what Broderick did, and so the battle was on, taking place in the hallway outside the locker room.

At the end of the day we were still 5–4–1, and the Cornhuskers stood between us and a bowl game. Nebraska was ranked first in the nation—which is where we were supposed to be according to Coach Schnellenberger's grand original plan. With our goals falling one after another throughout the season, we now had little but pride to play for. We didn't play terribly against the Huskers, but we still lost.

During my younger years, my family always spent the Thanksgiving holiday at my grandparents' house. Every year before Thanksgiving dinner, I would watch the Oklahoma-Nebraska football game. At that time, Oklahoma and Nebraska had a tradition as the giants of college football that went back to the 1950s. Oklahoma was national champion in 1955 and 1956, and Bud Wilkinson was the neighborhood hero, having attended high school with my aunt at the same school later attended by my mother and my uncle. As a child I sometimes wondered what it would be like to play in the OU-NU game. I never dreamed that when Thanksgiving came in 1995, I would be standing in the stadium in Lincoln, lining up against the Cornhuskers on their home turf.

Nebraska's home stadium is a throwback to the 1930s, enclosed at both ends and extremely steep on the sides. With its massive upper decks, it puts seventy thousand screaming people, dressed in a sea of red, right on top of the field. It was even more intimidating than I had imagined. This was the last game of the season, so they introduced all of the Nebraska seniors to a roaring standing ovation before the start of the game. They were the undefeated defending national champions. How could you create a more exciting and intimidating event?

The Huskers did win, 37–0, and even though the game was out of reach for most of the fourth quarter, Coach Schnellenberger was true to form and stuck grimly to the starters right up to the bitter end. After all my years of watching this rivalry and imagining what it would be like to play in it, I really should have had the chance, but I didn't. As it turned out, I would miss the game in Lincoln two years later because of an injury to my Achilles tendon. It was really a shame that during my entire career at OU I didn't get to play a single down against the Cornhuskers on their home field.

I had set my home VCR to tape the Nebraska game before I left Norman, and I was anxious to see how it looked. The television tapes were always more exciting than the game films, which had no continuity because they were split into separate tapes of the offense and defense. Watching the tape was fine until late in the game, when sportscaster Brent Musburger launched into a description of Howard Schnellenberger, comparing him to Captain Kangaroo from the old TV series for kids. Shortly after that quip, OU's left tackle, J. R. Conrad, jumped the snap count, and Musburger used the opportunity to describe the Sooners' weight coach, Joe Juraszek, as Mr. Green Jeans, Captain Kangaroo's sidekick. I still believe this bit was planned in advance, because as he was talking the network aired comparison pictures of Coach Schnellenberger and Captain Kangaroo. Maybe the viewing audience thought it was cute, but for me it was the absolute worst-case example of a network deliberately targeting a football program for embarrassment.

Another announcer who hurt OU during Coach Schnellenberger's reign was ESPN's Lee Corso. At the start of the season it appeared that Corso was a good friend of the coach's, or at least a big fan. (If he was a friend, he was definitely of the fair-weather variety.) When OU started the season on a three-game winning streak, Corso was touting the Sooners as national champions and Coach Schnellenberger as the architect of OU's revival. By the end of the year, when OU's offense hit the skids, he couldn't say enough bad things about the Sooner players. Ironically, Corso's negative comments at the end of the season didn't hurt the Sooners as much as had the false expectations he fostered at the start of the season.

Those expectations were long gone by the time we played Nebraska. The *Tulsa World* called it right in a postgame headline: "OU Finishes with Bang, Shoots Self." That game's problems were the same kind of problems that had plagued us all season long: Fumbles. Interceptions. Missed blocks. Penalties. I think all of these problems can be traced back to a practice regime that favored military obstacle courses over football fundamentals. We simply hadn't been able to score; before that blowout in Lincoln was a string of ten straight quarters in which we'd been unable to score a single point. To make matters worse, the OSU and Nebraska losses were the first back-to-back shutouts in thirty years of Oklahoma football.

On November 25, sportswriter John Klein wrote in the *Tulsa World*: "It was a somewhat fitting end to a disappointing season. It finished like it started. OU was its own worst enemy."

We were through for the season.

HOWARD'S END

Upon reflection, 1995 was my worst year with the OU program. As I drove home to Arlington with my parents after the Nebraska game, I sat in the back seat and just stared out the window, asking myself, "What happened?" Our anticipated 11–0 or 10–1 season wound up 5–5–1, we won only two Big Eight games, we finished unranked nationally, and we had been outscored throughout the season, 273–233. Was coming to OU the worst mistake I'd ever made? What might have happened if I'd picked Arizona State or Texas A&M? Instead, I was with a team that had started out thinking it could win the national championship, only to wind up losing five games, tying one, and suffering two shutouts, one of which was at home to our archrival, the OSU Cowboys. You couldn't have written a worse script for the Sooners that year.

Even with all this, most of us on the team still felt OU would give Schnellenberger another year to prove himself. But we had been wrong before, and fortunately, we were wrong again. We were overjoyed when he announced his resignation on December 18, just as the season ended. By most signs, it was not a voluntary resignation, despite OU's official statement to the contrary at the time.

In a December 19 *Oklahoman* story, Bob Hersom wrote, "The resignation came two days after reports that some OU seniors had complained about practice sessions. The seniors claimed OU broke NCAA rules by sometimes practicing more than four hours per day and 20 hours per week." But OU President David Boren called the resignation "voluntary" and said it was in everyone's best interest. For his part, Coach Schnellenberger said, "In recent months a climate has developed toward the programs, understandably in some cases and perhaps unfairly in others, that has changed my outlook on the situation. A change would help improve that climate. My decision has nothing to do with any rules problems, because we have been diligent in adhering to the rules at OU and throughout our career."[24]

All of this was said by way of simultaneously released written statements from Schnellenberger, Boren, and Duncan. No news conferences were held. Schnellenberger did not make himself available for comment. The year of Howard Schnellenberger had simply ended as abruptly as it had begun, with the surprise announcement of his hiring.

The *Detroit News* reported his departure this way:

> Howard Schnellenberger resigned Monday, ending a one-year stay as Oklahoma's head coach that started 3–0 but dissolved into a 5–5–1 season. He made his unexpected announcement in a statement issued through the school's sports information office.
>
> University President David Boren said Schnellenberger's decision was voluntary and that the team's record was not an issue. Neither were rules violations, said Schnellenberger and Athletic Director Donnie Duncan. A Tulsa newspaper had reported that Schnellenberger often exceeded the NCAA's time limits for practices.[25]

Ray Buck, the national columnist for SportsLine USA, had a different spin, however, bringing up the drinking issue again in his December 23 column: "What we had heard through the rumor mill, and sadly suspected, now is being reported by an Oklahoma newspaper: Howard Schnellenberger is being investigated for allegedly drinking himself out of a job."

Buck continued,

> [And he did so] recklessly and stupidly. Right under the noses of the University of Oklahoma players, several of whom went off the record this past week in substantiating ugly rumors about their 61-year-old head coach with booze on his breath and virtually zero control of his team. Plain and simple, Schnellenberger had lost it.
>
> The former savior of football programs at the University of Miami and Louisville resigned from OU Monday after fulfilling just one year on a five-year contract that paid him $125,000 in base salary and close to $500,000 including radio, TV, endorsements and other perks.[26]

The *Tulsa World* estimated the value of his remaining contract at $2 million on the day he resigned. He settled for $107,500, which included his base salary through June 30 plus expenses.

About that, Buck wrote, "Now along comes an explanation. Why would anybody 'voluntarily' walk away from that? Answer: Anybody wouldn't. But Schnellenberger, contrary to reports of his resignation, was forced out. He swept out his desk, snubbed the media and agreed to a $107,000 settlement, plus moving expenses back to the Miami area where he and his wife reside."[27]

Sportswriter Pat Forde put a darkly humorous, yet accurate, spin on Coach Schnellenberger's career miscues in an article entitled, "Schnellenberger Made Another Bad Decision." It read, in part:

> LOUISVILLE, Ky.—All in all, you can envision worse career decisions. Taking a job in the buggy whip industry at the turn of the century. Or with the Communist Party in Eastern Europe in the late 1980s. Or with the Cleveland Browns' PR staff in 1995. But in the future there will be a catch phrase for professional suicide. It will be known as "Pulling a Schnellenberger." Howard Schnellenberger, hailed in September as the Supreme Commander of the Sooner Nation, was deposed in a

bloodless coup Monday. The powers that be at Oklahoma can call it a resignation if they want, but you can smell the gunsmoke from a firing all the way out here.

That stunning action gives Schnellenberger the dubious distinction of having made two of the worst career moves in college football history:

- In 1984 he left a burgeoning dynasty at Miami for a United States Football League team that folded before ever playing a game.
- Last year he left his hometown fiefdom at the University of Louisville for Oklahoma. He lasted 367 days on the Plains. Few Sooners have come and gone sooner. The man obsessed with carving out a niche in gridiron lore will have a small, ignominious one at Oklahoma. They name nothing after a coach with a 5–5–1 record.

Ego has been Schnellenberger's tragic flaw. It has spurred him from one bad decision to another, leaving behind programs that have gone on rather well without him. . . . He committed an astounding number of gaffes in his Year from Hell, the most costly of which was fielding a grossly underachieving team. But he deserved more than one season.[28]

Stories about Coach Schnellenberger's problems at OU did not disappear with his departure on December 18, 1995. Six months later, the *New York Times* reported in a June 17 story that he was fired for not winning enough games. The *Times* story, written by John Underwood, a former feature writer for the *Miami Herald*, was titled, "The Coach Takes a Beating . . . Howard Schnellenberger Did Something Unforgivable at Oklahoma: He Lost Football Games." Schnellenberger, breaking his silence in talking to the media about his time at Oklahoma, said he was still "very bitter" and called his last few weeks on the job "the worst time of my life anywhere." He also asserted that the OU officials did nothing to dispute rumors about excessive drinking even though they knew they were not true.[29]

Then the coach said, "Every other place I'd been, the administration, the fans, the players were behind me. This time I was an outsider, and an outsider didn't have a cut dog's chance . . . a no-win situation." To many of us on the team, however, Coach Schnellenberger had set himself up for a no-win situation by having his team drop 748 pounds of needed weight, running drills that had nothing to do with football skills, and bragging throughout the preseason about winning the national title in his first year.

Reacting to the *Times* story, OU President Boren told the *Oklahoman*, "It was a case that they [the *New York Times*] wanted to portray that, at Oklahoma, winning is the only thing that counts. But that was not a major factor in this decision. All Oklahomans care about is winning? That clearly is not the case. We have values that are very important to us. We do not exploit our players."

Boren continued, "Certainly I had two concerns that were paramount with me . . . the health and safety of our players, and second, I really wanted someone I thought was a players' coach. Someone who was really felt by players to take a deep interest in them not only as athletes, but also as students. There may be places where Howard Schnellenberger is the right fit. It just didn't work out here."[30]

To Coach Schnellenberger's credit, he had been responsive when President Boren insisted on changes in practice policies, including returning drinking water to the field. Hospital treatments and emergency-room visits virtually stopped after that. Boren also reiterated that the coach's departure was by resignation and not termination. He said, "The whole nature of the settlement indicated it was a voluntary action on his part. Had we made a termination, he would have had the ability for more compensation."[31]

Today Howard Schnellenberger is back in the coaching ranks, creating a new football program at Florida Atlantic University (FAU). The AP quoted him as announcing, "The old war horse has risen again, and he's ready for battle. This is the most important thing I've ever undertaken. . . . I recommended to Dr. [Anthony] Catanese [FAU's president] that he consider me for this position, [and] I'm delighted that he concurred with my recommendation."

The AP story added, "The coaching job is Schnellenberger's first since he spent one turbulent season at Oklahoma in 1995. Besieged by ugly rumors regarding his drinking and treatment of players, he bitterly resigned under pressure. Now, at an age associated with retirement, Schnellenberger is starting over."[32]

In August 2000, Rick Bozich, sportswriter for the Louisville *Courier-Journal*, wrote the following under the headline, "Howard Has New Team to Dream Over":

> Howard Schnellenberger started practice at Florida Atlantic University on Monday with 165 players, including walk-ons from Trinidad, Colombia and Brazil. He quickly cut the roster to 136, with only 20 on scholarship. Schnellenberger, 66, is working his guys as relentlessly as Joe Paterno and Bobby Bowden work theirs—2 1/2 hours a day in the steamy conditions of South Florida. Remember, he's getting his team ready for opening day. Never mind that the game is 12 months away and hasn't even been scheduled. . . . After an aborted jump to the United States Football League in 1984, 10 seasons at Louisville and the one-year sack at Oklahoma, Schnellenberger has returned to where people wondered what he packed into that trademark pipe.[33]

Coach Schnellenberger hasn't ceased his bragging, either, claiming to take the new Division I-AA FAU squad to Division I-A level within five years and asserting he has an understanding with the Big East Conference to take the team into its league at about that time. As his first season at FAU came to an end, Coach Schnellenberger told the AP he believed he had picked the right place to build another winning football program, such as the ones he had built at Miami and Louisville. And he seemed to be more willing to wait for it than he was at OU. Good thing, too, since his first-year team finished at 4–6 and went 2–9 in the second year when they were outscored 369–145.

But his rhetoric still reflects his military bearing and his hard-nosed approach to the sport. "It takes a lot of battle under fire, tempering of steel, experience, whatever you call it," he told the AP in a November 17, 2001, story. "You can't rush it, as hard as you try. You have to endure these things so that the team will become experienced and productive and fruitful."

In the coach's biography posted on "The Schnellenberger Zone" of FAU's online media guide, no mention was made at all of his year with OU as late as 2002. This is understandable, especially when you consider the OU coaching statistics: Only three head coaches have had one-year stays at Oklahoma. Jim Tatum coached the 1946 season but then quit and took over the head-coaching job at Maryland. Jim Mackenzie coached the 1966 season but died unexpectedly later that year. And Howard Schnellenberger, well, his story is told here.[34]

You could make the following argument, however: If Howard Schnellenberger has a huge ego, if he runs year-round, tougher-than-nails training programs for his teams, and if he blows off steam in various ways to release the immense pressure he's under, then he probably is not that much different from a number of other extreme college football coaches. There will always be the Woody Hayes (Ohio State) and Frank Kush (ASU) type of browbeating coach, and hard-drivers like Paul "Bear" Bryant and Joe Paterno.

Why? College football is huge money, alumni support is vital, and national prominence is key. Among the nation's elite football programs, some fifty or so are trying like crazy to claw their way to the top of the rankings each year. Waiting at the end of this rainbow is a possible $13 million big-bowl payoff and national fame. In so many ways college football is a business, placing unbelievable stresses on coaches and players alike. On the line for the coach is his reputation and in cases like Howard Schnellenberger's, a half-million-dollar annual recompense. On the line for the players is pride in themselves and their school and hope that their efforts might lead them into the ranks of professional football.

For us in Norman in 1995, so ended one of the most unusual and certainly the most gut-wrenching years in the University of Oklahoma football program. As Howard Schnellenberger left, the team was in a state of chaos. It was like a brand new jigsaw puzzle that had just been dumped out onto the table before the laborious task of piecing it together. That was the job awaiting our newest "savior"—whoever it would be this time.

CHAPTER 5

Coach Blake

THE EXPANDING PLAYBOOK

Like a circle in a spiral, like a wheel within a wheel . . .

MICELE LEGRAND

You could make a good case that any new coach would be a breath of fresh air to us after the 1995 season, when Howard Schnellenberger left Norman for the sand and surf of Florida. We were tired of the pointless boot camps, we were tired of Coach Schnellenberger's dictatorial and self-focused style, and we were tired of losing football games. Coach John Blake would bring immediate relief to those first two frustrations, but not the third.

I was home in Arlington, Texas, over Christmas break when I first heard the news that Coach Schnellenberger had resigned from OU. I immediately called my roommate Tim Macias, who played offensive guard. Like a lot of us on the team, Tim was happy about the resignation. I felt more of a sense of relief, which was quickly followed by apprehension; another change was in store for me. I wondered who the next coach would be and what system he would install. I was worried about having to fight my way back up through the depth chart again. I had been at OU for only seventeen months when the interviews for my third head coach began.

As much as we didn't want to be subjected to a new coaching staff, we realized that Coach Schnellenberger and his ideas hadn't been helping us reach our goals. Over the year we had lost at least ten players who walked away from all of this, and we didn't want to lose more. What we wanted was more of a chance to work on the fundamental skills that would bring us more victories.

Several months after Coach Schnellenberger's departure came the resignation of Athletic Director Donnie Duncan, who was moving on to become the commissioner of the Big Twelve Conference. Duncan was tainted with the problems surrounding Coach Schnellenberger because it had been his decision to confirm Schnellenberger's hiring in the first place. So when he got the opportunity to move into the administrative ranks of the new Big Twelve Conference, he left OU. This was a good opportunity for him, and he knew it.

To replace Duncan, OU convinced 1969 Sooner Heisman Trophy winner Steve Owens to take a leave from his successful insurance business in Norman and take the reins as athletic director. Owens was initially reluctant to take the job, but he said yes with the understanding that it would be temporary; he would just help get OU over its hump and put the program on sound footing. Owens had been a record-breaking running back under Coach Chuck Fairbanks, who had gone on to the Detroit Lions before retiring from football. While at OU, Owens was a two-time consensus All-American, and he scored more touchdowns (fifty-six) during his career than any other Sooner. He also holds records for most touchdowns in a season (twenty-three) and most points scored in a season (138). He is well-liked and was a key part of OU's effort to "bring the family together again."

Before Duncan left for the Big Twelve, OU immediately put together a search committee for a new head coach—our third in three years. The committee was staffed with members of the athletic department, the OU Board of Regents, and some outside consultants, but no players. One of the committee members was Barry Switzer, who recommended that OU hire John Blake.

Blake was defensive line coach for the Dallas Cowboys, and this was the second year in a row Switzer had encouraged OU to hire him. Mack Brown of the University of North Carolina was also on the list, and he seemed a strong candidate. But this time the school listened to Switzer, and the thirty-four-year-old Blake was announced as our new leader. (We would be seeing Brown again, since he moved on to coach the University of Texas Longhorns.)

John Blake was not only the youngest head football coach OU had ever had, he was also the first African American head coach at the school. None of us cared a whit about race; we just craved a coach who could guide us to victory. Blake had played for the Sooners in college, and with Switzer's recommendation, it seemed like the old family was coming together again. That was exactly the image the university wanted to convey to the fans.

THE TROUBLE WITH A NEW COACH

When Coach Blake stepped into the job at OU, he was faced with a number of problems. Any time you change coaches, a number of things happen that hurt your team. Most obviously, the players must learn and adapt to a whole new system and a new staff of coaches. This is a transition that often requires much more than simply memorizing a new playbook. Some players may need to make physical changes, and others may need to change their mental approach to the game. This can be quite difficult, if not impossible. For instance, if a player was recruited for a pro-set offense, and the new coach wants to run the option, it may not be possible for that player to physically change to fit the new system.

The players also have to adapt to a new coach-player relationship. If the player expects a teacher and mentor relationship with a coach, and the coach turns out to be an erratic screamer, it will be hard for the player to adjust psychologically. The more the philosophy of the incoming coach differs from that of the outgoing coach, the more difficult this situation will be.

Another problem is that younger players who have put out the effort to move up the depth chart and into starting positions must prove themselves all over again. This gives a second chance to the older players, who may have been sandbagging it throughout their careers. In some cases this is good, because there are always some deserving players who seemed to be permanent residents in the former coach's doghouse and merit a second chance. But in most cases this second chance only takes away from younger players the opportunity to refine their game by repeating plays and techniques in practice.

As time goes on, there is also a problem between the players the former coach recruited and the players the new coach brought in. The new coach's recruits are "his" players, and no matter how hard he tries not to favor them, believe me, it happens. In the same light, the new coach is bound to live up to his own recruiting promises, but not those of his predecessor. If the new head coach promises a recruit he will be a starter, but the position coach feels another player, recruited by the previous administration, is better, guess who is going to start?

There is also a lot of pressure on the head coach to do better than the guy he replaced. After all, that's why he was hired in the first place. This pressure for improvement often leads to a solution known as "the quick fix": the junior college transfer. Sometimes the JC transfer works, as it did at OU in 1999 and 2000, when Coach Bob Stoops recruited a group of outstanding JC transfers, including Josh Heupel himself, who contributed significantly to OU's success.

Junior college transfers can also work out well in established programs because the coaches in stable programs know what talent is coming up through the ranks and which glaring holes must be filled. They also work well when the coach is an astute judge of talent and has time to assess that talent. Coach Stoops did a masterful job of identifying those holes and finding talented players to fill them.

Linebacker Torrance Marshall, offensive lineman Howard Duncan, and of course quarterback Josh Heupel were all incredible JC transfers. But the gaps these players filled were readily apparent; Stockar McDougle and Matt O'Neal would be going to the NFL, and the offensive line was a good place to look for support. In contrast, Coach Blake didn't really know the potential of his younger players or understand which gaps needed to be filled. This lack of information was primarily due to the late start he got in the recruiting season following Coach Schnellenberger's departure.

Normally, however, relying on a junior college transfer is a bad decision for several reasons. In general, two years of experience at the level of competition provided by the junior colleges doesn't equate to two years at the Division I-A level. Often the result is that a player who looks great on film against other JC opponents gets handed his lunch in a Division I-A game. To complicate matters further, junior college transfers don't remain in the university program very long. With two years of eligibility remaining, they are only on the team for three semesters. Even if they are up to the level of Division I-A competition when they arrive, they are not going to be around as long as the players coming up through the program. The team doesn't even get the benefit of having them around for more than one spring practice unless they are picked up before the spring semester. The best example of this is Torrance Marshall: he was already gone in 2000, after only three semesters at OU, but Rocky Calmus, who had been at OU since 1998, still had another year to play. The quick fix of junior college transfers can also produce a vicious circle: once a coach starts filling in the gaps with JC transfers, he ends up filling the gaps they leave with more JC transfers. On the other hand, a player recruited from high school has the potential to be in the same program for five years (or even six, as in my case).

Aside from these player and team issues, a completely new organizational dynamic is introduced when you bring a new group of coaches together. During a time when they should be focusing on the players, the coaches are testing the waters among themselves to determine who can be trusted, who can build solid friendships, who might be a good mentor. Overall, the coaches are learning how to get along in a new environment.

Each of the new coaches must establish where they fit within the coaching hierarchy. For example, does the offensive line coach select the players who make up the starting offensive line, or does that decision fall to the offensive coordinator, or to the head coach? In a new offensive situation, if a player blows an assignment because the offensive line coach gave incorrect instructions, does the offensive line coach accept the blame? Or does he cover himself by letting the head coach think the player got it wrong? A new coach might be more apt to let the player take the blame. Once I blocked a play exactly the way Line Coach Denver Johnson outlined it in the team meeting. Unfortunately, it was not the way Offensive Coordinator Dick Winder wanted it run. When Coach Winder started yelling, which he was sometimes prone to do, Coach Johnson blamed me for his mistake rather than admitting he had diagrammed it incorrectly and losing face with Winder. Thanks, Coach.

Another problem with a late coaching change is that there is no time to teach technique. Whenever a program changes its head coaches and offensive coordinators, the players spend most of their practices learning the coaches' offensive and defensive systems, and there is very little time to work on actual technique. The result is a team that makes a lot of mistakes on the field, like penalties, missed blocks or tackles, and fumbles or interceptions.

Finally, when a team hires a new coach, the players are stuck with him. The NCAA rules on eligibility make it almost impossible for a player to transfer to another university should he find the new system not to his liking. During recruiting, players have the option of choosing their coach. But once the player commits, he has no recourse if the coach he chose is fired or opts to leave on his own. The NCAA rules are set up to punish the players, not the school or the coach, for transferring. This can produce a disgruntled group of players who are literally forced to remain at a school because they can't leave without giving up a year of eligibility. Just add them to the other group of disgruntled players who are displaced by the JC transfers.

Unfortunately, all these problems came into play with the coaching change that brought John Blake to the University of Oklahoma as head coach. No wonder the team struggled for the next few years.

A PLAYERS' COACH

The selection committee saw Coach Blake as a "Switzer man" and felt he could revive the Switzer's glory days at OU. When he came to OU as head coach, Blake had played or worked for Barry Switzer for eight years: he was a nose tackle for OU from 1980 to 1983 and served as a graduate assistant for Switzer in 1986–1987. He had been defensive line coach for the Dallas Cowboys for three years, the last two under Switzer. Many observers saw similarities in their coaching styles and felt they were both "players' coaches." And they were right: the team members felt that Coach Blake cared about them individually.

As Merv Johnson, who had been an OU assistant coach for sixteen years at the time, once told *Tulsa World* sportswriter Dan O'Kane, "That motivates the players because they know you care, and it makes you want to play hard. They know you have their best interest at heart, and that makes them want to perform."[1] Blake also had great recruiting abilities, especially among Black players. Not only was he OU's first African American head coach, but he was only the second Black football coach in the Big Twelve Conference.

Blake had gotten Donnie Duncan's nod over other top candidates like Bob Davie, assistant coach at Notre Dame; Mack Brown, head coach at North Carolina; and Jim Tressel, head coach at Youngstown State—all more experienced coaches. Since Coach Blake had no offensive or defensive coordinating experience and had never been a head coach before, the search committee wanted to buttress him with two men who had filled those roles well. They were Dick Winder, offensive coordinator from Texas Tech, and Bill Young, defensive coordinator from Ohio State.

The attitude in the off-season conditioning camp in 1996 was much better than it had been the year before under Howard Schnellenberger. It was a hard eight weeks of running and strength conditioning, but there was a lot of emphasis on football fundamentals instead of the unfocused grunt work that we'd done in 1995. So we concentrated on pass blocking, offensive line blocking, and tackling.

The biggest difference, however, was that we concentrated on putting on weight rather than taking it off, as we had under Coach Schnellenberger. Under Coach Blake's philosophy, we made a welcome 180-degree turn from the previous year. As assistant coach for the Dallas Cowboys, Blake was used to big, bulky, lumbering players instead of the lean ones Schnellenberger wanted. At mealtime, protein supplements were added so we could regain the weight we had lost. When Coach Blake arrived at OU, I weighed in at 270 pounds, although I played best at 285. I hit that weight quickly under the new program.

So here we were, running focused conditioning drills instead of just running around a track and leaping from one monkey bar to another. We were doing wind sprints, changing directions, doing footwork drills. And we liked it. We worked hard, we came together, we were excited about things. For his part, Blake talked about rebuilding instead of winning a national championship the next season. Communication with him and the other coaches was good. We knew what was going on and exactly what the coaches expected of us. Blake was a good people-person, and so he worked a lot on fan support and fund-raising while Merv Johnson, the tight end coach, ran the drills and headed the recruiting effort. Merv was also our link to the past and a good guide for Coach Blake.

For the second year in a row we had switched lead horses at a critical time in the recruiting season. Early February is signing time, and since we had lost some players who bailed out under Coach

Schnellenberger's dictatorial style in addition to normal graduations, we needed several new additions. But between Merv Johnson's recruiting efforts and John Blake's winning personality, we did okay that year.

When we got into formal spring practices, we continued to work hard under the good direction of the coaches. The practices were hard but much shorter than before. Whereas Coach Schnellenberger had his assistants run three-and-a-half-hour practices, Blake's ran only one hour and forty-five minutes. The practices began with football fundamentals rather than wind sprints, then we did inside drills and then teamwork. We took time to learn the plays under Coach Blake's new offensive and defensive schemes.

Just as Howard Schnellenberger had been the opposite of Gary Gibbs in so many ways, so John Blake was strikingly different from Coach Howard. Blake was the classic player's coach, sometimes to a fault. He liked to spend time with us, and we were always welcome at his home on Norman's west side. He was not a screamer, and when we started to lose during the 1996 season, he spoke to us like we were his sons. "Everything will be okay," he'd say. His communication skills with the team were much better than we'd experienced with Coach Schnellenberger, and he would often invoke his Christian values when any of us seemed to deviate from good moral behavior. "What you do in the dark will eventually come to the light," he would often say to us. But he had his lighter side as well; he would often joke with us and was fond of greeting us with, "What's up Freak, Freak?"

Blake's goal for the season was also vastly different than Schnellenberger's had been. He made sure we all understood that this was a rebuilding process and that it might take a couple years to have us winning consistently again.

If there was a down side to Coach Blake's philosophy as a player's coach, it was that he sometimes deferred to his players' wishes and whims too much. I remember one time when he even canceled practice because one of the guys was complaining that we didn't have enough days off. As a result, there wasn't a whole lot of discipline on the team, and a few of the guys carried their behavior a little too far and wound up in trouble. It was nothing like the trouble that Barry Switzer's teams got into off the field, but things were a little too lax at times for the players' own good.

By spring practice I had moved up to the number one tackle and was eager for the next season to begin. Barry Giles was our other tackle. Harry Stamps and J. R. Conrad, the previous starters at tackle, had both gone on to the NFL. Justin Fuente was our redshirt freshman quarterback, vying with Eric Moore for starting position.

Justin, who was a pure drop-back passer, soon moved into the starting position at quarterback and gained a great deal of confidence during the spring. More important, Justin would stand up in the pocket (the space that the blockers create, from which the quarterback tries to pass) and was willing to take a hit. Eric Moore, who had played quarterback up to that point, had a tendency to look great in practice when he was protected by a red jersey, but when he played in the games he would get "nervous feet" and never set himself to throw the football. The results were breakdowns in the pocket, sacks, and wild passes. Eric's low throws were incomplete, and his high and wide throws were often intercepted.

It is important to understand that a quarterback who "sets up" in the pocket and "stays set" makes an offensive lineman's job of pass protection much easier. When the quarterback is set, a good offensive lineman will develop a sense of where the quarterback is and use that sense to get into position to set up the block on the pass rusher. If the quarterback moves around in the pocket, the pass blocking becomes much more difficult. If the quarterback moves far enough out of position, the linemen may actually assist in the sack by blocking the pass rushers right into the quarterback.

Offensively, we ran the ball more under Blake than under Schnellenberger, and Blake inaugurated a multiple offense, at least for the first year or two. We threw the ball and ran the draw (a play in which the quarterback drops back, seeming ready to pass, and then hands the ball to a running back), but those plays were used to open

Jay and his mother, Ann Smith, at spring ball, 1996.

This picture was taken at a Saturday Scrimmage during spring practice, with more than three hundred fans watching from the sidelines of the practice fields. John Blake had just recently been hired from the Dallas Cowboys to bring the Sooner family back together. As one of the top offensive linemen during spring practice, I was started at the left tackle position. I was twenty years old at the time. (Photograph by Bruce Smith) up our chances at running. We used a one- and a two-back set, running and passing about an equal number of plays.

Spring practice ended, and as we headed home at the end of the semester, we felt good about the coming season.

SUMMER 1996: THE CONFUSION BEGINS

The summer turned out to be somewhat of a mystery. I was scheduled for the second summer session so I could spend July and August in Norman, working out with the team. Expecting that classes would start the Monday after the Fourth of July holiday, I spent the week before on vacation with my grandparents in Appleton, Wisconsin. Over the holiday, on Wednesday, I received a call from one of the players with a message that Coach Blake wanted to know why I wasn't in Norman. I said I was planning to be there Monday for the start of classes, only to find out that classes had started on the previous Monday, *before* the Fourth of July. By then, Coach Blake was also out of town for the holiday, so to provide damage control I called Merv Johnson. I explained that we had messed up the start date and that I could fly down to Norman that very night. I would have missed only three days of class, which I could make up, and everything would be back to normal. The class was a repeat of one I had received a D in during the fall term, and catching up would not be difficult.

However, thinking it over, I realized that although I had planned to repeat the class to improve my grade, I didn't really need to. So I asked Coach Johnson if I could drop the class. Then I could stay in Wisconsin for the holiday weekend and drive back to Norman, saving the cost of an airline ticket, and still be present at the next workout on Monday. Coach Johnson agreed to this arrangement and said he would pass the information on to Coach Blake, and we went back to setting off fireworks.

I reported to Norman on the Monday after the holiday, only to find that no one was there—no coaches and no players except the few who were enrolled in summer school, and they were in classes.

Summer workouts were voluntary according to NCAA rules, and it turned out that no formal workouts were planned, so I came back to Arlington. From my perspective this was better, because I would get more intense workouts at home with my brother Allan pushing me. However, when Coach Blake returned to Norman, he didn't see it that way. In his mind, even though workouts were informal and not structured, if I wasn't in Norman, I couldn't possibly be working out.

Merv Johnson knew how much Allan contributed to my workouts, because he was familiar with Allan's work ethic and his success at Angelo State. For my part, I thought that since I had cleared my decision to drop the summer class with Coach Johnson, it would be all right if I spent the rest of the second summer session at home. When I returned to campus for pre-fall practice, I was in the best condition of all the offensive linemen, but Coach Blake seemed to consider me out of shape because I hadn't been in Norman all summer. It was an impression that I had trouble overcoming.

THE START OF THE 1996 SEASON: INEXPERIENCE ALL AROUND

Things still looked good as we headed back to OU to begin fall training. All the major university football programs were running summer training programs by now, including Tennessee, Ohio State, and Florida. Our philosophy was one we could live with: we would rebuild from the shambles of the program left in disarray when Coach Schnellenberger left. We were going to put the best team on the field that we could and play as hard as we could. The media bought into that philosophy, too, and the resulting pressure was much less than it had been the year before, when the press was told we would be winning the national championship that year.

This was also the first year of the Big Twelve Conference. The legendary Big Eight had evolved into a new and expanded set of teams. The old members remained the same: OU, OSU, Kansas, KSU, Nebraska, Colorado, Iowa State, and Missouri, but now there

Jay and his father, Bruce Smith, at Media Day, 1996.

1996 would be my redshirt sophomore year (junior year of college) under new head coach John Blake. I was twenty years old and six feet four inches tall and 285 pounds, and I was a projected to be the starting left tackle under Dick Winder's new offense. There were about one thousand Sooner fans on this hot (one hundred degrees plus) Saturday afternoon in August, and both my parents made the trip to Norman for Media Day. (Photograph by Ann Smith)

Head Coach John Blake and Jay at Media Day 1996.

    John Blake was always able to make his players laugh and feel comfortable around him, treating every player like his own son. A former player for OU, Blake was excited about being the new head coach, and everyone thought that by hiring him, the athletic department was bringing the Sooner family back together again and to the top of college football. At this point, not a single game had been played under Coach Blake. He and Jay were laughing because Coach Blake had a line of kids waiting for his autograph and had to sneak away for this picture. (Photograph by Bruce Smith) were also four Texas teams: Texas A&M, Texas Tech, Baylor, and our old nemesis, the University of Texas.

Another big difference was that the conference was split in half, into the North and South Divisions, and we wound up in the South with the Texas teams and OSU. That left us with only two other conference teams we could play in any one season, meaning that our annual, historic grudge match with Nebraska would no longer be an annual affair. The Cornhuskers would have to rotate into our conference schedule like everyone else. It was in our favor in the coming 1996 season that Nebraska would not be a regular-season game.

Although we wouldn't be playing Nebraska every year, the possibility existed that in some years we might actually play them twice: once in the regular season and again in the conference championship game, which was a new addition when the Big Twelve was born. In this title game, the winners of the North and South Divisions would square off to decide the conference winner.

With Coach Blake had come a new menu of assistant coaches. I've already mentioned Dick Winder, our new offensive coordinator from Texas Tech, and Bill Young, defensive coordinator. Winder was an older guy from West Texas, had been around Texas high school football for years, and was a real cowboy with a wide grin and a big West Texas personality. He had taken average players at Texas Tech and done well with them there, fashioning strength by putting together good teams that were greater than the sum of their parts. He would do the same for some of the average players at OU. The challenge with Coach Winder was that his offensive scheme was very complicated, and he had to spend so much time teaching the plays and the system that we didn't have enough time left over to work on football fundamentals. That lack of preparedness would show in our early games of the upcoming season.

From what we could tell, neither Winder nor Young had been among Blake's inner circle of friends before he took the OU job. Although they were fine coaches, they never seemed to be embraced by Coach Blake, who wanted to exchange them for closer friends. That move would have to wait until the end of his second year, however.

Also among the new coaches was Denver Johnson, my third offensive line coach since I signed on with OU. He was a very emotional coach but one who would give you honest feedback on your performance, and generally a nice guy.

At the end of my second year I had a good spring practice and established myself at the starting right tackle on offense. Everything seemed to be falling into place for the Oklahoma football program. Coach Blake had installed a pro-set offense, and offensive coordinator Dick Winder was well known for creating an offense that could put points on the board. The offense had looked good in the spring game, and everyone was looking forward to the fall schedule.

Unfortunately for me, Coach Blake had brought in two junior college transfer offensive linemen. It didn't seem to matter that neither of these players had been in Norman over the summer, or that they finished in last place in the fitness tests. They were going to be the stars. Initially, this decision didn't have a great impact on me, but later it had a dramatic impact on the offensive line's ability to perform as a cohesive unit.

One of the junior college transfers fell by the wayside, but the other, Sammy Williams, did have potential. From the onset of pre-fall practice, Sammy was listed as the starter at right tackle. This meant I was moved over to play left tackle. This move was OK with me because left tackle is where I wanted to play in the first place.

This all went along fine through the first two weeks of our two-a-day pre-fall practices. The offensive line seemed to be coming together as a cohesive group, and I was settling in at the left tackle position. Then the dreaded two-a-days ended, and the team was beginning to prepare for the season opener against TCU.

But what happened during the week before the TCU game was inexplicable. The coaches changed the entire makeup of the offensive line, moving Sammy to left tackle and me back to the right. To this day I have no idea why the coaches panicked and changed the offensive line, especially in the week prior to our game with TCU, a team that the Sooners should have handled easily. My best take on this is that, for some unknown reason, Coach Blake was concerned that I simply wasn't ready to play left tackle. I had played on the right side of the line for three years in high school and two in college, and I had only been in the left tackle position for two weeks—not much of a chance to prove myself. Coach Blake was more focused on blaming me for my absence from campus that summer. He was left with the impression that I simply dropped out of summer school and spent the summer loafing at home in Arlington.

Then, in yet another change in the week before the TCU game, Coach Blake panicked again and decided to move Sammy back to the right side. Apparently he believed that Sammy Williams was a great player and that I couldn't handle a "bull-rushing lineman." I was now listed as the second string right tackle on the depth chart, behind Sammy.

The events that followed gave me the impression that the offensive line coach, Denver Johnson, stood up for me in an odd way. Even though I was listed as second team on the depth chart and I wasn't listed in the program as the starter, I still started at right tackle in practice throughout the week before the TCU game and in the game itself. However, it was clear that this decision was based not on whether I could play better but on the fact that I knew the offense better and was less likely to make a mistake. My feeling about this came from Coach Johnson's comment to me prior to the TCU game. He said, "You're starting at right tackle, but if you make one f—ing mistake I'm going to yank your ass out of the game." I can somehow picture Coach Blake saying to Coach Johnson, "If you want to start Jay ahead of Sammy, that is up to you. But if he makes one mistake, Sammy is going in there to play."

So there I am, a sophomore going out to play in my first Big Twelve college football game in a new offense and in a position I have played in practice only during the three days prior to the game, and the line coach tells me he is going to yank me the first time I make a mistake. Well, guess what? There is no football player on earth who is going to go out and play under those conditions and *not* make a mistake. So sure enough, toward the end of the first quarter, I missed an assignment, and so Sammy came into the game. At this point, the offensive line was in shambles. Remember that Barry Giles, who was now the starting left tackle, wasn't moved up to start until the coaches moved me over to right tackle. So he also had only three practices in which to prepare. The result of all this player shifting was a loss to TCU for the first time in the history of OU football since the dropkick gave way to the kickoff.

In a broader sense, there was no need for the coaches to panic. Thanks to Howard Schnellenberger's Stone Age approach to grooming new players and the all-senior offensive line of the previous season, the offensive line in 1996 was brand new, the rest of the offense was new, and the players had no college game experience. What can you expect? You simply can't build an offensive line under those conditions in two weeks. So switching positions didn't help; in fact, it made things worse. If you disrupt the offensive line by shuffling players into new positions, you can't expect the team to recover in three days. Even under much better circumstances than ours, the offensive line doesn't begin to come together until the week prior to the first game, and the most dramatic improvement occurs between the first and third games of the season. If the coaches had just left well enough alone, we would have been all right; we would have had a chance to get off to a much better start that season.

Playing football is similar to performing in show business in some respects. In both cases, the old adage holds true: "A bad dress rehearsal means a good opening night." Whenever you are learning a new skill, there is a point where the pressure of the deadline for an upcoming event detracts from your normal performance. After you get past that point, performance continues to improve. The experienced director, or coach, recognizes the dress rehearsal for what it is—an anomaly that he pretty much ignores as he continues to prepare for the main event. On the other hand, an inexperienced director might panic during the dress rehearsal and try to make changes that only make matters worse and absolutely guarantee failure on opening night. In the case of the Sooner offensive line, someone should have provided our inexperienced head coach and our inexperienced offensive line coach with another adage: "No matter how badly the offensive line performs at the end of two-a-day practices, don't mess them up any more than they are at that moment. Just pat them on the butt, focus on your first opponent, and press on with what you've got."

Our offensive line had been set up correctly at the start of pre-fall practice. By the end of the season, in fact, the offensive line had returned to its original configuration, with me at left tackle and Sammy at right tackle. Unfortunately, in the meantime and as a direct result of the coaches' panic and subsequent switching, Oklahoma lost some games it should have won.

After the position moves, our line didn't jell for some time. We felt like our two weeks of two-a-days had been wasted, and that the progress we had made was blunted. When you're not working as a team, there's a problem. And we had a big problem. Moving from the left to right side, or vice versa, is a big deal for an offensive lineman; everything gets reversed when you move to the other side of the line. When you're blocking right, you have a totally different set of rules than when you're blocking left. For example, a draw play is different on the right side than on the left; if I move from left tackle to right tackle, I'm going in the other direction and have to mentally flip the play over to figure out who I'm blocking. We had run our plays over and over in spring practice and fall two-a-days. Now those plays were changed, and this just a few weeks before the season was to start. It was dangerous because if one player makes a mistake on the offensive line, the play is over and you've lost it.

So Coach Johnson had us going through the playbook throughout our meetings early in the fall season, trying to learn the plays over from the other side of the line. That was time that could have been spent on mastering some fundamentals.

But football season schedules don't wait for problems like these to be ironed out, and before we knew it, the season was upon us, ready or not. Unlike the year before, however, there were no predictions that we would win the national championship, or even the conference championship for that matter. We were unranked nationally, and the sports world seemed to be taking a wait-and-see approach with us.

Our first game was at home against TCU, and you could see our lack of preparedness right there on Owen Field on opening day before a hopeful crowd of 65,569, about 10,000 short of a home sell-out. You know OU fans aren't expecting much of your team when you start at home in Norman with less than a sellout. Maybe the fans sensed our own apprehension. On that September Saturday we weren't making plays and we weren't making blocks, but we were making plenty of mistakes. We managed to score only one touchdown and lost the game, 20–7. Our 1996 season was off to an uninspiring 0–1 start. Losing any game in the season is tough for a team, but losing your opener—especially at home—rubs salt in the wounds.

Still, as unpleasant as the loss was, it was not the disaster it would have been under the weight of Howard Schnellenberger's goal of winning the national championship. We reminded ourselves that our goal under Coach Blake was to rebuild, win as many games as possible, and try for a bowl game. We were more relaxed than in 1995, and we were enjoying our practices more.

We had a bye week the Saturday after the TCU game, so we spent the next two weeks just working on plays. We finally learned the plays, but this required us to focus less on fundamentals and so we made other mistakes. There were penalties, fumbles, missed blocks, and missed tackles. The mistakes spread through our season like an Oklahoma prairie fire. They went with us to San Diego on September 28 against the San Diego State Aztecs, where they paved the way for our 51–31 loss to a team that most earlier OU squads would have chewed up.

Next up was cross-state rival Tulsa, another team that usually doesn't give OU much trouble. But this was no normal year for the

Sooners, and although we played them in Norman, we lost to them for the third time in a row, 31–24.

This was a game we could have at least tied, if not won. But one of those pesky mistakes that had plagued us during the first two games hit us at exactly the wrong time, as we were pushing for the tying touchdown. We were running a "36 Power O," where the right guard and the center block inside and left and the left guard pulls to the right to block the end. The running back goes through the hole where the end is blocked. On this play, however, De'Mond Parker got the ball, six feet from the goal, then lost the ball on a fumble at the one-yard line. We were finished for the day, and we were 0–3 for the season.

The struggle between the head coach and the offensive line coach over my position continued on into the season. I remained on the second team on the depth chart and in the game programs, but I still started every game. We didn't know until the pregame warm-ups who would actually start, however. During the warm-ups, each offensive unit runs a series of plays. If I was assigned to the first unit during warm-ups I felt fairly certain I would be starting. By the time we played Kansas, I was listed as starting right tackle on the depth chart and in the game program, and then the coaches switched me back to left tackle.

After the third game of the season, the coaches began substituting the entire second string line as a unit. Of course, the first time they did it, the second line promptly marched down the field and scored. That posed a problem for the coaches: do they play the second line ahead of the first? The coaches never seemed to realize that because they had lower expectations for the second line, it was running a more basic offense than the first line. They just assumed the second line was more motivated to play. Meanwhile the first line was struggling just to keep up with all the complexities of Dick Winder's dazzling multiple offense. Playing the second line was also effective in that it gave the first line a breather, so it could come back rested later in the game. As the season continued, the coaches gave up this shuffling approach altogether when injuries started to blur the distinction between the first and second lines.

After the Tulsa game we offensive linemen were settling into our positions, and we were missing fewer assignments. However, we still weren't playing as a unit, and mistakes in individual technique were now becoming more apparent. Some linemen were stepping with the wrong foot, putting their heads on the wrong sides of their blocks, and losing body position on pass blocking. As a unit, we were missing blitzes, suffering breakdowns in pass protection, and having difficulty picking up the defensive line's diverting tactics, like curls and stunts.

Next up was our conference opener with the Kansas Jayhawks. For the second week in a row we'd be playing at home, and we were hopeful heading into the conference matchups. Although we played well against the Jayhawks, they blocked our crucial field goal, leading to a Jayhawk touchdown. We went downhill from there and lost by a lopsided 52–24. This is when I first sensed our players were giving up. It was the same thing that had happened to us mid-season last year, and it was disheartening. We had now played four games, lost them all, and three of those losses were in front of our own fans. Was there anything that could give a boost to this dismal season? We didn't have to wait long for that answer to come.

HOPE FOR RECOVERY

After the Tulsa game, Coach Blake had asked me what I thought was wrong. I told him that we hadn't taken any time to work on fundamentals. We needed work on basic things, but we were particularly weak in our ability to pick up the curls and stunts. So he had us work more on those things in practice, and the offense began to improve as a unit and so did our stats. He must have asked the same question of a number of other players, because the other units started to improve as well. Oklahoma football was beginning to show a faint glimmer of hope for recovery. As faint as it was at that moment, it marked the turning point. It would still take another two years to return to prominence, but from that point forward Oklahoma football was on its climb back to the top.

Our next opponent after Kansas was the Texas Longhorns, who were having a much better year than we were. We made our annual trek down to Dallas as twenty-one-point underdogs with an urgent need to win a game. We practiced in the Cotton Bowl on Friday afternoon, and some of our enthusiasm seemed to be returning. It is hard not to get excited about this longtime rivalry with the Longhorns. To some, this one game is a season unto itself. Sure, it's great to win a conference championship and a bowl bid, but then there is winning the Texas game. In the years when the Sooners have gone 9–2 or 10–1 but lost to Texas, there was a kind of asterisk next to the season record. You can almost hear the players say, "We did well that year, but we just couldn't beat Texas. Wait till next year."

On the morning of the game, Coach Blake was excited because Deion Sanders and Leon Lett of the Dallas Cowboys had agreed to join us in the locker room and on the sidelines. Sanders and Lett were friends of Blake from his time as assistant coach with the Cowboys. He thought they would give us some spark in this important game. As it turns out, he may have been right.

We hit the floor of the Cotton Bowl between the huge throng of orange-clad Longhorn fans and red-clad Sooner fans. The noise, as always, was deafening. No matter what either team's season record is, this game always draws a raucous sellout crowd. The game comes after a night of serious partying in the streets of Dallas, and a large percentage of the fans are still recovering from hangovers when the referee blows the game-opening whistle.

We played very well that October day, cutting down on the high number of penalties and fumbles that had plagued us. Although we fell behind, we kept fighting. Still down eleven points going into the fourth quarter, we scored on a punt return and a two-point conversion to cut the Texas lead to three. Texas was looking tired and, curiously, a little out of shape as the game ground on.

Then we got the ball back and drove down the field behind quarterback Justin Fuente, who made a great sixty-yard play. Unfortunately, the yardage was lost on a flag—another penalty at a crucial time. Had the play not been nullified, we would have won the game in regulation with a touchdown. As it was, we settled for a field goal to tie and send the game into overtime.

This was the first year the NCAA allowed overtime play, and we were glad to have a chance to win. In college overtime, each team gets the ball at least once; it is not sudden death like in the pros. If both teams score an equal number of points on the first exchange, you both go at it again until one team puts up more points than the other.

We won the coin toss and elected to start on defense. Teams routinely do this because it lets them see how many points they must score to win. If Texas were to kick a field goal, then a touchdown from us would beat them. That kind of knowledge would be vital if OU faced a fourth and short yardage later. Instead of risking a loss, we could tie and go into another overtime. The point was moot here, however, because when we got the ball it took us only five plays to score a touchdown. On the last play of the drive, James Allen took the ball to the right and scored off of my block. We beat Texas, 30–27, and the place went wild. There was a huge pileup of red jerseys in the end zone, and I was on the bottom of it, not minding a bit. I still remember linebacker Broderick Simpson "borrowing" an OU flag and running around the field with it. It was a definite Kodak moment, and a much-needed boost for our team.

So here we were, sporting only a 1–4 season record thus far but feeling pretty good about it. In fact, our morale was better than the year before when we were 4–1–1 after the Texas game. Why? Well, for one thing, this was the first time we'd beaten Texas since I'd been at OU. It was a great feeling, especially since I was playing in front of some of my former high school fans and friends. For another, we were just 1–1 in conference play and still in the running for the Big Twelve Conference title. For another, our morale was much better under Coach Blake than under Coach Schnellenberger. And finally, there was a general feeling that after five games we had worked out our kinks as a team, and maybe we were now ready to start playing more seriously.

Whatever the reasons, we felt good. The fans were happy, we had a great celebration in the locker room, and many of us spent the night in Dallas that night and drove back to Norman the next day. This time, all the banners and flags on I-35 proclaimed us as the victors, not Texas.

The next week we traveled to Waco to take on the Baylor Bears, who were not having a very good year. Our teams seemed pretty evenly matched, given our own level of play for the year. We played well on their field, simply going out and executing our plays. We made some mistakes on the first drive but still drove downfield and scored. It seemed like we had started to believe we could play well and score. We won the game, 28–24, and despite the narrow margin of victory, we felt good about it. We were now 2–1 in the conference and ready for our next opponent.

Unfortunately, our next opponent was high-powered Kansas State, and we were on the road for the third straight week. Memories of the Wildcats' 49–10 win the previous year were on our minds as we flew to Manhattan. We knew we would have to reach down deep for the kind of focus and execution it would take to beat them.

We began inauspiciously on our own five-yard line after losing the coin toss. Justin Fuente was quarterback, and I was over at left tackle. In this game I allowed the only sack of my lifetime. We wound up punting from our goal line, and K-State got the ball on our thirty. They steamrolled the rest of the first half, going up to 35–3 by halftime. In the halftime locker room we vowed to do better in the second half. We roared back, scoring twenty-four unanswered points and cutting their lead to 35–27. We would score another eight points before the game was over, but the Wildcats woke up in time to score their only second-half touchdown and slide past us, 42–35.

At 2–5 overall and 2–2 in conference play, and with Nebraska and Texas A&M up ahead, we knew we were effectively finished for the year as far as a conference championship or even a bowl game was concerned. Still, we had regained our pride in the Texas and Baylor games and had come from a long way back in the K-State game to lose by only seven points. So we decided to play for that pride and just go out and enjoy ourselves in doing it.

NEBRASKA

Our pride would take a beating the next Saturday against the top-ranked Nebraska Cornhuskers, and it would happen again before our home fans on Owen Field. We matched up well against the Huskers in the first half and kept the game in reach. But things fell apart in the third quarter, when Nebraska scored off a Justin Fuente interception and scored another touchdown. That was really our first mistake of the game, but then we fell apart. We lost control of the game, and there didn't seem to be anything we could do about it.

When the game ended, we had lost by a humiliating score of 73–21. To my knowledge, the University of Oklahoma had never lost a football game to anyone by fifty-two points, and it was not a record anyone wanted to create. But we did. After that game I remember thinking that now I understood the difference between being No. 1 in the country and being on the bottom, which is exactly where we were. I realized we were rebuilding as a team, but I also realized how low this program had sunk over the past few years. We were not even close to being a contender for the conference. We were 2–6 and out of contention for everything now.

After the game, Nebraska's offensive coordinator, Turner Gill, came up to me on the field and said, "Keep your head up, keep working hard, and you will be fine." It meant a great deal to me. Coach Gill had worked very hard to get me to attend Nebraska, and I had always felt he was truly a class act. This gesture proved it to me. Later that week, my father sent a note to Coach Gill thanking him for taking time to talk to me. Coach Gill then sent a return message to my parents that read, "Dr. and Mrs. Smith, I have often thought

Jay and Grant Wistrom (#98) of Nebraska, fall 1996.

In this picture, I am playing left tackle on the offensive line. I am trying to pass block Grant Wistrom away from OU quarterback Justin Fuente (not pictured), who is trying to throw a pass downfield. Grant Wistrom was an All-American defensive end for the top-ranked Cornhuskers. The Sooners played well in the first half but ended up getting beat, 73–21. This game was played under first-year Head Coach John Blake. Grant Wistrom continued on to the NFL and now plays for the St. Louis Rams. I started all eleven games in 1996. (Photograph by Lisa Hall) about Jay in the last year or two. . . . I wish Jay all of the success in the world . . . on the field, in the classroom, and all of the endeavors he chooses to go after." I will always keep that letter.

Sometimes people ask what makes Nebraska so great, year after year. To begin with, college football is a passion in Nebraska, much as it is in Oklahoma. It's maybe even more popular there, given the little variety in entertainment available in the central plains states. Second, there are a lot of gifted athletes in Nebraska and only one Division I football school: the University of Nebraska. Third—this is pretty unique—understand that just about every local school district in Nebraska sponsors a kid to attend NU, enabling him to walk on and try to make the team. Whereas a normal Division I school may have twenty such walk-ons, Nebraska has often had fifty or more. And most of them are players who could win scholarships at other schools.

Because walk-ons don't receive scholarships, at least not right away, this allows the university to use its football scholarships for more out-of-state players. As a result, there are extra players all over the place in Lincoln. Although the NCAA allows teams to suit up 105 players at two-a-days, when these practices are over coaches can suit up as many as they want for home games and up to sixty-two for away games. At Nebraska home games, they have players standing three deep on the sidelines. This is a pretty exciting sight for the fans, and pretty intimidating for the opposing team.

The Nebraska coaches put their players through intense weight training and high-level practices and feed them mass and weight gain supplements. Add to all this the great coaching traditions at Nebraska, capped by the legendary Bob Devaney and Tom Osborne eras, and you have the recipe for success.

Armen Keteyian, in his book *Big Red Confidential*, said the following of the Husker football phenomenon:

> [Cornhuskers are] (n)ot so much football players as they are survivors of a finely tuned, fiercely competitive, complex program where depth charts run ten deep, strength and conditioning

have been elevated to art forms, and acres of athletes battle each year. About 60 percent are in-state kids, walk-ons mostly, prized players from places like Kearney, Gering, Broken Bow, and Burr, who grow up dreaming of wearing the scarlet and cream. The remaining 40 percent define what Nebraska football has become in the late 1980s: the second home to speedy blue-chip black athletes from the inner cities of Chicago, Los Angeles, Houston, and New Orleans. Defensive backs, linebackers, running backs, split ends, strangers in a strange land, all struggling to adjust—socially and otherwise—in predominantly white Lincoln. Trying to cope. Struggling to understand the pain, the pleasures . . . and the pressures of big-time football in a state where, as one former player found, "You get brainwashed. Nebraska football is everything—you eat, sleep, and drink it."[2]

And that is Nebraska football in a nutshell. It's ironic that in the late 1980s, about the same time OU was having so much highly publicized trouble with some of its football players off the field, the same thing was happening to Nebraska. It's just that they didn't get the spotlight that the Sooners did. Keteyian goes on to describe "the big-time money and pressures that come with being the winningest team in college football: a suicide, widespread ticket scalping, the use and abuse of cocaine and steroids, and the lucrative 'pay for play' system where star players were secretly paid for passes, tackles, and TDs."[3] So the team that has somehow had such a clean reputation over the years has also had its darker moments as well. But through it all—man, are they a tough team to beat!

FINISHING OUT THE SEASON

Next up for us was Oklahoma State, in Stillwater. Still smarting from the memory of our 12–0 shutout the previous season, we were determined to win this game. Coach Blake had been shuffling our starting quarterback position between Justin Fuente and Eric Moore. But a two-quarterback situation can sometimes create problems for the offensive line. Each quarterback has his own pacing, and it's easy for a line to get thrown out of sync. It also can create a bit of a leadership problem on the field because there are two field generals instead of one. Both Fuente and Moore had their strong points and weak points: Moore was jittery and would run out of the pocket easily, whereas Fuente wasn't that mobile and would stand back in the pocket and throw the ball.

We met the Cowboys on a beautiful Saturday afternoon in November, and they didn't make it easy on us. The game was close throughout, but we finally beat them near the end on a long run, when James Allen ran a draw over my side and broke it for sixty yards. We won, 27–17.

We were buoyed by the win because no matter what else had happened to us this year, we had accomplished two of our goals: beating Texas and beating Oklahoma State. So we were confident when we headed to College Station the next week to take on Texas A&M. It was a really humid day, and we were playing the Aggies in a close game. Down by a couple of touchdowns in the first quarter, we came back and knotted the score by halftime. But in the second half our mistakes showed up again in penalties and fumbles, and we lost, 33–16.

One of my more frustrating moments of the season came in the waning minutes of the A&M game. Throughout the year, Coach Denver Johnson had continued to threaten to pull me from the game for making a mistake, and in this game it finally happened. Unfortunately for me, Coach Denver often had no clue who was making the mistakes. In this play our quarterback was sacked from the left side. I was promptly yanked and didn't play the rest of the game. However, I hadn't even been on the left side of the line. The play was a tackle-over-right, where the left tackle lines up in an unbalanced line on the right, outside the right tackle. The tight end on the left is the one who missed the block, and Denver blamed me even though I was on the opposite end of the offensive line. That week I was rated as one of the best linemen for that game, but I ended up on the bench because the line coach couldn't keep the plays straight.

The final game of the season was at home with Texas Tech. Rain pelted Owen Field as the game opened, and we immediately ran into a problem. Not only were the ball and the field slippery, but even worse, the Red Raiders' defensive line seemed to know what we were going to do offensively before we did it. Why? Because Dick Winder had come to OU from Texas Tech, and he was running the same offense here that he had at Tech. We even had the same snap count, which was, "Go," or "Go, Go." Texas Tech's defensive line knew this and would sometimes yell out our snap count, causing us to jump offsides. This happened several times during the game, and we lost our final contest of the season, 22–12.

We finished the year at 3–8 and headed home for the holidays, far removed from any bowl game. It was not exactly what we had in mind when the season started, but we were looking forward to improving in our second year with Coach Blake.

MY ACHILLES HEEL

We came back to Norman in January to help with recruiting. At OU, as at most schools, the players host the recruits who come to campus for recruiting weekends in December and January. It's a big social affair, where we sell the program and the university and feed the young guests every time they turn around. Seriously—no one ever gets close to going hungry during a recruiting weekend at OU. The coaches are around at all meals, talking it up with the recruits. Then there's an academic meeting, a campus tour, a basketball game, parties on Saturday night, and a Sunday meeting with the coaches. These are the formal visits, and the NCAA lets each recruit have a maximum of five.

Officially, I was a sophomore at the time, although this was my third year at OU. We had a young team, and we really hadn't lost anyone in key positions recently. But teams always have openings and usually bring in an average of twenty-five freshmen on scholarships. Being in the Big Twelve Conference helps a lot in recruiting efforts, because it's an important football conference. Coming off a 3–8 year made it a little harder for OU, but Coach Blake had a winning personality and was good at recruiting.

Some people wonder whether OU's "bad boy" reputation from the last years of Barry Switzer's tenure made parents hesitate to send their sons to play for the Sooners. As far as I could see, this concern didn't exert any influence on our recruiting efforts, at least not any more. It was 1997, and the problem days for Switzer's OU players, a few of whom had wound up in jail, had ended back in 1989.

A new addition for our team—and an important one for me— was Sam Pittman, who came from Cincinnati to be the fourth offensive line coach in my three years at OU. (Denver Johnson had left to coach Murray State, a Division I-AA program in Kentucky.) Now we were surrounded by positive reinforcement from Blake and his coaches. Everything was upbeat. Coach Blake wanted us all to get bigger and stronger, so he didn't run us as much. Instead we lifted weights. This was great, because most players would rather lift than run. For one thing, you get stronger faster that way. For another, lifting is easier than running, especially for big linemen.

Overall, we worked in a more relaxed and positive environment, and our goal was to make ourselves better as players by working on techniques. Off-season proved to be a real joy. We still had to get up at 6:00 A.M., but that was OK. I worked my way up to 290 pounds, 50 pounds more than my lowest weight under Coach Schnellenberger, and I played much better at that weight. When we got into spring practice, all the players knew the plays for a change, and even though I was moved from tackle to guard and back again, I did well. We had developed a great offensive line, and I was looking forward to the fall. Justin Fuente was our quarterback, everyone was excited, and the future was looking fine. Coach Blake even gave out awards for academics and achievements at our intersquad game. For the first time in over a year, it seemed like we had time to go to school and do well.

Spring semester ended, and I headed home to Texas for a short three weeks, during which I worked on my speed. When June came, I was back at OU with sixty other guys, lifting weights and running, prepping for fall camp, which would start in August. Summer training is always hard work, especially with the Oklahoma heat. This was a typical Oklahoma June, with the thermometer edging toward one hundred degrees on most days and topping it on a few. But I was psyched up about fall practice and the regular season beyond that. Our offensive line had jelled, I was getting my second season as a starter, and only good things seemed to be happening during this summer of 1997.

Good things were happening, that is, until June 24. We were doing a drill invented by the weight coach: we'd run up an incline, weaving our way through a shuttle-run laid out with construction cones. The cones were set about ten yards apart, and the object was to sprint to a cone, pivot around it, and then sprint to the next cone, proceeding up the incline. On the fifteenth of sixteen repetitions, I was pivoting around a cone and pushing off to sprint uphill to the next cone when I felt a sharp object pop against my left calf. I have never been shot, but if I ever am, I suppose it will feel exactly like that. I fell to the ground and grabbed my lower leg, thinking I had sprained it. The reality was worse. As the trainer and doctors soon diagnosed, I had torn my left Achilles tendon. Most people imagine this must be the worst pain an athlete can feel. Usually it is, but really, my tear didn't hurt that much.

What hurt more was knowing that few athletes ever regain their prior abilities after tearing their Achilles tendon. Often it's a career-ending injury. After the diagnosis, I called my folks to share the bad news. My dad knew how serious it was from his days of playing for the University of North Dakota.

The Achilles tendon is a thick band of tissue that attaches the muscles of the calf to the heel bone—the key to the foot's ability to flex. The tendon enables the athlete to push off the foot. It's what gives an offensive lineman the firepower to explode off the ball.

Usually the result of a stop-and-go or backward-to-forward motion, an Achilles tendon tear is a serious injury. According to Dr. James Barnett, a member of the Association of Professional Team Physicians and team physician for the Orlando Magic, "It can happen very suddenly, without warning, and it is almost always a season-ending injury for the individual."[4]

An athlete can injure the tendon in a variety of ways. Dr. Barnett describes one possible injury trigger called an eccentric load. This is when a load or stress is applied to a tendon that's already being stretched, as when an athlete is running backwards. An eccentric load is the opposite of a concentric load, in which you are applying a load to a muscle that's being shortened, as when you are doing toe raises while walking up a flight of stairs.

Doctors believe a number of Achilles ruptures are caused by stopping and starting or moving backward-to-forward quickly. In this case, you have a concentric load followed quickly by an eccentric load, or vice versa. This might occur when a quarterback drops back to pass and then steps up into the pocket. That is similar to what happened to Vinny Testaverde when he fell with an Achilles tear in the second quarter of a New York Jets' opening game, clutching his leg in obvious pain.

So here I was, just elected as one of the team captains for the season and named as preseason All–Big Twelve. I was excited about a really great season in my junior year. I would be starting, and the junior year is when you're really given the once-over by the NFL scouts. But instead of all that to look forward to, I was facing surgery in two days. This surgery was an option on my part, but without it I would have had no chance of ever playing again. Nevertheless, the local sportscasts and ESPN were all reporting that the Oklahoma Sooners had just lost their best offensive lineman for the entire year.

I wasn't that pessimistic; I was mentally determined to recover and rejoin the line in time for the Texas game, a little over three months away. But at the time I really didn't know the impact this kind of injury can have on your body. In Achilles surgery, the two ends of the tendon are sewn together and the foot and lower leg are placed in a cast, with the foot pointed down to lessen the tension on the repaired tendon. Normally it requires a six-to-twelve-week recovery period, and that's if you recover enough to play again, which is not guaranteed.

I spent four weeks in a cast. When it came off, I was feeling pretty good, so under the guidance of the trainers, I started slowly by walking, using a walking boot. After two weeks of walking I was able to jog and do some light running. In order to provide additional support for my Achilles and to provide a margin of safety, the doctors and trainers fabricated a brace for my ankle. Over the course of the next two weeks, I started to build up a little speed, and I thought I might even beat my own timetable for returning to the team.

Then the unthinkable happened: on the very first day that I stepped up the intensity of my running, eight weeks after surgery, I tore the tendon again. I really wasn't running that hard—it was more like warm-ups, where you are going about half speed to stretch and get loose. This time I felt a snap, and I thought it was just scar tissue that had popped. I didn't realize that it had torn again, and with the support of the brace I was able to finish the rehab session. But if you pushed down on my Achilles with your fingers, you could feel a gap where it had separated. I went back in for an MRI, which confirmed that I had indeed torn my Achilles again. The first tear had apparently healed, but in overcompensating and trying not to tear it there again, I pulled too hard, put too much strain on the rest of my leg, and tore it all over again a little lower down.

The experts were saying if the first tear didn't end my career, this one would. But again, I opted for surgery, and the coaches and doctors told me I was the first player ever to have the surgery done twice. OU brought in an ankle specialist to perform the surgery at the Oklahoma Health Sciences Center in Oklahoma City.

The surgery seemed successful, but even so I knew my season was over. This time I was in a cast for ten weeks instead of four. I was facing my first year at OU without playing football, and the prospects looked dim.

Now Coach Blake had to make some quick adjustments. He had lost much of the momentum our offensive line had gained up that point. I had been playing guard at the time of my injury, and they had to prepare a younger and more inexperienced player to start an expanded season of twelve games (the season was expanded from eleven because we were on tap to play in the Pigskin Classic in Chicago's Soldier Field). The job of replacing me actually fell to two players: Adam Carpenter and Jason Bronson, both redshirt freshmen.

Coach Blake was facing other problems, too. We all knew he wanted to fire Dick Winder and Bill Young, the offensive and defensive coordinators whom OU had handpicked to buttress Blake's inexperience as a head coach. Neither was in Blake's inner circle of friends, and in coaching, it's important for a head coach to feel close to his assistants because he must trust them to do so much. Blake's offensive philosophy, which changed often, didn't mesh well with Winder's, and there were several disagreements between the two coaches as a result. Blake wanted his own people in those key slots, but during his first year he hadn't been afforded the opportunity to make the changes he wanted. So the team went into the 1997 season with conflicting coaching philosophies on how best to get the ball downfield.

Before the team knew it, fall practice was over and the season was upon us. The Pigskin Classic was held on August 23 against still-strong Northwestern University, who in 1995 had played its best season ever, won the Big Ten Conference, and had gone to the Rose Bowl. I was able to travel with the team to Chicago, but obviously I did not suit up. I just watched from the sideline with the ever-obtrusive cast smothering my left leg. The Sooners didn't stand a chance that day, and we were shut out, 28–0. It was an omen of things to come for yet another season.

I spent my time lifting weights with my friend and teammate Joe Carolla, trying to get stronger. Since I was in a cast, I couldn't use my whole body for lifting, so I bench-pressed weights as Joe handed them to me and worked on my upper-body strength. I can't say enough good things about Joe and his help. Without him, I doubt I could have come back from those twin Achilles tears.

People asked me if I was worried about not being able to come back or if I was worried that Adam or Jason would replace me on the offensive line. My answer, then as now, was that I didn't worry about coming back because I knew I could do it. What did worry me was that my absence left a hole in the line, and a redshirt freshman had to take my place. As the losses starting piling up for OU that season, I worried I might be partly responsible for the bad season the Sooners were having. I felt they really needed me out there.

I was also worried about being distant from the team that season. When you are injured and are in rehab, you are cut off from the team; you don't practice or play with them. In some ways, you feel like you're not a member of the team anymore. You're taken out of the whole team picture. You may travel with them, but that is more a ceremonial gesture than anything else.

So I stepped away from football not only for that fall, but also for the spring, as it turned out. Two things kept me focused: strength training and academics. Every day I felt myself getting stronger, and I saw my grades rise dramatically. I had my best grades ever, with my GPA for the year hovering around 3.5. As bad as being cut off from the team was, it was great to be able to be a full-time college student for a change. One day I realized, "Wow! I really have time to go to class and study now!" I also had a chance to make new friendships among nonathletes. I had pledged Phi Gamma Delta fraternity during my freshman year, but I never had the opportunity to be a real member until the year of my injury.

I took part in more campus activities, going to plays and concerts and fraternity parties. It was a good chance to build friendships outside of football, and now, as an alum, I often see some of my fraternity brothers in Oklahoma City and Tulsa. Many college football players say that they enjoy playing football, but they wish they could go to college a second time to see what being a college student is really like. Football is a year-round business for the team, and there just isn't much time left over to behave like other students. Now, because of this disappointing injury, I had that chance.

I was living in an apartment off campus on the $450 per month the university gives its football players for housing expenses. When you start to pay your own way, you realize how little that is, even in Norman, Oklahoma. After 1995, the NCAA outlawed dorms devoted exclusively to college athletes. They instituted a 50–50 rule, under which a dorm can be comprised of no more than 50 percent student-athletes. The rest have to be nonathlete students. Another change under current OU rules is that only freshmen athletes can live in designated dorms. Bud Wilkinson House, the "football dorm," was converted to that 50–50 ratio in 1996. From then on, Bud Wilkinson House would house only the twenty-five incoming freshmen players, who roomed together in thirteen of the dorm's rooms. Abolishing exclusive athletic dorms forced athletes to move off campus sooner than the coaches would have liked them to. I had lived in athletic dorms for two years.

While I was enjoying my year as a college student, the football team was not having much fun on their way to a 4–8 season record. Although the Sooners rebounded from the Northwestern shutout with a 36–34 home victory over tough Syracuse two weeks later, in another two weeks they turned around and lost to California, 40–36, in Berkeley.

On the Saturday of that Syracuse game, a terrible thing occurred that changed management at the top for the Sooners. On the very day of the game, Steve Owens's son committed suicide, stunning us all and leveling our athletic director emotionally. Owens resigned the next week, and the university was crestfallen, both at the tragedy and at the loss of its former playing legend and athletic director. Once again, as he did after Coach Schnellenberger's abrupt departure in December of 1995, Larry Naifeh filled the gap as interim director until the university brought in Joe Castiglione the following spring.

Back on the field, however, the Sooners were showing they could score some points, and that was important. At 1–2, they tackled Louisville at Owen Field and won, 35–14. That win not only evened the season record at 2–2, but it was especially sweet since Louisville was Howard Schnellenberger's old team, which he had coached for a decade before bringing his act to Norman.

But two losses would follow that victory, to Kansas (20–17 at Lawrence) and to Texas (27–24 in Dallas). There was no last-minute miracle this year when it came to the UT game, and now the Sooners stood at 2–4.

Under Coach Blake, the players improved, but they quickly realized the offensive scheme was not set in stone. Quite the opposite: it evolved on a weekly basis. First-year players struggle with their team's offensive scheme, but by the second year they are generally used to it. Not so under Coach Blake, however. The scheme changed all the time, and it became apparent the coaching staff wasn't working well together. Coach Winder was running his multiple offense, which uses a complicated assortment of formations, while Coach Blake and Joe Dickinson, the running back coach, were pushing the option offense, an offense that had not been run at OU for years in which the ball carrier has the option of either passing the ball or running with it. They were two vastly different philosophies, and the confusion was showing up on the playing field.

The team began the trek back to .500 the next week with a close home win, 24–23, against Baylor. But that was followed by a three-game string of losses against Kansas State (which was vying for a No. 1 ranking at the time); Nebraska, and Oklahoma State. These last two losses were especially stinging, because second-ranked Nebraska, who had beaten us by fifty-two points the year before, absolutely torched us this year at Lincoln, 69–7. So we obliterated the record we set in 1996; this year we lost to the Huskers not by fifty-two but by sixty-two. Heaping coals of humiliation on that loss was an Owen Field thrashing at the hands of Oklahoma State, 30–7.

Given those flamethrower weeks, it is amazing the Sooners found any way at all to win their final game, especially since it was on the road. But traveling to Lubbock to play Texas Tech, the team reached down and pulled up enough spunk to hand the Red Raiders a 32–21 loss.

Season number two with Coach Blake was now history, and it had been almost identical in record to season number one. The only reason we were 4–8 this year instead of 3–8, as in 1996, was because of the extra Pigskin Classic game. It's interesting to note that those, like John Underwood of the *New York Times*, who had said that Coach Schnellenberger was fired after a single season simply because he won only five games would have to deal with this fact: Coach John Blake had gone two seasons winning a total of only seven games, and OU was bringing him back for yet a third season.

THE 1998 SEASON

Not only did I miss the regular season in 1997, but I also missed spring ball in 1998. My Achilles was too tight and my leg was not secure enough to go through the footwork drills required during those practice sessions. I spent the off-season walking, working on my rehab, and doing a little jogging every day. I spent time in the weight room building up my strength, but it was now a more gradual process because I had been away from the team for a year. I didn't want to do the kind of drills that would result in yet a third Achilles tear. I rode the stationary bike, did upper-body conditioning, received massage therapy, and hit the swimming pool every other day. So my fall experience as a "real" college student stretched into the spring as well, and I was enjoying myself in that respect.

Meanwhile, Coach Blake had finally gotten his wish to replace Winder and Young as offensive and defensive coordinators. He moved in his friend Joe Dickinson as offensive coordinator and brought in Rex Ryan (son of famed pro coach Buddy Ryan) as defensive coordinator. So now Blake had his friends installed as assistant coaches and hoped for a more unified overall coaching philosophy. Everyone was on the same page.

Blake continued to be loved by the players, probably allowed himself to be influenced a little too much by their likes and dislikes, and engendered what some players called a "country club atmosphere" in the off-season. Players often came and went as they liked and sometimes did whatever they wanted. Coach Blake tried to be the moral compass for the team, as a few players made some bad decisions in their off-time. He would often invite players to his home and counseled us by resorting to his favorite mantra: "Whatever you do in the dark is going to come to the light." He said if you believe in and follow God, you'll be fine. One of the ingredients missing under Coach Howard Schnellenberger had been the feeling among the players that he really cared about them. That was not missing with Coach John Blake. The players knew he cared about them, and cared a lot.

Coach Blake's slogan for the team was, "Performance Is Reality." By that he meant that the players who perform will play—playing the game being the truest reality for a football player. But he often seemed to deviate from that philosophy in deciding who to start in our games. He seemed to have his favorite players and would start them, no matter what. Some of this can be chalked up to his inexperience as a head coach, some of it to his closeness with players, and some of it to bad advice from his friends, the new assistant coaches. Coach Blake wanted his players to be happy and enjoy themselves. But there is a fine line between having fun and losing discipline, and the team didn't have much discipline under the beloved Coach Blake.

When I first joined a running group again with some of my teammates, it had been a full year since my 1997 injury. I realized quickly that I wasn't as fast as I had been before the injuries. I wasn't as agile, either. To an offensive lineman, the thing that matters most is what's called your "explosion," or your acceleration off the line. You must act before your defensive opponent can react. That explosion is tied directly to your Achilles, which controls how fast you can move your

Allan and Jay Smith at Owen Field in the fall of 1998.
The Sooners had just completed their last scrimmage of fall camp on an evening that reached 106 degrees. The practice was late in the evening, and the lights had to be turned on to finish the scrimmage. This scrimmage was set up for the fans, and some twenty-five thousand showed up that day. This was Coach John Blake's third season as head coach. I was twenty-two years old and weighed 295 pounds. My brother Allan had made the trip from Michigan, and my parents had come from Arlington to watch the scrimmage. I finished fall camp as the starting left guard. (Photograph by Bruce Smith)

feet. We call it foot speed. It also affects your sense of balance, especially in the down position. So I knew it would take a lot of work to get back to the level I was used to.

Since my injury, I had dropped from starting position to fourth on the depth chart when two-a-days began in August. I would have thirty-one practices to prove myself and try to regain my previous starting role, and it wouldn't be easy. I had also lost my role as co-captain. It seemed that Coach Blake didn't want me as one of his captains at all. I sensed he didn't care that much about me because I had been absent from the team for a whole year, and now he wanted to play his own recruits ahead of me. These were sophomores, and in 1998 I was listed as a senior.

I had a tough time with two-a-days, getting back into the routine and playing like I used to. Plus, the "country club" atmosphere extended to the practices, and the players weren't worked hard enough to allow any real competition, which took away my opportunity to shine and move up on the depth chart. So I started the regular season in fourth position. I would get a lot of playing time, but I would have to hustle to start or move into starting position if someone ahead of me got injured.

The 1998 season began at Owen Field on September 5, when we hosted North Texas, beating them easily, 37–9. The next week we followed up with a squeaker win against TCU in Fort Worth, 10–9. That game was played in a driving rainstorm, and it showed us we had developed some character over the past few years. We initially fell behind the Horned Frogs, 9–0. I was playing well and was making my blocks, although playing in the rain you always have to be more cautious in firing off the ball for fear of a leg injury. But my Achilles held, and we started to climb back late in the game. We scored a touchdown with about 1:40 left in the game, hit the extra point, then recovered our onside kick. We blunted our effort momentarily when we fumbled it on the first play, but we got the ball back and Jeff Ferguson kicked the winning field goal on the last play of the game. That sparked an outburst right after the game from one of our former tight ends coaches, Charlie North, who was now with TCU. After the buzzer sounded, North started a fight with one of our players, grabbing his helmet and swinging it around in a wide arc and starting a brawl on the field.

North's resentment aside, it was the first time under Coach Blake that we had opened a season with two wins, and things were looking up. Although I hadn't seen much playing time in those two games, I seemed to play well whenever I was inserted, and that boosted my confidence in the rehab process. At 2–0, I thought the team was doing even better than my preseason prediction that we would finish 7–5.

I got into the third game early when the left guard in front of me on the chart, Adam Carpenter, stretched the medial collateral ligament in

Jay (#71), Mike Skinner, Rocky Calmus, and Roger Steffen celebrate after the 1998 victory over TCU.

The Sooners traveled to Fort Worth for this game. We had been losing, 9–0, with two minutes left in the game, when we managed to score a touchdown to bring the score to 9–7 with 1:40 left to play. OU recovered the onside kick, and Jeff Ferguson kicked the winning field goal as time ran out. The Sooners won, 10–9, and the celebration began. (*Daily Oklahoman*)

his elbow on the very first play from scrimmage. This was a home game against California, which we narrowly lost, 13–12. We missed one field goal, but our kicker, Jeff Ferguson, had mononucleosis at the time, and he was the only person who could do the job. Added to that weakness was a series of fumbles and penalties that we made throughout the game. Nonetheless, my play was good enough for the coaches to keep me in the starting position for the next two games.

Next up was Colorado, and we drew them at home. We were getting tired of losing to Colorado; we had not beaten them since 1988. We were well-matched this year and it was a game we should have won, but we fell two points short, 27–25. Again, under Coach Blake and his assistants our playbook was expanding and changing a little too quickly for us to feel confident in our blocking assignments.

We now had experienced back-to-back losses, but the worst was yet to come. We would lose three more times before another victory. Those losses were to our old nemesis Texas (34–3) in Dallas, to Missouri (20–6) in Columbia, and—for the second straight year—to Oklahoma State (41–26) in Stillwater. These last two losses were especially hard. It was the first time Missouri had beaten us since 1983. As for Oklahoma State, we were penalty-crazy that day, and the referees set us back a total of almost two hundred yards as a result. So we lost, despite a shining performance by tailback De'-Mond Parker, who rushed for 220 yards. As the AP reported after the game, "Parker shouldn't have been surprised. He has topped 200 yards three times in the past three seasons, and Oklahoma is 0–3 in those games." More than any other telling statistic, that one shows that even with some great plays, we found ways to beat ourselves with way too many penalties and fumbles. And those miscues were often a direct result of an evolving offensive scheme that often changed from week to week.

Now sitting on a 2–5 season record and 0–4 in the Big Twelve, we knew that once again, we wouldn't be going bowling. So we were back to playing only for pride, and we pulled out our next game at home against Iowa State, 17–14. Unfortunately, that was followed by a humiliating 29–0 shutout in College Station against the Texas A&M Aggies, the game that officially kept us from winning the required six games to go to a postseason bowl.

The season did end on a winning note for us, however, and I think that helped our momentum for 1999. Our last two games were against Baylor at Waco, and at home against Texas Tech. We beat the

Bears, 28–16, and the Red Raiders, 20–17, to finish the year at 5–6, our best record during the Blake years.

YET ANOTHER CHANGE

As our problems mounted during the 1998 season, especially during our five-game losing stretch, the inevitable speculation about Coach Blake's future reached a crescendo in the press. The AP reported in October that "John Blake's third year has proved no better than his first two, which were awful. That has prompted widespread speculation that Blake will be let go with two years remaining on his contract." The AP went so far as to say, "Oklahoma fans are so hungry for a return to glory that, after the Sooners lost to Texas a few weeks ago, it was widely reported that a group of heavyweight backers were putting together a package to lure Barry Switzer back."[5]

When Switzer reported he had no desire, at age sixty-one, to return to college coaching, the AP turned its attention to other possible replacements, including Georgia's Jim Donovan, Tulane's Tommy Bowden, Oregon's Mike Bellotti, Northwestern's Gary Barnett, and the defensive coordinator of the Florida Gators, a man named Bob Stoops.[6]

Athletic Director Joe Castiglione refused to discuss Blake's future during the season. But the AP reported that, "The prevailing feeling last week was that if Blake was to have any chance of saving his job, the Sooners would need to beat rival Oklahoma State. They lost, 41–26, while committing 19 penalties for 177 yards."[7]

Still, Coach Blake remained popular with the players. Senior defensive tackle Kelly Gregg said it was the team that was failing to execute plays, not Blake. "I don't think the coach should catch all the blame," Gregg said. "Coach has never thrown a block, never made a tackle. It's unfair for him to catch all the criticism."[8]

However, the AP observed that our team had "been in disarray on the field, particularly the offense." The article noted that Blake initially preferred a multiple offensive scheme, but then changed his mind and went to the option game. "That has proved disastrous," the AP article continued. "The Sooners worked on the wishbone extensively during spring practice and fall two-a-days, but now run out of the I-formation. Brandon Daniels, who was moved from defensive back to quarterback to run the option, is now the No. 3 choice at the position. The starting quarterback against Oklahoma State was Eric Moore. He had played the position for three years but moved to receiver in the spring because the coaches didn't feel they could win with him running the offense."[9] As a telling vignette of the confusion our offense experienced during the Blake years, that one's not bad.

The bottom line for the 1998 season was we had outgained six of seven opponents but wound up being ranked a lowly ninety-seventh nationally in scoring, at only seventeen points per game. We were also among the nation's leaders in penalties (we had committed eighty-three during the first seven games alone that year). And the biggest indicator of all was this: after three seasons under Coach Blake we were 12–22, which was the worst three-season record in OU football history.

As far as I was concerned, the more important win-loss record was 23–33–1, which was the overall, five-year record of the team since I had joined them in 1994 under Coach Gibbs. This is not what I had envisioned for myself when I turned down all those other football programs back in my senior year at Arlington Lamar High School. However, because of my injury year, my application for a sixth year of eligibility had been submitted by OU to the NCAA, and I was hoping I could salvage at least one winning year before I had to leave the team.

With all that had happened, none of us on the team was really surprised when we heard that the OU regents voted 4–2 on Sunday, November 22, the day after the Texas Tech game, to terminate John Blake's contract. "This is a wrenching decision for all of us, but as president of the university I want to express feelings of appreciation we have for John Blake," OU President David Boren told the media.

Jay at the regents meeting in 1998, where the regents voted to fire John Blake.

A few days after the end of the 1998 season, the regents met at the OU Student Union and voted to fire coach John Blake. He finished his term as head coach of the Sooners (1996–1998) with a record of twelve wins and twenty-two losses. I answered questions from the media after the decision was announced to the press. (*Daily Oklahoman*)

The regents opened their Sunday meeting at 3:00 P.M. in the Oklahoma Memorial Union Ballroom on the OU campus. A large crowd had gathered for the meeting, including many football players. The board opened the meeting, then promptly went into an executive session that lasted four hours. When they emerged, they announced their decision to terminate Coach Blake's contract.

Tight end Jason Freeman, who had played his last game the day before, told the AP that the players were shaken by the announcement "because of the kind of person Coach Blake is . . . the kind of character he has instilled in us. There are a lot of people hurt by this decision."[10]

After the vote, offensive coordinator Joe Dickinson praised the way Blake had handled himself during the season. "He's been a rock," Dickinson told the AP. "There's been a lot of attacks on John for three years. He is a lot better coach today than he was three years ago, and he's getting better every game. He's great for these kids. They love him and they proved that (against Texas Tech). We were supposed to lose this game."

For his part, Coach Blake displayed the same class that he had evidenced throughout his three-year tenure at OU when he told the press, "This program is headed in the right direction. We came here for a purpose: to get the foundation established to be a winner. Most of all I want to thank all those who stuck by me . . . who knew what I stood for, and I would never change that."[11]

So ended the three-year chapter in OU history under John Blake, the third head coach in my five years with the team. Now, with one precious, final year left, I would be proving myself all over again to coach number four. We had no way of knowing it at the time, but this next choice was going to a very good one indeed for the University of Oklahoma.

CHAPTER 6

Coach Stoops

TARGETED DISCIPLINE

If I could change the world . . .

ERIC CLAPTON

I was twenty-two years old when John Blake was fired as the head coach at the University of Oklahoma, and at the time I remember thinking, "I can't believe it's all happening again." We were to have our fourth head coach in my five years at OU, and I would again have to prove myself all over again to Lord knows who. But I was older and more patient now.

Before I left school for Christmas break, OU announced that our new coach would be Bob Stoops, defensive coordinator at the University of Florida. So at least I didn't have to wonder and agonize over the holidays about who we'd be facing when we returned in January. However, I didn't know much about Bob Stoops at all, so I still wasn't sure what to expect when I returned to campus four weeks later.

By this time I had become very interested in management science and was nearing completion of my marketing/management degree, so I was honestly interested in how the new coach was going to manage the Sooners. Would he be able to pull us out of our slump

Left to right: Coach Bob Stoops, Lee Allan Smith, and Barry Switzer.
This picture was taken around December 1, 1998, at an on-campus press conference
announcing that Stoops was the new head coach of the Sooners. (Daily Oklahoman)

and bring us together as a team? I wanted to see what management strategy he would use, and this time I was even more interested in that than in the depth chart. Not that I didn't want to start; I did. But I had another hurdle standing in the way of my playing another year for the Sooners: technically, I had used up my eligibility after five seasons, and I had to get the NCAA's permission to play a sixth year.

Before I went home for Christmas, I had filed the application, explaining that my injuries had wiped out my junior year on the team. But the NCAA approval was not automatic in these cases, and I wound up having to wait until spring to get that approval. So I had to go through all the rigors of January and February conditioning without knowing whether I was going to stay on the team. Finally, the NCAA approved my petition, and I was allowed a sixth year with OU. I breathed a deep sigh of relief and looked forward to yet another new beginning as a Sooner.

OUR INTRODUCTION TO TARGETED DISCIPLINE

Coach Stoops had managed to address the team once before we left for Christmas break, and I liked what I saw and heard. He told us we would build the program on the long and successful OU football tradition, and then he told us to enjoy the break and be ready to work when we came back. He seemed energetic, young, very intelligent, clean-cut, and sharp. He had the right coaching credentials, having coached with a national championship program at Florida, and he exuded a great deal of confidence in what he could do and how to do it. The next day I chatted with him in his office. I told him I was a senior and was here to do whatever he needed. He said the team would need the seniors to take the leadership reins and steer the team in the right direction. It was music to my ears.

Another thing I liked about Coach Stoops was that he interviewed every assistant coach on the team and gave everyone a shot at staying. Most left, however, and Stoops started with an almost completely new slate of assistants. Mark Mangino was the new offensive line coach—my sixth at OU. Mike Leach was our new offensive coordinator, and Mike Stoops (Coach Bob Stoops's brother) and Brent Venables would share the defensive coordinator position. As I recall, one defensive coach from the previous year, Derrick Sheppard, did stay until summer. We also had a new strength coach to replace Joe Juraszek, and that was Jerry Schmidt.

On the academic side, I actually graduated from OU that December, having been on campus four and a half years. I decided to begin graduate school as an MBA student in marketing and management. When we returned to campus in January, it was business as usual in the off-season conditioning program, with a couple of exceptions.

The first day back we had our first team meeting, where the new coaches were introduced. Then we scheduled the morning runs, and for the first time, we had scheduled times for lifting. Coach Stoops told us we were going to start rebuilding right then. He said he didn't care what our positions were—he'd seen the team's films and knew what we could do.

"We're here to teach you how to be disciplined football players," he said, and there was no question he was going to direct the program. It also became apparent that there was a new coaching philosophy in town and that it could be boiled down into two words: targeted discipline.

We started our first day of morning conditioning with ten fifty-yard wind sprints, which was another new wrinkle. Up to this point, we had only run half that many on any given day, and they always came at the end of the workout session. Now they came before the workout, they were double the number, and the coaches called them simply "a warm-up." Any idea we had that we were still in shape after a month off evaporated that day. Half the team immediately fell out from exhaustion, gasping for air.

Coach Stoops called us into a meeting and said he was very disappointed in us. It was obvious we needed work. From that point, this off-season program was more intense than anything we'd had before. We ran four days a week, which is something linemen hate to do. We're used to quick movements in a relatively small area; we're not used to running distances or sprints, although we'd done our share of it at OU over the years.

This program would prove to be as tough as Howard's off-season conditioning, the difference being that this prepared us to play football. Every one of the conditioning drills, tough as they were, related directly to improving our football skills and increasing foot speed, which is so important for a lineman. So we jumped rope, we jumped hurdles, and we ran bungee cord drills. The way Stoops's assistants did the bungee cord drills was interesting: two guys would be tied together waist-to-waist with a twenty-five-foot elastic cord, and then the pair would set off running in the same direction. Inevitably, one guy is pulled while the other guy pulls. So your goal is to increase your speed and reduce the tension on the cord. We also pulled sleds with weights attached to them, dragging them thirty to forty yards from belts strapped around our waists. This helped us increase our explosion off the line. Then we ran shuttles back and forth, constantly changing directions. At the end of the workout we'd run four to six two-hundred-yard dashes to work on the last part of conditioning.

Hard as the running drills were, our mornings didn't begin there. Prior to running, we did sit-ups. A lot of them. We started out with three hundred every morning and wound up doing eleven hundred by the end of the eight-week program. It took us forty-five minutes each day just to do our sit-ups.

I knew this conditioning program—especially the running drills—was the kind of training I needed to get my Achilles back to 100 percent. I felt good, my tendon felt good, and I didn't worry about injuring it again. So I gave 100 percent at work-outs and ran these conditioning drills four days a week for eight weeks in the off-season.

Complementing our running and other conditioning drills was our lifting program. Everyone was scheduled in the afternoon for lifting. We lifted weights from one station to the next, and a couple of players fell out of lifting for the day from exhaustion. This was intense, fast weight training, and it was new to us. Again, however, every lift we did had something to do with improving the targeted strength we would need on the football field.

The program worked well for me. My weight wound up at 296, and although I gained 10 pounds, my body fat dropped from 22 to 14 percent. For a lineman, putting on weight while still dropping fat is a great combination. Linemen usually shoot for a body fat range of 12 to 18 percent, while linebackers try for 10–12 percent, and the backs and smaller guys look for 8–10 percent.

We were also put on individually targeted diets. Strength Coach Jerry Schmidt met with each of us during the off-season program and told us what our individual diets should be and what our individual weight goals should be. This was quite a change from Howard Schnellenberger's broad-based one-thousand-pound team weight loss goal.

All of this was evidence of something very important to Coach Stoops and his staff: targeted discipline, or discipline directly related to improving our football playing skills. We had weekly goals, instead of simply a season-long goal of winning a national championship. We could check ourselves each week to see if we were hitting those goals, and if we weren't, we could find out why.

When spring practice started I was moved to first team, left tackle. That was my favorite side of the line, and the fact that I am right-handed made no difference. We had very few tackles on offense at this time, and it was great to be filling an important hole and to know I had come all the way back from my injuries a year before.

It was on the line that we learned the offensive scheme of Mike Leach and Mark Mangino. It was on the line that we were put under a microscope like never before. From the moment each starter walked out onto the practice field to the moment he returned to the locker rooms, one of several video cameras trained on the field recorded his every move. Players would get individual feedback on every play, and some of that feedback was not pleasant. I have to say that playing for Mangino was not easy. He was a tough mentor and expected a lot from his offensive linemen. There was a lot of in-your-face yelling, although he would later smile and say he was simply "telling us" what we were doing wrong. Either way, the important thing is he was exact in his critiques, so we knew exactly what we had to do to improve our performance. Mangino also has a lot of heart and works with his players to get the desired results.

When you think about it, at a program like OU's, you get a lot of individual attention as a starter. There are so many coaches, and only twenty-two starters on offense and defense, so the player-coach ratio is small indeed. Five starting offensive linemen are coached by the offensive line coordinator and his graduate assistant. If you try to get by with slack performance, you get noticed, and you pay. If the coaches don't catch it at the time, they will see it later when they watch the tapes of the day's practice. One way or the other, as Coach John Blake used to say about our personal lives, what we would try to do in the dark would eventually come to light. And since I had been around the longest, it seems like Coach Mangino would always reserve a little something special for me in the way of "feedback." One of the things he used to say to me was, "You've been here since Bud Wilkinson, and you *still* can't get it right!"

SMARTS, SIZE, AND STRENGTH: PREPARING THE SOONERS FOR VICTORY

For the first two weeks of spring practice I played at left tackle, and then Coach Mangino moved me inside to left guard to help with some of the line blocking calls and to help a new player, Al Baysinger, feel more comfortable in his position at left tackle. The blocking calls, which are used to designate the blocking assignments for the offensive line, are vitally important for linemen, and they must be relayed from someone on the line to the running back and blocking backs within a matter of seconds between breaking from the huddle and hearing the quarterback start his snap count. The signals are based on the defensive formation currently staring at you, and they are conveyed by way of hand signals, pointing, or calling out numbers to the backs. As you can imagine, there is a lot of chatter on the offensive line before the snap count begins.

When I played as either right or left guard, the man playing center on our line was very important to me. We were blessed to have great centers like Matt O'Neal and, later, Bubba Burcham. The guard and center work in tandem on the offensive line to block a down blocker and a linebacker.

The center is so named for several reasons, not the least of which is that he is the center of activity on the line, with at least three duties to perform simultaneously. First in importance is getting the ball cleanly to the quarterback, of course. Second, he must snap and step forward at the same time in one fluid motion to block the oncoming lineman. And third, the center usually calls out the defensive pattern to the rest of the line, who then use hand signals or verbal calls to relay the set to the backs. Usually a team will bring in a different center for deep-snap situations like punts. The theory is you don't want to risk having your normal center injured while running downfield to tackle the punt receiver. Additionally, that center can concentrate on making long snaps, while the regular center can specialize in short and shotgun snaps.

Sometimes fans wonder if there is much trash talking on the line of scrimmage. Perhaps surprisingly, there isn't. Offensive linemen are way too busy assessing the defensive set and relaying information to each other and the backs to engage in intimidation tactics. The same is often true of the defensive line, although any trash talking that might occur probably originates from that side of the line.

People also wonder about how much holding actually goes on after the ball is snapped and the two sides butt heads. No one wants to draw a holding penalty that will blunt a drive, but sometimes holding is the lesser of two evils. If you see a lineman or linebacker getting by you to sack your quarterback, as an offensive lineman you may well reach to stop him. If you do it the right way, holding doesn't often catch the attention of the referees. As long as you keep your arms in front of you and not out to the side, there are certain techniques you can use to slow the advance of the would-be tackler that will escape the referee's eye.

In the end, however, nothing works as effectively as size, strength, conditioning, and quickness. Whenever you see a poorer team staying close to a better team during the first half and then falling behind in the second half, it's usually because of differences in size, strength, and conditioning. For linemen in the 230–280 pound category, weight is also important. A 230-pound lineman won't last long against a 270-pounder. When both linemen are above 280 pounds, however, conditioning is the determining factor. The better-conditioned athlete will last longer. Good conditioning also improves quickness, which ensures a lineman's explosiveness. Linemen must be able to fire off the line in an instant. If they are just a step behind the onrushing defenders, it will be too late.

Oklahoma fielded the best-conditioned teams in the Big Twelve during the 1999 and 2000 seasons, and that was a key to our success. Whoever is strongest at the end of the game will probably win the game, and that's why we won like we did. Sometimes people think it's tradition that pulls a team through in the tight spots. Tradition may be a factor, but only if the team is making its own tradition at the present time. You can't make much headway simply by borrowing from traditions past. Certainly it helps to have motivational speakers like Barry Switzer or Brian Bosworth in the locker room, but in the end, it's going to be the team's willingness to make the plays happen and execute them. That often comes down to conditioning, and sometimes it simply comes down to luck. In addition to their talent, conditioning, and dedication, the 2000 National Champion Sooners were sometimes just flat lucky.

Some people wonder about the effect that crowd noise has on the ability of players to hear each other and the ability of the quarterback and linemen to call the plays and blocking patterns. In truth, if you are disciplined, as most major-college players are these days, you don't even notice the stadium noise. You are working in something of a repetitive mode—you've run these plays so many times in practice that your timing and movements become instinctive. Still, to get us accustomed to stadium noise, sometimes the coaches would try to simulate it in practice situations. For the practices leading up both the Texas and Texas A&M games, they brought in loudspeaker systems, popped in CDs of the A&M and Longhorn fight songs, and turned them up to high volume. These are just two examples of how Coach Stoops tried to cover every possible base in preparing for our opponents.

Spring ball finally ended, and we had three glorious weeks off to take finals and enjoy two weeks of summer break. Then we reported back to campus in late May for twelve weeks of summer conditioning. Tell me college football isn't a year-round job! I should point out that the summer conditioning program was officially voluntary. The coaches couldn't require it. But the reality is that if you want to impress the coaching staff and have a chance to play during the coming fall season, you show up.

The first few weeks of summer conditioning were pleasant enough. We pretty much repeated the routine of the winter conditioning program; the drills were held outside, and the June and July weather wasn't that bad for Oklahoma. Players also lifted weights five days a week and took a class to keep their stipends coming in and cover their room and board. During this particular summer, however, I elected not to take a class, and my parents covered my living expenses. So I enjoyed the summer, living in an apartment by myself and not in university housing. I was just lifting and running, and for a short time I got a feel for what it must be like to be a professional athlete. I liked the feeling, but it was bittersweet because I knew my torn Achilles had put a dent into my plans for playing in the NFL.

Before fall practice started, each of us on the team had to pass a conditioning test, and it was one of the toughest tests I've ever seen. The test consisted of two three-hundred-yard runs on grass. Each run was broken up into five sixty-yard lengths. We had to run a sixty-yard course five times for one three-hundred-yard run, then immediately turn around and do it the second time. To pass the test, an offensive player had to complete these two shuttles in an average time of fifty-two seconds. And I'm talking about 296-pound linemen!

What is so hard about that shuttle is that every time you turn back to start another sixty, you lose your momentum and your muscles tighten up. You have to fight your body to keep moving. It was one of the most physically and mentally demanding drills I've ever run. We ran the test on the game field before two-a-days began in the heat of August. Fortunately, the hard work paid off and I passed it on the first day. If you didn't pass the first time, you had to run it until you did pass before you could start practicing. If you didn't pass after three tries, you ran sprints after practice. No one was allowed to get away with anything. Some players quit the team as a result, including offensive tackle Adam Carpenter, who had replaced me during my injury year.

We had a big team meeting before fall camp, and part of the agenda was to honor those players who had participated in at least 95 percent of the summer conditioning program of lifting and running. If you made it, you got a black T-shirt that said "Sooner Iron" on the front and "Commitment" on the back. These shirts were handed out in front of the entire team on the last day of conditioning during a nice breakfast, and I was among the 60 percent of the team who got a shirt. It was a great feeling.

ANTICIPATING THE 1999 SEASON

We were given a week off before August practices began. I went to Atlanta for five days to see my folks, who were living there at the time. I sensed this was the calm before the storm, judging from what the summer conditioning program was like. Could fall camp be even more rigorous than that? Probably. I wasn't sure what to expect, but I knew I was in great shape both mentally and physically. In fact, I was in my best shape ever except for the slight edge on athleticism removed by my Achilles injuries. Still, I weighed 296 going into fall camp, I felt great, and I was excited.

Fall camp started with twelve days of two-a-days on the intramural fields, southeast of the stadium. We would be working in temperatures as high as 108 degrees, which wasn't all that unusual for an Oklahoma August. Each day would begin at 7:15 A.M. with breakfast. We'd get taped up in the locker room at 8:30 and then hit the field from 9:15 to 11:30 A.M.

Once at the intramural fields, we would work our way into practice. How? Well, from the very first the coaches had the offensive linemen jump rope in pads and cleats. Then we'd stretch and do warm-up running. The coaches kept us moving the whole time, all two hours and fifteen minutes of practice time. They'd be talking to us constantly as well, especially if they thought we weren't doing the drills right. At the end of each morning practice, we would do what we called fourth-quarters, which were alternating thirty-second sets of push-ups and sit-ups over a ten-minute period.

Morning practice would end at 11:30, after which we had three hours to relax and eat. Then we'd tape up again and go back to practice about 4:30 P.M. I remember there wasn't all that much actual grass on the practice fields during this particularly hot summer, and dust clouds would rise from the field as we ran our plays. The guys practicing for Arizona State in the desert had nothing on us!

Practices would end with wind sprints called four-gassers: four sprints of fifty-yards each and totaling two hundred yards. After we left the field, we still weren't through. We then had to lift weights, finishing our daily workout at 7:30 P.M. Then it was dinner, a short team meeting, and time for everyone to hit their bunks. We needed no encouragement for that.

At first Coach Mangino liked to experiment a lot with the offensive line, so he shifted us around quite a bit, trying us out in guard and tackle positions on both ends of the line. A few weeks into practice, however, he had decided who belonged where and had solidified our starting positions.

Some people wonder how you can function in 105-degree heat while running strenuous drills in thirty pounds of football gear. But for me, the hotter, the better. I'd much rather work out or play in hot weather than cold weather. My body just seems to function better in heat. We had plenty of Gatorade and plenty of water, so dehydration wasn't a problem. At one point the coaches did try adding salt surreptitiously to the Gatorade to fortify us against the extreme heat. But it didn't work. You could taste it immediately, and the drink lost its soothing effect. So many of us just opted for water instead.

By the end of fall practice, I was slotted in at the left guard position, with Al Baysinger next to me at tackle. On the other side of center Matt O'Neal were right guard Bubba Burcham and right tackle Stockar McDougle. We were all about the same size, with the exception of Stockar, who towered over everyone at six feet, eight inches and 358 pounds. He was huge, yet very nimble and quick. He would wind up going to the Detroit Lions in the first round of the draft in 2000.

Everyone was talking about going to a bowl that year, which would be a first for everyone on the team but me. OU hadn't been to a bowl since 1994, and I was the only one who had been around that long. But we were realistic. Knowing that we were still rebuilding, we anticipated a 7–4 or a 6–5 season.

We established a lot of team rules and goals during fall practice. About ten of them were specific offensive and defensive goals, and they were all set up so that we could check our progress each week to see whether we were on track. Gone were the days of the sweeping, all-or-nothing national championship goal. Of course we would love to be national champs, but we knew we had to work our way up to that level.

Looking back on Coach Stoops's off-season conditioning program and the spring and fall practices, I would have to give him high marks as a manager and a coach. Players were scrutinized in every way possible for their performance; there was good, precise communication between players and coaches; and it was all about to start paying off as the 1999 season—my last—was about to unfold into a new era of OU football.

In August, the national press was touting us at having a pretty good chance for a winning season, given our improved air attack and the fact that we had a highly regarded junior college transfer quarterback in Josh Heupel and a highly regarded head coach in Bob Stoops.

THE LOCKER ROOM ON GAME DAY

What transpires in a team's locker room on the day of a game? Well, it depends on whether it's before the game, during halftime, or after the game, and it also depends on who wins. But whenever it is, the locker room is a hotbed of emotion.

At OU our pregame routine was always the same. On Friday night the players and coaches would attend a movie together, and then there was a curfew and room check at 11:00 P.M. (I usually had no trouble sleeping the night before a game.) On Saturday morning, we'd eat a light breakfast, attend chapel, and then hold offensive and defensive meetings. About two hours before the game, we'd head to the locker room, where a fleet of trainers would be ready to tape us. They would target our ankles, wrists, fingers, and any other vulnerable areas we each might have. I would usually get my fingers taped at the knuckles because that's the most vulnerable trouble spot for a down linemen perched upon his fingertips. Man, would my fingers get messed up during a game!

All around the locker room, players would be wearing their stereo headphones, listening to every variety of music imaginable, but mostly some kind of rock. For me, Metallica and Ozzy always seemed most inspirational. After taping, we'd have an hour to get dressed, and our adrenaline would start building slowly for the game ahead. Then we would hit the field for pregame warm-ups, going at about three-quarters speed and getting a good sweat started. We'd head back to the locker room, don the headphones again and start downing some Gatorade. This is where you really start pumping. Players start bouncing off the walls and smashing into each other, testing their rigging.

At some point before the game, there would be a motivational talk by the coach or occasionally someone like Barry Switzer. This was followed by the team prayer, which the coach always started with the players kneeling around him. Then there would be an explosion as the prayer ended and the team sprung to life, each player jumping around and rushing toward the exit. On the way out of OU's locker room, we each passed under an overhead sign that read, "Play Like a Champion Today." We would reach up and slap that sign on the way out of the locker room. Tradition dictates that you try to hit it in the same place each time. Superstition is a big thing among football players and coaches alike. For my part, I always ate of box of candy Dots at the Friday night team movie and tried to get taped by the same trainer each time.

The OU locker room is just outside the stadium, on the south side. We'd cue up just outside the stadium, in a passageway underneath the south end-zone seats, then hit the tunnel that led out onto Owen Field. Under Bob Stoops the team still takes the west side of the field. Here we'd meet the screaming roar of the Sooner fans. There is no other feeling in the world like running out of the tunnel and onto the field to that massive greeting. It's a feeling that will probably stay with me my whole life.

The visiting team, which hit the field first, didn't have it so good. OU fans are polite but not overly gracious toward teams opposing their Sooners. It must be intimidating to play in this legendary stadium, especially when looking up to the press box area and seeing the seven national championship titles and thirty-seven conference championships the Sooners have won. Making it even more depressing for the visitors is the fact that their locker room is on the west side of the stadium, and I'm told it is the smallest and worst visiting locker room in Division I-A college football. I'll have to present that as hearsay evidence, however, because in six years with the Sooners, I never set foot into the visitor's locker room.

At halftime we hardly had time to catch our breath in the locker room. The time went by very quickly, and we were busy getting fresh T-shirts on under our pads and downing Gatorade, bananas, and oranges. The coaches held their own five-minute meeting first, then came in and usually gave a motivational talk before offensive and defensive coordinators started talking to individual players about what they needed to do in the second half to improve their performance. I suppose you would call the atmosphere one of relaxed tension: we were eager to get back out onto the field and finish the job, but our bodies were also tired and would have liked just a little more rest before doing it. The whole halftime scene in the locker room lasted only ten to fifteen minutes, however, so before we knew it we were exploding back onto the field for the second half.

When the defense was on the field, I spent very little time standing around and watching the game. The offensive line would usually sit together, taking instructions from a coach as we tried to conserve our energy for our time back on the field. So many isolated vignettes and dramas were being played out on the sidelines during a game, and all these pieces were meant to fit together to produce a winning team effort on the field.

After the game, the locker room mood ranged from elation to frustration, depending, of course, on how the game came out and the importance of the win or loss to the team's goals for the season. Most of my coaches would be encouraging even after a loss, trying to get us to shake it off and move on toward the next game's effort. But if we won, the locker room would be Party Central, especially if we'd just won a big game or cinched a bowl bid, or, as the Sooners did in 2000, won a conference championship and then national championship.

In any case, the locker room can be a great scene of male bonding where friendships take hold that will last a lifetime.

THE 1999 SEASON

The team we were supposed to start against was Arkansas State, but they had to back out and we began with Indiana State instead. That was the first-ever meeting between our two teams. The Sycamores play in Division I-AA, and from the moment they showed up at Owen Field in their bright blue uniforms, they didn't look like a good match for us. Their stats alone would indicate the discrepancy. Back home in Terre Haute, their stadium seated a maximum of only 12,764 fans, and they were starting this season with a sophomore quarterback who stood only five feet, nine inches and weighed only 170 pounds. Still, it was a sold-out night game in Norman. I love playing at night, maybe because it brings back memories of Friday night lights at high school games. And the crowds always seem to be a little louder at night than in the day. Anyway, night or day, we were ready to play, and I would describe us as confident but not cocky. We had a little trouble getting untracked, we were uneasy at first, but then we settled in and won, 49–0.

It was Josh Heupel's first game as a Sooner, and he did well. We on the offensive line knew what we were doing as the center called out the defensive front and we relayed the information by hand signals to the backs. We had a game plan going in, and we stayed with it. Mike Leach's offense was beautiful. It was set up so we could score on almost every play Heupel called. Leach's philosophy was to get the ball to a back or a receiver—mostly on short passes—and then let him run and make plays. Leach loved blitzes because when a defense blitzes its players, it leaves holes open, and that's where Heupel would throw the ball to one of our receivers. All in all, this offense had a logic that we hadn't seen before, and the logic made sense.

On the next Saturday there was another home game, this time a late-morning start against Coach Kevin Steele's Baylor Bears. Before a sold-out crowd dressed in a sea of crimson, we buried our second team of the year, 41–10. We were throwing all over the field, and by the end of the game we were ranked in the top three teams nationally for total offense, averaging 450 yards per game.

Our third game was interesting because it was our first trip to Louisville to play Howard Schnellenberger's old team on the road. Although we had played the University of Louisville in 1997, this was our first chance to see the "house that Howard built" there. It is an impressive stadium, especially for a team the size and quality of Louisville. But this team was deceptively tough, and we had an even battle with them through three quarters. By the end of the third quarter, however, we opened things up on a special third-down play. We used a false snap count and they jumped offsides, so we scored a

Bob Stoops with punter Jeff Ferguson at a preseason intersquad scrimmage in the fall of 1999. The temperature that day in Tulsa reached 107 degrees, but over five thousand Sooner fans attended this scrimmage, held at a local high school. (*Daily Oklahoman*)

touchdown and rolled over them through the fourth quarter. We won, 42–21. Clearly we were not having problems scoring points this year, averaging forty-three points per game through the first three games. Our defense was of some concern; we didn't like giving up twenty-one points to a team like Louisville. Still, we were undefeated and excited about the rest of the season.

That excitement peaked the following week as we prepared to head to South Bend, Indiana, for a highly publicized matchup with Notre Dame. Anyone familiar with Oklahoma football history knows how significant Notre Dame has been. The last team to beat Bud Wilkinson's Sooners in 1952 before they started their forty-seven-game winning streak was Notre Dame, in a 27–21 game. Four and a half years later, the team that ended that winning streak was—you guessed it—Notre Dame, beating OU, 7–0. Add to that history the fact that, like the Sooners had been in years past, Notre Dame was a perennial powerhouse, coming off a 9–3 season in 1998. Then toss in the facts that these two teams had not met on the playing field since 1968 and that in eight lifetime meetings between them, Notre Dame had taken seven. All told, you had the recipe for a real media event.

ESPN did not disappoint. They assigned a camera crew to the Sooners for the entire week leading up to the game. Since I was the oldest starter on the team, they miked me all week and the crew followed me through practices and around campus, telling the story of the rejuvenated Sooners through my eyes to a great extent. The Saturday game would be the ESPN game of the day, and they followed me right up through the pregame warm-up in Notre Dame Stadium.

The huge stadium (capacity 80,012) is filled with the spirit of football tradition, and you can almost see the ghosts of past Irish greats like John Huarte and Joe Montana dancing around the field, dodging oncoming defensive linemen. I got first-rate goose bumps when we ran out onto the field. A lot of OU fans showed up for that game, so there was plenty of support in the stands. Among those fans were my mom, dad, and brother Allan.

Notre Dame scored first, but we came back with a long kickoff return by Brandon Daniels. We tied it 7–7 and were playing well, going ahead in the third quarter by sixteen points. But we relaxed too early, and Notre Dame rallied to catch us and move ahead. We tried a fourth-down play late in the game, didn't make it, and lost the game, 34–30.

We were so focused on executing our plays and individual assignments in this game that it wasn't until after the game that I really noticed the bright gold helmets of the Irish. As I was walking off the field after the final play, the significance of this day hit me and I said to myself, "Holy Cow, I'm playing against Notre Dame in this stadium and with this crowd!" I knew we had played well through most of the game against a strong team, so the loss was not as hard to take as it might have been. Overall, the day was bittersweet, but we were still 3–1 for the season, and 1–0 in the Big Twelve Conference.

Next up was Texas and our annual trek to the "neutral" site of Dallas and the Cotton Bowl. Coach Stoops didn't appear to know all that much about the OU-Texas rivalry, and as we prepared for the Longhorns he tried to convince us it was just another conference game. During the week he ordered the UT fight song played over and over again on our practice field so we'd get used to it. It was an intense week as we tried to get the bitter taste of defeat out of our mouths. We really wanted to turn it around, and to do that, we'd have to beat the team that held a lifetime 54–34–5 advantage over us. The Longhorns were coming off a 9–3 season and a 38–11 Cotton Bowl victory over Mississippi State, and they weren't doing badly in this year's early season, either. Texas was quarterbacked by sophomore Major Applewhite, who had been the 1998 Big Twelve freshman of the year with almost 2,500 yards in passing. So we knew we had our hands full.

Frank Romero had been brought into left tackle next to me, and the whole line was jelling again. Coach Stoops brought in Barry Switzer for practice one day, and the legendary coach delivered a great motivational speech that really fired us up. As for me, I knew this would be the last time I would walk down that tunnel and walk onto the Cotton Bowl field.

We did our pregame warm-ups and were feeling great on this October afternoon. Then Mike Leach pulled a great ploy: he left a fake script of our first fifteen plays on the sidelines. As if on cue, someone from the UT staff picked it up and took it into their locker

Left to right: Bubba Burcham (#59), Matt O'Neal (#60), and Jay Smith (#71) in the 1999 game against Texas.

In this picture, Matt O'Neal is making line-blocking calls by pointing out the linebacker that the offensive line will block if the defense happens to blitz its linebackers. These calls were made on every play of the game by the offensive line. Texas was playing a 30 defense that day to try and stop the pass. The Sooners took an early 17–0 lead in the first quarter against Texas but would lose the game by the score of 28–38. Bubba was a junior, and Matt and I were both seniors. (Photograph by Randy Bennett)

room, thinking it was the real thing. Suffice it to say, the trick worked like a charm and we looked utterly amazing during those first fifteen plays, which obviously were dramatically different than what Texas thought we would run. So we went up 17–0 before Texas knew what hit them. We threw, we ran, we did whatever we wanted.

For their part, the Texas coaching staff began making adjustments by rushing only three down linemen and substituting their big defensive linemen to keep them fresh in the one hundred– degree heat. We were still short on offensive linemen and really only had one line that could match them. The adjustments worked, and the

Longhorns caught us and wound up winning, 38–28. I remember walking off the field and up the ramp, turning to face the field, and realizing that OU had only beaten and tied Texas once in the past six years I had been with the team. It was a stinging thought, but when I looked over and saw the big "OU" painted in our end zone, my face eased into a smile.

I wound up doing the postgame interview, and for the first time I can ever remember, I felt edgy and jumpy with the press. I guess I was pretty upset; I knew we were now 3–2 and had lost our last two games after being up by sixteen and seventeen points. It seemed we were so inexperienced at being successful and had so rarely been ahead by so much, that we simply didn't know how to handle it or finish games. I got dressed and sifted through the crowd to find my parents and brother. Looking back, I don't think I could go through another Texas loss emotionally. You could not get me to play on that field again knowing I'd come out a loser. I'd had enough of it.

After Texas, we got a little relief with a bye week and had two weeks to prepare for our next opponent: always-tough Texas A&M. This was the team that had creamed us, 29–0, in 1998 and finished the year at 11–3 after taking the Big Twelve Championship Game from Kansas State in two overtimes. The Aggies had then gone on to the Sugar Bowl, losing to Ohio State, 24–14. They were having another good year in 1999. At least we had the comforting knowledge that we'd play them in our own Memorial Stadium.

At practice that week, it became clear that we were determined to beat these guys. This would be our homecoming game, and we wanted to please Coach Mangino because he had just come to OU from Kansas State, the team that was blindsided by A&M in the 1998 Big Twelve Championship Game. A&M had knocked Mangino's team out of a Bowl Championship Series game and sent the Wildcats to the Holiday Bowl instead. More than once that week Mangino said, "Boy I'd like to beat these guys!" We realized we'd like to beat them, too; we remembered the shutout the Aggies inflicted on us the year before. In that game A&M had stopped us on nine consecutive drives.

Coach Mark Mangino and Jay during a time-out at a 1999 home game.
   Coach Mangino giving positive criticism was a constant sight for all offensive linemen during the 1999 season. His favorite saying to me was, "You've been here since Bud Wilkinson and you still can't get it right!" (Photograph by Randy Bennett)

A&M was another night game and another sluggish start for our offense. So the coaches resorted to some trick plays, and we started scoring points. Actually, we scored a lot of points but never felt we had enough. Over on the sidelines we were telling each other, "We gotta keep scoring! They're gonna come back. Let's keep rolling!" Coach Stoops repeated that mantra in the halftime locker room, so we came out and scored more points in the second half. I wound up playing both ends of the line, moving over some to right tackle for a change. Everyone got to play that day, and it's always a great feeling to see the all the guys get in. Our fears of an Aggie comeback were not realized, thankfully, as we buried the team from College Station by an incredible 51–6 score. Along with much of the rest of

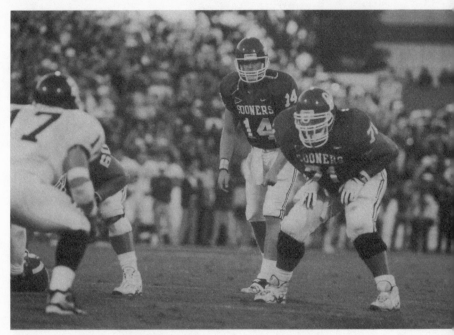

Left to right: Josh Heupel (#14) and Jay (#71) in the 1999 Texas A&M game.

Josh and Jay are driving down the field as part of the offensive unit. This picture was taken just before the snap that would lead the Sooners to a touchdown and a 17–0 lead on the Aggies. The Sooners continued to roll and ended up winning this game, 51–6, handing Texas A&M its worst loss in over ninety years. This game was played under the lights for a sold-out crowd at Owen Field. (Photograph by Randy Bennett)

the nation, we had to blink when we read that score in the papers the next day because few people thought we'd even win the game, coming off of back-to-back losses as we had. Everyone was celebrating after the game, and that Saturday night Norman was the biggest party town I've ever seen.

Now we were six games deep into the season and stood 4–2 overall and 2–1 in the Big Twelve. It was much better, we thought, than where we'd been the past few years. Only two more wins and we would be bowl-bound for the first time since 1994. The next five games were all conference games, and by this time, we felt winning the Big Twelve was not out of the question, especially since we didn't play Kansas State or Nebraska in the regular season this year. If we got to the conference championship game we'd have to play one or the other, but then, if we got that far anything could happen.

Whatever hope we entertained of a conference championship, however, was put to rest a week later when we traveled to Boulder to play Coach Gary Barnett's Buffaloes. Barnett had just come to Colorado after his successful tenure at Northwestern, where he had taken the Wildcats to the Rose Bowl. In fact, his name had been tossed around as a possible head coach at OU, so we knew he was good, as was his team, which had won the Aloha Bowl in 1998.

We had trouble from the start against the Buffs. They knew our hand signals on the line as well as Heupel's hand signals. They shifted their defensive line and seemed to know what we were going to do before we did it. Although we managed to score twenty-four points, we gave up thirty-eight to Colorado's offense and lost the game by two touchdowns. I would have to say this was the first game of the season that we'd really lost. In the Texas and Notre Dame games we were close enough toward the end to pull them out if we'd had more time. But not on this day. After the game, Coach Stoops said it was right that we got beat, because we just didn't execute well. Chalk up our second conference loss for the season. Four games were left, and we needed two of them to get to a bowl.

The following week we got help from Missouri, the team that had snapped a long losing streak by beating us the year before, 20–6, in Columbia. But that was then, this was now. We were facing them in Norman, not Columbia, and this time we had our offense moving. On this November 6 we showed up not only with a strong offense but also with an equally strong defense, and we shut out the Tigers, 37–0, to move within one game of bowl contention.

Iowa State made us bowl-eligible the next week. We rolled into Ames to play Dan McCarney's Cyclones and rolled out a 31–10 winner a few hours later. This win was great for me because my parents came to Ames for the game, and it was the first time my cousin

Ryan Smith got to see me play. Ryan had been to Angelo State to see Allan play, but he had never been to a Division I college game.

After the game, we erupted into an impromptu dance party in the locker room. Everyone was ecstatic about going to a bowl game, the first for everyone on the team but me. Coach Stoops was one of the most excited men in the locker room as he shouted, "We're going bowling!"

Not only were we going bowling but, with two games left, we had a chance for an 8–3 regular season. At least we had that chance the week before we traveled to Lubbock, Texas, to play Texas Tech. I think that under normal circumstances our 1999 team would have beaten the Red Raiders, but this was coach Spike Dykes's thirteenth and final season as head coach there, and Tech wanted to give him a good send-off in his final game.

We ran out into Jones Stadium before about fifty thousand Red Raider fans on an extremely windy day, which wasn't great for the passing team we were. We managed to score well enough, but we fumbled the ball more than usual. We went to the half-time locker room with the lead, but we came out and fell flat in the second half, losing 38–28. So much for conference championship dreams that year; we stood 6–4 overall and 3–3 in the Big Twelve. As if losing the game wasn't enough, our charter jet broke down in Lubbock and we had to take a bus back home to Norman. This was major punishment, as it gave us eight long hours to relive the loss.

We closed out the following week with Oklahoma State at home. The OSU game is always a special game no matter where it's played. The folks in Oklahoma just choose up sides and don either the red or the orange of their respective heroes all week long. But this was an especially important game to me because it would be my final home game at Memorial Stadium as a Sooner. My long career was about to come an end on the campus I so dearly loved. There would be a bonus game, as we were also headed for the Independence Bowl in Shreveport, Louisiana, but this was it for playing on Owen

Jay and others warm up before the 1999 Texas Tech Game.

    The Sooners had traveled to Lubbock to play the Texas Tech Raiders. This was a typical west Texas day: the sun was shining, and the wind was blowing in from the west. The Sooners led at the half but were unable to complete passes in the second half, which led to their loss. (*Daily Oklahoman*)

Field. It was an afternoon game, and my parents and brother made the trip to see me close out my regular-season career.

    The team really wanted to beat OSU, a game that had not been so easy for us in recent years. Coach Bob Simmons and his Cowboys had matched our 5–6 record in 1998, and we didn't want to lose to them this year. So we came out throwing and quickly went ahead. We took it to them the entire afternoon, and they never got close.

Two odd things happened during that game. One involved our starting right offensive tackle, Stockar McDougle, who was put in our backfield by Coach Mangino to run one play. In so doing, Mangino was giving our biggest offensive lineman (six feet, eight inches tall and 358 pounds) a chance to run the ball. We had practiced it earlier in the week because Kansas State had done the same thing the previous week and had then announced they had the largest running back in the nation. So Mangino, who had come to us as offensive-line coach from Kansas State, now decided to show that we had the largest running back in the nation. So he called the play, lined Stockar in the backfield, and told his offensive line to block and get out of the way quick. "You don't want to have 360 pounds falling on you," he said. Stockar was running off of my block, so I was very concerned about getting out of the way. Stockar got the ball, broke through the line of scrimmage, and then a 180-pound OSU safety tried to stop him. Stockar dragged that guy about ten yards before going down.

The second odd—and sad—thing happened toward the end of the game. We were going to receive the ball on an OSU punt with 1:40 left on the clock. Coach Mangino had decided to put the seniors out on the field for one play even though we were ahead by four touchdowns at that point. The idea was that Stockar, Matt O'Neal, and I—the three senior linemen—would lock hands after the play, then throw our arms into the air and walk off the field as cameras captured our final departure from Owen Field. The plan called for freshman punt receiver J. T. Thatcher to let the ball drop untouched to the ground, and then for our offense to hit the field for the ceremonial final play. But no one in the stands that day would see this, because it never happened.

Instead of letting the ball drop, J. T. decided to catch that punt and raced it back seventy yards for a touchdown. When he came to the sidelines afterwards, instead of receiving congratulations from the coaching staff, J. T. was hit by complaints for screwing up our plan.

As Rocky Calmus watches, Trent Smith dumps a bucket of water on OU Coach Bob Stoops after the 1999 victory over OSU.

Under new head coach Bob Stoops, the Sooners had just defeated the OSU Cowboys at home and finished the regular season with a 7–4 record. The Sooners finished the 1999 season with a home record of 5–0. (*Daily Oklahoman*)

Left to right: Josh Heupel and the offensive line on Senior Day at Owen Field, 1999.

Under new head coach Bob Stoops, the Sooners had just defeated the OSU Cowboys at home, finishing the regular season with a 7–4 record. This was my sixth season as a Sooner, the only season with a winning record. For the seniors this was the last time to play on Owen Field under the lights. This offensive line gave up only fifteen sacks out of some four hundred pass attempts to break an OU record. The starting offensive line was Frank Romero (#63), Jay Smith (#71), Matt O'Neal (#60), Bubba Burcham (#59), and Stockar McDougle (behind #63). Matt O'Neal would end up playing for the Atlanta Falcons, and Stockar McDougle would end up playing for the Detroit Lions. Josh Heupel (far left) would end up being drafted by the Miami Dolphins and then traded to Green Bay. Frank Romero would also have an excellent chance to play in the NFL. (Photograph by Derek Lester, Style Shop, Norman, Oklahoma)

The game ended with us winning, 44–7. Afterward, I sat down on the bench and slowly tried to take in my six years as a member of this team, playing on this legendary field. Everyone was celebrating the victory and our shiny new 7–4 season—the best since I'd arrived six years before—but I just kept thinking, "Boy, I would have loved to have that picture of Matt, Stockar, and me coming off the field for the final time."

I did get a consolation prize, however, when the offensive linemen all went back on the field with Josh Heupel and someone on the staff took a big picture of all of us out there. That picture is one of my prized possessions today.

THE LAST GAMES OF MY CAREER

After the game we took a few weeks off for finals and Christmas break, leaving for Shreveport on December 26 for the Independence Bowl, where we would meet Ole Miss in a night game on New Year's Eve. We did two-a-day practices for three or four days and felt good about our chances against the Rebels, whose 1999 regular season record was similar to ours at 7–4. New Year's Eve was also special for me because I turned twenty-four on that day, the last day of the millennium.

It was a surprisingly humid night when we took to the field in Shreveport, and the grass was wet. As the game began we found ourselves slipping and sliding a lot, and we fell behind early in the game. We didn't seem to be playing in sync and went into the locker room at halftime trailing the Rebels. Josh stood up and encouraged us to just go out and play and enjoy ourselves in the second half. Coach Stoops said the same thing, and that's just what we did when the second half began. As a result, we started rallying and scoring points, taking the lead late in the game and still holding it with a minute left when one of those gut-wrenching things happened. We hit a bad kickoff, and the referees tacked a penalty against us on top of that. The result was great field position for Ole Miss, and they won the game on a field goal, 27–25.

That loss notwithstanding, we knew we had begun our comeback as a new edition of the Sooner football tradition, and we seniors felt we were leaving the team in good hands for continued success in the year ahead. If only we had known how good it would be! Still, I was pleased with the way things had turned out that year, and I celebrated with my parents out in the parking lot with champagne and a cigar. It was now just after midnight, and I realized my college football career had ended in the previous century.

As it turned out, I was not yet through as a college player because Stockar, Matt, and I were all invited to all-star games after the season ended. I went to the Gridiron Classic All-Star Game, held the end of January in Orlando, Florida. It was a great experience to represent OU among all the other talented players from other schools there. The emphasis was on the positive, and I got to play under famed pro coach Buddy Ryan and beside Notre Dame quarterback Jarious Jackson. I played well, and my team won the game to boot. You can't ask for a better afternoon than that. I knew this would be my last afternoon in a college football uniform, but I still had hopes of being drafted into the NFL.

I signed with an agent in expectation of such a call, but it never came. I guess the pro teams figured I was too much of a risk with my twice-torn Achilles. The other two OU senior linemen had better luck that year. Stockar McDougle went to Detroit, and Matt O'Neal went to Atlanta. I wound up getting invited to the NFL Combine, where the NFL coaches gather to survey the graduating college talent, but that was it for me and the NFL. A year later, when the X-treme Football League (XFL) began recruiting, I again had hopes of playing, but no calls came.

I was later offered a chance to play as a center with the Oklahoma City Wranglers of the Arena Football League, but I declined. I was also invited to a tryout with Montreal of the Canadian Football League (CFL), but they wanted me to report at 320 pounds, which was impossible for me to do. Besides, I was ready for the next phase of my life and decided to put my efforts into the MBA program at OU and a job with a Norman marketing company. I didn't know it then, but I would spend a lot of time the next fall watching my teammates take our 1999 level of play to new heights and reclaim the glory of Oklahoma past.

CHAPTER 7

That Championship Season

Somewhere out there, out where dreams come true . . .

JAMES HORNER

This chapter is a little hard for me to write because I must admit to at least some envy of the 2000 edition Oklahoma Sooners. It would have been nice to see the fruits of six hard years of labor pay off in this national championship. As it is, I must content myself with the fact that I was a part of the rebuilding process, and as a senior, I helped lead the Sooners to their 1999 comeback season, which set the stage for the greatness of the 2000 season.

And wasn't it a great one indeed?

I got to sample some of the team spirit in the 2000 off-season because I started working out with the team after the guys returned to campus in January following the Independence Bowl. I still had my all-star game to play and needed to stay in shape for it. After that game I busied myself with my MBA classes and began lifting and running on my own. Gradually I started putting a little distance between myself and the team because I knew I needed to move on to a new phase of my life.

Early in my post-OU days I still entertained hopes of playing pro ball. I was one of 360 college seniors invited to the NFL Combine for the coaches to assess, but my Achilles was deemed too risky for any team to draft me. It's a little-known fact, I believe, but even though about 200 of these 360 seniors in the Combine get drafted each year, only about thirty-eight on average actually wind up making one of the NFL teams. The Canadian Football League is an option for the guys who don't make the NFL, and I had a chance to play for the CFL but declined. The money they offer is not that great when you consider it is paid in Canadian dollars. Also, I didn't want to become one of those guys who just spend their time hanging around on the fringes of the pro teams, hoping one day to make it. So I decided to call it a career, hang up my pads, and go do something else.

Given the decade of adversity preceding the 2000 National Championship Sooners, given the years of wondering if this team would ever come back or return to its glory days, given the Sooners' bad-boy image and its three-year probation, and given the string of four head coaches in six years, this may have been the most important OU national championship to date. It would mark a new era: the Stoops era.

How did the year start? What were the expectations of the team, the media, and the fans going into the year? How did the team react to each week's challenge and victory? These are some of the questions this chapter addresses. Although I had graduated from the team in 1999, I continued my friendships with the players who made up the 2000 Sooners. I roomed with punter Jeff Ferguson, who played with the team through the 2001 season, and I spent part of the year working out with the team. This is the story of the greatness the team achieved following all those years of turmoil.

EARLY PROSPECTS FOR THE 2000 TEAM

In terms of player personnel, the Sooners were in pretty good shape to open the 2000 season. The team's biggest loss had come in its offensive line when Matt O'Neal, Stockar McDougle, and I finished our eligibility in 1999. Back-up guard Ryan Allen had also graduated.

That left OU with some big holes to fill on the offensive line. To fill my position, the Sooners brought in Howard Duncan from a junior college. Bubba Burcham replaced Matt at center, and back-up guard Mike Skinner was moved into the starting position. Scott Kempenich was a back-up guard who moved up to starting right tackle, and Frank Romero was over at left tackle. So that would be the new offensive line that would lead the team to glory this year.

Other losses from graduation included receivers Brandon Daniels and Jaraill Jackson, but the team was deep in receivers so their departure wasn't that damaging. On defense, nearly everyone was back.

From what I observed and what my friends still on the team told me, the 2000 off-season was a little tougher than the 1999 program because the coaches really wanted to take the team to the next level. The guys were getting used to the Stoops's off-season program, and Coach wanted to keep it challenging by throwing in some new wrinkles in 2000. But the conditioning program and spring ball went well. I'm told the coaches encouraged the players to take it easy on tackles so they wouldn't get anyone injured. The 2000 offensive line had to go pretty far to catch our 1999 line; in the spring game, the offensive line gave up more sacks than we had in 1999.

The team broke for a couple weeks for spring finals and a little rest, and then they were back in Norman for another summer of volunteer conditioning, for which 70 percent of the team showed up. The conditioning went well, as did fall camp, and before they knew it, the Oklahoma Sooners were facing the 2000 season. They felt ready; they were expecting a 9–2 season, with two losses probably coming at the hands of either Texas, Kansas State, or Nebraska, whom the Sooners had to play back-to-back in October. If they finished at 9–2 and won the South Division of the conference, they'd play in the Big Twelve Championship Game in Kansas City. All that seemed like a realizable set of goals for this year.

The national media wasn't so sure. The Sooners seemed to have the right team, but they had no superstars, which the media dearly love. The Sooners were rated near the bottom of the Top 25 polls. As

Sports Illustrated noted later, "When the season began, the Sooners were barely on the fringes of the national polls. When it ended, they were basking in the limelight of No. 1."[1] But Bob Stoops convinced most fans and media that after showing a lot of heart in the 7–5 season of 1999, his Sooners were going to be an even better team in 2000. The season opened up with a 106-degree night kickoff on September 2 against the University of Texas at El Paso (UTEP) on Owen Field.

Senior center Bubba Burcham may have said it best when he told *Sports Illustrated*, "It would be kind of stupid to expect to go seven-and-something or eight-and-something. We want to be the best."[2]

A PROMISING BEGINNING

The sell-out crowd of 74,761 who braved the record-breaking heat for a Sooner game that evening sensed they were in for a good year. I was there, too, but I was still having trouble believing that my career had ended, and it was difficult to let go. I had to accept the fact that I could no longer suit up and play. In one way it was like the time I had in rehab, except that then I still had the feeling that I would return to the playing field. This time I knew I wouldn't be back in uniform. Although I wanted to see the team do well, it was hard to get truly excited. I watched the season from afar; the only other game I attended during the regular season was the Oklahoma-Nebraska game in midseason.

The Sooners began the season opener slowly and were ahead 27–7 at the half, but they rolled over UTEP in the final quarter on their way to a 55–14 rout. This came despite a series of penalties (nine for a total of seventy yards), fumbles, and missed opportunities that led players like sophomore strong safety Roy Williams to say after the game, "We know we didn't play up to OU ball."[3] But it was good enough for a decisive forty-one-point victory in which freshman tailback Renaldo Works scored three fourth-quarter touchdowns to take the game from a Sooner win to a runaway. That victory came even though OU failed to take advantage of many of the seven UTEP turnovers. This was clearly a game in which OU could have scored in the eighty-point range if the players had been more alert to their chances. Still, the defense played solidly, even scoring one of the OU touchdowns on a Roy Williams interception and a thirty-five-yard return to the end zone.

Daily Oklahoman sportswriter George Schroeder likened much of OU's offense that night to a jalopy clunking along on bad gas.[4] Stoops chided the offense for being out of sync in the second quarter. But Heupel wasn't doing badly, completing eighteen of thirty-six passes (with seven straight incompletions in the sluggish second period) for 274 yards and two touchdowns. He was intercepted only once.

The next Saturday found the Sooners back home again for the second straight week, this time against Arkansas State. Coming off the opening-week win over UTEP, OU was ranked twentieth in the AP Top 25 College Football Poll, and it was nice to be moving up that ladder, rather than down. Once again it was an evening game, and once again the thermometer soared as the State of Oklahoma was on its way to its worst string of rainless days at one hundred degrees plus. But once again the stands were filled, and almost seventy-five thousand fans went crazy as the Sooners opened up the first period by reeling off twenty-eight unanswered points against a team that, frankly, looked a little lost on Owen Field. About the only similarity between these two teams, in fact, was that both had red and white uniforms. I'm sure that after that game Arkansas State Coach Joe Hollis wished he hadn't pleaded with Coach Stoops the year before to have this game moved to the 2000 season. Maybe in 1999 they would have had a chance against us, but on this night, the game was probably over shortly after the opening coin toss, when OU took the kickoff and moved eighty yards in fifteen plays to go ahead, 7–0. Then, later in the quarter, J. T. Thatcher returned a line-drive ASU punt up the middle and down the sidelines sixty-six yards for a score.

Altogether the Sooners mounted 533 total yards. Impressively, 208 of those came on the ground. And this time there would be no second-quarter slump for Josh Heupel, who torched the air above Owen Field for twenty-four of thirty-two passes, 302 yards, and three touchdowns. And Renaldo Works, the hero of game one, ran for 109 yards on twelve carries, with 75 yards on one marathon touchdown run. Again, penalties dogged the Sooners (eleven for a total of ninety-five yards), but the offense appeared to find its rhythm at last.

As for the defense, it turned in another great performance, holding Arkansas State to 275 yards running and passing, and giving up only one touchdown. Although most fans had their eyes on Heupel and the offense by now, the defense was quietly becoming the power behind the Sooner throne. They would draw a higher profile in the weeks to come when the offense slacked off at critical times.

Next up was the Sooners' second Texas team of the year, Rice University. So far, scheduling was about as good as it gets, because this would be OU's third consecutive home game and the team had two weeks to prepare for it. Since the Sooners were 2–0 going into battle with the Owls, and since Rice was not considered a powerhouse by any stretch of the imagination, the Sooners were feeling pretty good about their chances of going 3–0. They buttressed that optimism with sweat and hard work in practice, and Coach Stoops covered the last base by inviting former Sooner great Brian Bosworth (the Boz) into the locker room to give the team a pep talk before the game. Bosworth told the squad they couldn't expect a winning tradition to just happen because of the past efforts of Sooner teams; they would have to make it happen themselves, on this day.

I guess the Boz's speech much have had some effect, because the Sooners—now ranked sixteenth nationally—led, 21–6, by halftime. Center Bubba Burcham told the *Oklahoman* after the game that this margin had been unsatisfying to many on the team, who felt they were relying too much on tradition in the first half and not enough on execution. So they added two more touchdowns late in the third quarter and a third in the fourth to seal the victory. Again, OU stacked up more than 500 yards of total offense, 324 of those coming off of Heupel's arm and some great catches. This was also the first game in which sophomore running back Quentin Griffin really established himself, eclipsing Renaldo Works, who had starred in the first two outings. Griffin ran for 117 yards on fourteen carries and crossed the goal line three times.

The defense did its part again, keyed by linebackers Torrance Marshall and Rocky Calmus, who combined for twenty-five tackles and helped hold Rice to just 145 total yards. With both the offense and defense running in sync, OU had managed to win its first three nonconference games since the 1993 season.

The Sooners, now ranked fourteenth, began Big Twelve Conference play the following week against Kansas, and for the fourth straight week OU played at home. Given the choice between playing the first four games at home or ending the season with four games at home, I suppose most teams would prefer starting out before the home fans to get up a head of steam for the season. So whoever the scheduling gods were for this year, they were with the Crimson and Cream.

Although the Jayhawks traditionally have offered little trouble for the Sooners, the game had not been a cakewalk for several years. Kansas has a habit of surprising opponents, and the Jayhawks came into this game with a 2–1 record. Although this would be OU's fourth win of the season, it didn't come easy. Another sell-out crowd watched and waited for the Sooners to open the game up, but the halftime score had the Sooners ahead by only eight, 24–16. Relief finally came in the third quarter, when Heupel hit receiver Andre Woolfolk for a touchdown to give OU a 34–16 lead, which is the way the game ended after a scoreless fourth period.

Kansas did its part in helping the Sooners win by turning the ball over seven times. Still, agile KU quarterback Dylen Smith presented a challenge to the OU defense, throwing the ball for 216 yards during the first two quarters. In fact, Kansas actually led twice in the first and second quarter, 6–3 and 16–10. Oklahoma could have fallen even further behind in the second quarter, when OU tight end Trent Smith fumbled and gave KU the ball deep in Sooner territory. But in a couple more plays, the Sooners got the ball back when Ramon Richardson took it away from Dylen Smith.

This was one of those quiet turning points in the season. Had OU gone down, 23–10, and allowed KU's momentum to build, there's no telling how the game would have come out. As it was, the team kept it to a six-point margin and added a couple touchdowns of our own before the half. Then our defense adjusted in the second half, and limited Smith to only forty-two yards over the third and fourth periods. On the Sooner side of the line, Heupel connected on twenty-nine of forty-three passes against the nation's top passing defense at the time. On this day, Josh threw no interceptions.

As September came to a close, OU was 4–0 overall and 1–0 in the Big Twelve. The fans thought they had really seen something during the hot month of September, but the team was still having trouble getting respect from the national media. There seemed to be a feeling among the media that OU would self-destruct. Then came October.

RED OCTOBER

The month we all came to call Red October began on October 7 with OU's annual grudge match against the Texas Longhorns. Going into the season, the Sooners knew they would have to face Texas, Kansas State, and Nebraska back-to-back. Realistically, they were hoping to win any one of those games, which would put them in good shape for a 9–2 season. Each of these teams was very strong this year. Texas had opened with early wins before taking a surprising stumble against Stanford in Palo Alto. They were ranked eleventh in the nation.

But OU had risen to tenth position, despite the fact that most experts considered the team untested up to this point. This would be the game that would show whether we had the right stuff or simply looked good at the expense of much less talented teams. The question was answered unequivocally by the second quarter of the Texas game, when the Sooners vaulted to a 42–0 lead on their way to an astounding 63–14 rout. Heupel was hitting his targets, but the big story of the day was Quentin Griffin, who rushed for three touchdowns in the first half and three more in the second half. Although he totaled only eighty-seven yards for the day on twenty-three carries, Griffin was a real workhorse in picking up the needed yardage for those six scores.

On defense, the Sooners held Texas to minus 7 yards rushing and 161 yards passing. In comparison, OU's offense totaled 534 yards. About the only negative for the Sooners was the loss of 127 yards on thirteen penalties and the loss of two fumbles. Those miscues make the final score even more amazing—a classic example of how this year's edition of the OU Sooners overcame their own mistakes to win anyway.

How big was this win? Well, for one thing it was our biggest rout since a 1992 win over Arkansas State, 61–0. And it was the most points scored by a Sooner team since 1989, when OU beat New Mexico State, 73–3. And most importantly to the OU players on this October day, it was the worst whipping an Oklahoma football team had ever inflicted on the University of Texas. You have to go back to the famed 1956 Sooners under Bud Wilkinson to find a spread even close to this forty-nine-point OU win. In that championship season forty-four years before, the Sooners had beaten Texas, 45–0.

Berry Tramel of the *Oklahoman* put the game and its significance into perspective when he wrote the following:

> Suddenly, nothing seems out of OU's grasp. Not Kansas State next week. Not Nebraska the week after. Not the Big 12 title. Not the Orange Bowl. A total embarrassment for the university of a state that prides itself on pride. Here's the sobering truth for Longhorn fans: Bob Stoops took over a bigger mess at OU than Mack Brown took over at Texas, got started a year later than Brown and now has passed his foe. By 49 points. . . . This game made Oklahoma football fans feel better than they've

felt since the Barry Switzer days. No one wanted to leave. The south end of the Cotton Bowl—OU's end—remained full 15 minutes after the game. OU band members flooded the field for post-game revelry, complete with cameras for snapshots in front of the scoreboard. Seniors Ryan Fisher and Reese Travis commandeered the Ruf-Neks' massive OU flag and planted it on the cotton boll at midfield. Another giddy senior, Al Baysinger, hopped aboard the Sooner Schooner for a ride around the Cotton Bowl's north end. Stoops ordered his troops back to midfield for a group photo. He plans to give each a copy, "to keep with them to remember the moment."[5]

To top things off, somewhere during all that partying, OU President David Boren announced to the media he was canceling classes for students at OU on Monday. This was the first time that had happened since the days of Barry Switzer.

Things just don't get much better than this for a college football team. The players would have loved to bask in the afterglow of this rout for weeks. It would have been nice if the Sooners could have had more time to savor the historic victory over Texas and enjoy their newfound eighth-place rank in the national polls. But they had to compress that feeling into a twenty-four-hour period because up ahead loomed an even tougher opponent. This rival was bearing down on the Sooners like a huge truck whose loud horn was blasting a hole into their revelry. It was one of the top five teams in the nation and maybe the toughest in the nation. Some thought it was even tougher than Nebraska.

It was the undefeated Kansas State Wildcats. They were ranked second in the nation. We would have to play them in their own backyard.

The Saturday of the Kansas game, October 14, seemed to arrive too soon. Before they knew it, the Sooners were hitting the field in Manhattan, Kansas, as a purple-clad, record-breaking crowd of 53,011 roared approval of their hometown heroes, who were behind only the Nebraska Cornhuskers in the national polls. The Wildcats

Coach Stoops and others celebrate during the final moments of the first 2000 game against Kansas State.

The Sooners were on the road in Manhattan, Kansas. The Sooners and the Wildcats were both ranked in the top ten. It was a cold, snowy day, and the Sooners beat KSU. (*Daily Oklahoman*)

planned to tend to the Huskers later, but first they had to deal with these white-clad jerseys with the crimson numbers from down south, these upstart Sooners who seemed to be feeling their oats this year. As usual, on this day the Sooners were the underdog in Kansas. But they didn't stay there for long.

The Sooners were on the scoreboard first with a forty-yard Tim Duncan field goal, but Kansas State came roaring back with a drive capped by a fifteen-yard run by their starring quarterback, Jonathan

Beasley, to pull ahead, 7–3. That would be the Wildcats' last lead of the day. OU came right back with a ninety-three-yard kickoff return and Josh Heupel's passing prowess to go up 17–7 at the quarter. The Sooners added two more touchdowns in the second quarter after K-State narrowed the gap to 17–14 on another Beasley run. One of those second-quarter touchdowns came on a nice seventeen-yard run from sophomore running back Quentin Griffin.

With the halftime score at 31–14, I knew there would still be a certain degree of apprehension in the locker room because the team knew they could still lose this game, as we had in 1999 when we lost back-to-back games after leading by seventeen and sixteen points. So to help seal it, Heupel hit receiver Antwone Savage in the third quarter on a seventy-four-yard pass play to put OU up, 38–14.

That's where K-State woke up and made the rest of the game interesting, scoring seventeen unanswered points and pulling the Wildcats to within seven points with 10:31 left in the game. This was really the first time all season the Sooners faced the possibility of losing a game. Had that happened here after the team had mounted a twenty-four-point lead, the rest of OU's season might have turned out dramatically different than it did. But the Sooner defense stiffened, overcoming a threatening K-State interception on a halfback pass. Blunting the Wildcats' effort to tie or go ahead, the OU offense found enough in reserve to get Duncan close enough for a twenty-four-yard field goal that widened the Sooner lead back to ten at 41–31. The score stayed that way, and the Sooners had won their sixth straight game of the season.

Following the game, Sooner Assistant Coach Steve Spurrier, Jr., said, "The history of being able to win on the road is huge for any team. And what a sign that deep down inside, I can go play about anywhere."

Heupel finished the day completing twenty-nine of thirty-seven passes for 374 yards with no interceptions. It was not a day for our rushing offense, as K-State kept us to only eleven yards on the ground. This was the first time in the 2000 season that the Sooners really had to go deep to find ways to win the game. And this would become a pattern for the season: if the ground game was blunted, they'd attack through the air; if the lead dwindled in the face of an aggressive offense, the defense would find itself in time to save the game; if the normal plays weren't working, there would be a break-through kick return or long-gainer off a short pass. From this game in Manhattan through the remainder of the season, the Sooners were nothing if not creative in the ways they would win football games. No point deficit would intimidate them, and no lead would prove fail-safe until the end of the game. It had become a very inter-esting season, and we were only halfway through.

Up next was a two-week break to prepare for the only team in the country the pollsters felt was better than K-State: our arch-enemy Nebraska—the country's other Big Red.

The Sooners continued their season-long rise in the polls and were ranked third in the nation after the K-State victory. As for their team goals, they had more than they had expected at the outset of the season. So far OU had beaten not one but two of the dreaded three giants in October. Now the Sooners trained their sights on the third. If they won against the top-ranked Huskers, they would be ranked first. That had not happened in thirteen years.

How were the players taking in their success? Bubba Burcham probably expressed it best when he said, "It's still all a blur."

At kickoff in Norman on October 28, eleven fans shy of seventy-six thousand saw Nebraska take the ball and steamroll down the field on their way to a 14–0 score by the end of the first quarter. They wrapped up 167 yards on just eleven plays. Was disaster striking on Owen Field? Was the Sooner bubble ready to burst? OU had been behind by as much as a touchdown only once during the season; now they were down by fourteen and had put nothing up on the board in response.

"We had everything going our way early on," Nebraska coach Frank Solich would say after the game. "But the test of a good foot-ball team is when your backs are to the wall like that and how you respond. [Oklahoma] responded very well."[6]

Very well indeed. After that challenging first quarter, the Sooners adjusted, and their defense held the Cornhuskers scoreless on their last eleven possessions of the game while the Sooner offense put up thirty-one unanswered points. The second quarter was big for the Sooners, who scored three touchdowns and a field goal to go up 24–14 at the half. The second half turned into a tough defensive contest as the Sooners put up a lone touchdown in the third to end all scoring for the day. Final score: OU 31, NU 14. Oklahoma scored on a Quentin Griffin one-yard run, a Curtis Fagan reception and run, a Tim Duncan field goal, a Josh Norman eight-yard run, and a Derrick Strait thirty-two-yard interception return.

Senior linebacker Torrance Marshall pronounced the Sooners' second touchdown as the game's turning point. It came on a Josh Heupel pass to receiver Curtis Fagan that pulled the Sooners even at 14–14 with about eleven minutes left in the second quarter. "When we got that score," Marshall said, "we didn't look back."

Once again, the Sooners had used both their offense and their defense to turn in great performances and win the day, propelling them into first place in all the national polls. Although the Sooner offense had been held uncustomarily to fewer than 450 total yards, and although Heupel had connected on only twenty of thirty-four passes, it was more than enough to produce the necessary points.

Had the defense not stopped the Huskers cold after the first quarter, this could have been a repeat of the famed 1971 Oklahoma-Nebraska game, which OU lost, 35–31. In that historic game, which prevented the Sooners from having a perfect season, it was a given that whichever team touched the ball last—with enough time left—would win the game. In 2000 it was OU's defense that spelled the difference and prevented a wire-to-wire shoot-out. And how tough was that Sooner defense? Nebraska had entered the game with a 398-yard per game rushing average. It was tops in the country in that category. But the Sooners shut them down to just 195 yards for the day.

The following week, OU hit the cover of *Sports Illustrated* with a shot of Quentin Griffin, who had fifty-two yards rushing, outracing a Husker defender. The headline read, "Back on Top."[7] With the back-to-back wins over three of the best teams in the country, OU had turned the Halloween month into Red October.

NOVEMBER 2000

The week after the Nebraska game, the Sooners headed south to take on their third Texas team of the year, the Baylor Bears. This team was not having a good year, but some feared the Sooners might be over-confident and looking past Baylor toward the next opponent: Texas A&M. Then there was the infamous *Sports Illustrated* jinx to ponder: being featured on the magazine's cover has often proved fatal to a team's next game. Not so this time, however. The Sooners came to Waco to play, and the game was over by the end of the first quarter when OU went ahead, 28–0, en route to a 56–7 romp. The Sooners racked up thirty first-downs while allowing Baylor only seven, and OU mounted a crushing offensive yardage lead of 516 to just 94 total yards for the Bears. Clearly both offense and defense were clicking on this first game of November. Individual Sooner stars were Heupel (313 passing yards), Thatcher (a 60-yard punt return), and three different receivers: Seth Littrell, Curtis Fagan, and Antwone Savage. As had become customary, Heupel spread his passes among several receivers; he really had no favorite because OU was blessed with many good ones.

So the team now stood at 8–0 overall and 5–0 in the Big Twelve. Clearly the Sooners were marching toward a conference championship, although to win the championship game they would have to beat either Kansas State or Nebraska again. But characteristically for this edition of OU's team, the Sooners were thinking only about the next game and not what might happen down the road. And that next game was in raucous College Station against the always-tough Texas A&M Aggies.

This game would be closer than any other thus far, and to win it, OU would have to reinvent some of its old Sooner Magic. Once again, OU would have to find a way to win a football game after stumbling over its own mistakes and winding up in a deep hole in front of eighty-seven thousand Kyle Field fans urging their Aggies on to victory.

Headed into this game, Texas A&M was ranked twenty-third nationally, but on that day they played like they were in the top five. The Aggies led at the end of each of the first three quarters: 7–3, 17–10, and 24–13. At one point the Sooners found themselves down by two touchdowns, and things looked bleak.

It seemed the Aggie defense had learned some lessons from the way previous opponents had blitzed the Sooners. Every team before A&M had seemed to think the best way to break up OU's passing attack was to blitz its linebackers and hurry Heupel into making bad throws. But the Sooner passing attack actually worked best when facing a blitz because Heupel would simply throw short to a receiver who was standing in the hole just vacated by the blitzer. In some ways it was like Heupel was taunting the linebackers to charge him, like Rocky Balboa did to Apollo Creed in the movie Rocky. In charging him, Creed left himself open to body blows, just as OU's opponents would leave themselves open to the short pass.

But A&M didn't do this. Fearing the long pass, they decided to leave the defensive line soft and drop back defenders to cover more receivers. The strategy worked for much of the game, and it was helped by three OU turnovers (including two Heupel interceptions) and one blocked punt, all of which led to twenty-four Aggie points. After halftime, Oklahoma adjusted to the soft defense and called upon its backs to produce 110 yards in the second half as opposed to only 6 in the first half. Leading that rushing charge was Quentin Griffin, who carried the ball seventeen times for seventy yards.

"No one's head was down," said offensive coordinator Mark Mangino after the game. "Some of those kids were over there smiling and winking at each other, because they felt like, 'Hey, we'll get these guys.'"[8]

The Sooners' comeback brought them to within three points of the Aggies, 31–28, with almost eight minutes left in the game. Then, on the Aggies' ensuing drive, OU linebacker Torrance Marshall dropped back and intercepted a Mark Farris pass, returning it forty-one yards for the go-ahead touchdown. OU led for the first time since early in the second quarter, 35–31. But the Aggies weren't through and had plenty of time left to score the winning touchdown. On one of their remaining two possessions, A&M made it to the threshold of scoring, only to have the drive die on a fourth-down incompletion from the OU four-yard-line when Ontei Jones broke up a Farris pass. The Sooners managed a first down on their next possession, punted, and withstood another Aggie surge, which fizzled with thirty-six seconds left on a fourth-down pass play that ended five yards short of a first down. The Sooner Magic had held. As right tackle Scott Kempenich shouted to a friend as he left the field after the game, "Don't forget the Sooner Magic, Buddy!"

Now it looked like OU had cleared all the daunting teams on its schedule and had only two contests remaining before what appeared to be an inevitable matchup with Kansas State in the championship game, since the K-State Wildcats had knocked off Nebraska in their big game. But OU's two remaining opponents were Texas Tech, which had upset them the year before, and their old bedlam opponent, Oklahoma State.

Tech came first, and the game was back on Owen Field in Norman. This could be the day OU could wrap up the Big Twelve South Division title and a trip to Arrowhead Stadium in Kansas City for the conference title game. But the Sooners had trouble getting untracked in this game, mounting only a 7–0 lead at the end of the first quarter and going into halftime with a 14–3 lead. Indeed, it wasn't until Heupel found Renaldo Works in the end zone for a third-quarter touchdown that OU could breathe a little at 21–3. Tech came back with ten fourth-quarter points to close the gap, but Quentin Griffin scored on a three-yard run for OU, to give the Sooners the final 27–13 score.

The national media did not see this as an impressive perform-ance by the Sooners. Tech had blistered the Sooners for twenty-two first downs and 330 total yards, and they had held the ball for over 33 minutes to the Sooners' 26:25. But the Sooners' defense rose to the occasion on key plays and helped the offense seal the victory. In the end, the win meant a 10–0 record, a Big Twelve South title, and a trip to the conference title game.

Texas Tech coach Mike Leach, formerly of the Sooner staff, had praise for the Sooners following the game: "They're real consistent. They don't have any blatant weakness. They just keep coming every time. They just beat you."[9]

Now the Sooners had only their annual grudge match against Oklahoma State left, and the game's outcome would have no effect on OU's chances of going to the Big Twelve Championship Game— they were headed to Kansas City either way. But a loss would be dev-astating to Sooner pride, especially a loss to the archrival Cowboys. This game was all about in-state bragging rights, and it was also a chance for the Sooners to prove to the national media that they were better than their effort against Tech had indicated.

OU was still clinging to its No. 1 national ranking but not as strongly as before. An OSU loss would drop them a few notches in the polls and make it harder—if not impossible—for them to lay claim to the national championship. After all, Florida State and Miami were still going strong nationally. So even if the Big Twelve title was secure, a lot was still riding on the outcome of this game. The Sooners were favored by twenty-five points going into the game, which was to be played on November 25 at Stillwater. It would be OSU Coach Bob Simmons's final game with the Cow-boys; OSU had already announced he would step down after a 3–7 record with one game remaining. The team wanted nothing more than to win this last game for him, and they came very close to doing that.

Although the Sooners scored first on a short Fagan reception from Heupel and went up 7–0 at the end of the first quarter, points would be very hard to come by from then on. OU managed only a field goal and a safety in the second quarter and was shut out entirely in the second half. Winning a Big Twelve game while scoring only twelve points is not easy, and when the Cowboys' Tatum Bell unleashed a sixty-yard run in the third quarter, OSU pulled to within five points of OU, at 12–7. It looked like the Cowboys might pull a major upset when they drove to the OU twelve-yard line with 3:15 left to play in the game. The drive ended when a fourth-down pass from OSU quarterback Aso Pogi to tight end Marcellus Rivers was knocked down in the corner of the end zone by Derrick Strait, allowing OU to escape with a surprisingly tough 12–7 victory.

"I was waiting," said Derrick after the game. "I already had my mind right that I wasn't going to let him catch it. It just came down to me and him going to get the ball."[10] Shorter by five inches than Rivers, Derrick leaped and got it first.

OU's sputtering offense had managed only 309 yards on the day, although Quentin Griffin once again took advantage of soft defensive coverage to scramble for big yardage. Today he ran for 115 yards on twenty-one carries and also caught five passes for 59 yards.

As the afternoon sun set over Stillwater, the Sooners knew they had tapped once again into that Sooner Magic, which some people would just call luck. But anyone who has ever played football knows that luck is often the twelfth man on the field for your team. Before the Sooners' next two games were over, the team would have to tap into it again and again.

THE BATTLE FOR THE CONFERENCE CHAMPIONSHIP

Beating a team like Kansas State once in a season is difficult. Beating that same team twice is almost an impossibility. They've seen you in action, they know what you can do, and they know how to adjust to you. They have no desire to go down twice, and they especially don't want to do that when the conference championship and a Bowl Championship Series game are on the line. Since our victory over them back in October, the Wildcats had stumbled only once, and that to Texas A&M, the team that nearly derailed us. Add to all of this Arrowhead's location in Kansas City, just a short drive north of Manhattan, and you could make a case this was a home game for the Wildcats.

This is what the Sooners faced when they showed up at Arrowhead Stadium on December 2 to take on the Wildcats. As for OU, our conference title hopes were on the line as well as a shot at the national championship game in the Orange Bowl. In short, this was a pressure-packed game, just the kind of game that a player dreams about when he comes to Division I-A college football.

Just shy of eighty-thousand fans showed up at Arrowhead on a cold Saturday to watch what promised to be a great game. I had gotten tickets from friends of my father who were Nebraska fans and had expected the Cornhuskers to be the northern division representative. I watched the game from the upper deck with my agent, Greg Stoneberger.

The game began as a defensive battle, and the Sooners managed only a thirty-three-yard Tim Duncan field goal in the first quarter. Kansas State came back in the second quarter with a ten-yard touchdown scamper by quarterback Jonathan Beasley and then added a twenty-two-yard field goal to go up, 10–3. OU knotted it at halftime, however, on a short pass by Heupel to Trent Smith.

OU came back in the third with Heupel dancing seven yards for the go-ahead touchdown, making the score 17–10. Kansas State tied the game later in the third quarter on a fifty-eight-yard punt return by Aaron Lockett. The Sooners then tacked on back-to-back scores on an Andre Woolfolk seventeen-yard reception of a Heupel pass and a Tim Duncan forty-six-yard field goal, to go ahead, 27–17. For two crucial plays, Coach Stoops dipped into Barry Switzer's old playbook and came up with a great option play. The first sent Quentin Griffin racing twenty-two yards to the Wildcat seventeen-yard line during a seventy-nine-yard touchdown drive and the second had him advancing twenty-nine yards for a field goal.

The 2000 Big Twelve championship game at Arrowhead Stadium in Kansas City.
The Sooners were 11–0 going into this game, which was played on a cold day in
December 2000. OU beat Kansas State for the second time this season and was
invited to play in the national championship game in Miami against Florida State.
(*Daily Oklahoman*)

"That was just some Oklahoma football of old," Stoops said. "We haven't forgotten totally about the option."[11]

Duncan's field goal came from the Wildcats' twenty-seven yard line on a fourth-and-three play with 1:25 left. Stoops said later he was about to go for the first down but instead went with his intuition that Duncan would hit the field goal. He did. Kansas State then mounted one more touchdown drive with a sixteen-yard pass from Beasley to wide receiver Quincy Morgan to bring the Wildcats within three points of a tie, at 27–24. But there were only six seconds remaining on the clock, and there would be no last-minute miracle for K-State.

Looking back, it's clear that the game belonged as much to OU's defense as to its offense. They held the Wildcats' offense to just seventeen points, far below its season average, and they allowed the gifted Beasley only 12 of 28 passes for the day, for a total of 106 yards. On offense, Heupel hit on 24 of 44 passes for 220 yards, but he threw three interceptions. For his rushing efforts, Griffin managed eighty-seven yards on thirteen carries to round out the Sooner attack.

After the game, Heupel summed up the season as well as the game when he said, "We just find a way to win. We just do enough to win. It's something special."[12]

So for the first time since 1987, OU had won its conference championship, making it the thirty-seventh such title in the Sooners' trophy case. Better yet, they were on their way to the Orange Bowl and a shot at the national championship against Florida State. The Oklahoma boys were back in town. I was excited and proud, but at the same time disappointed that I couldn't play. My dream was coming true, but it was one year late for me.

THE ORANGE BOWL

All season long the Sooners had trouble getting respect from the national media. They were the underdogs going into every major game, and even as they continued to win, the press seemed to pick apart what they didn't do as opposed to applauding what they did. The close Texas Tech and Oklahoma State games didn't help the media's image of a team ready to falter. The second K-State win solidified the Sooners' hold on the No. 1 ranking in the nation, but few national media outlets gave them a chance of winning it all at the Orange Bowl.

Interesting, isn't it? The same group of journalists and coaches who give a team the country's top ranking also make them the underdog when they go against the No. 3 team in the country. That's exactly what happened when OU faced off against Florida State University on January 3 in Miami: No. 3 was favored over No. 1. Miami was ranked second in the AP poll but FSU has a higher BCS ranking. Oklahoma had turned in a fine season, but now the media seemed to be saying, "They're playing a real national powerhouse in FSU. They really can't be expected to win against the Seminoles."

A couple of weeks before the game, Josh Heupel and FSU quarterback Chris Weinke had gone toe-to-toe in New York City for the Heisman Trophy, with Weinke coming out the winner. That's just how the national press expected Weinke's team to do against Heupel's in the Orange Bowl.

Of course they were wrong.

As they had done three times this year at home, once again the Sooners were playing under the lights before almost seventy-seven thousand fans in a southern climate. But this time the lights were those of Pro Player Stadium, the city was Miami, and the opponent was Florida State. It just doesn't get any bigger than this, and you could have sliced the tension with a steak knife. The Sooners were a double-digit underdog to the defending national champs as they rushed out onto the floor of the stadium that night. Oklahoma was thought to have less speed, less strength, and less experience in big games like this. Florida State, in contrast, was here for the third straight year. But as *Oklahoma Daily* student writer Matt Franklin reported later, "Instead, the Sooners proved to have more heart, a better game plan and better execution."[13]

Of the many predictions that went wrong on this night was the idea that this would be an offensive battle. The opposite proved true and remained true all night long, as OU controlled the game on defense. Chris Weinke, the new Heisman winner, found himself up against a brick wall and was unable to score all night long. The Sooners, on the other hand, were scoring when they had to, making their way to a 13–0 lead that lasted until the last minute of the game, when OU punter Jeff Ferguson downed an errant snap in his own end zone, giving the 'Noles their only two points of the night.

Still, this game was anyone's to win for a long, long time. The Sooners held only a 3–0 halftime lead, managing to inch up to 6–0 when Duncan hit his second field goal of the night in the third quarter. But then Florida State drove the ball to the OU thirty-five-yard line and had a first down there with more than twelve minutes left in the game. That's when Weinke started passing bricks as he threw four incompletions, including a bomb into the end zone that was almost caught for what would have been the go-ahead touchdown. After a short OU possession, the Sooner defense again rose to the occasion. After OU's punt pinned Florida State on its own five-yard line, junior linebacker Rocky Calmus forced a Weinke fumble. Sophomore safety Roy Williams scooped it up, and OU had the ball deep in Seminole territory. Two plays later, Quentin Griffin got the call and hammered it home from ten yards out to put the game out of reach at 13–0.

Once again, it wasn't a great night offensively for the Sooners, and few experts would have predicted thirteen points would be enough to win this game. But the Sooner defense played magnificently, shutting out the high-powered Seminole offense and Heisman winner Weinke.

The Sooners had just won their seventh national championship, and their first since 1985. Reflecting on the game, Heupel spoke for the team when he said, "It's a dream come true. We don't care what the media or the oddsmakers think. We believe in ourselves. This team knows who and what it is."[14]

WITNESSING THE RETURN TO GLORY

Finally, everything had come full circle for me. I reflected on all that had happened from the time I started playing football in junior high school, to the national championship game in January 2001—the game that I had always dreamed about, OU versus FSU for the national title. This game brought it all into perspective—all of those years of playing college football, all the ups and downs that came with changes in coaching staff, all the daily work in the weight room and training room, all the rehab with the hope of getting another chance to play. All of this was just the prelude to greatness. My total football experience, starting with my first day of football practice in junior high school through my last play as a Sooner in the Independence Bowl, had now culminated in the Sooners' return to glory.

And no one is prouder of them than I am.

After the end of that game, I remember thinking that this was the greatest moment I would experience in OU football. Of course, I was the poster boy of mixed emotions. On the one hand, I was thrilled because of the victory, I was relieved because the Sooners were back on top, and I was proud of what I had been able to accomplish and what the seniors from the 1999 team were able to contribute. On the other hand, I was sad that it was over. That single moment put my whole football career into perspective. Every play, every snap, every sprint, every push-up, every injury, every ache and pain, every mistake, every scrimmage, every game, every drop of sweat—suddenly it was all worthwhile. That victory was something that I had dreamed of but never really expected to happen, and I will look back and relish everything that led up to that moment.

EPILOGUE

So You Think You Want to Play College Football?

OK, so there you sit. You've stayed with me this far, you've heard the stories and shared the experiences vicariously. Maybe you're playing high school football and dreaming about playing in college. Or maybe you're a parent whose son is doing that. Either way, you're asking yourself: Is it worth it? Is college football worth the personal sacrifices it takes? My answer, in a nutshell, is yes, but only if you love to play the game. Even then, you will still have to face the kinds of ups and downs this book discusses.

I loved to play football, so from the outset I dreamed of playing at the highest level possible. Let's face it, it is a thrill to be considered by the schools with great traditions that play in front of tens of thousands of live, cheering fans every week in addition to the other millions watching on TV. I would have played anywhere just to play, but to have a chance to play NCAA Division I-A at a school with the tradition of Oklahoma was a dream come true.

I also wanted to play for a team that had a chance to contend for a national championship. Of course, I was realistic, knowing that only one team finishes at the top at each season's end. Still, if you play for a program like OU, which had already won six national titles (now seven), your chances are better than in a program without such a tradition.

I also went to Oklahoma thinking I had an excellent chance of playing beyond the college level. This was not totally unrealistic since coming out of high school I had the size and notoriety that one might expect of a future NFL-level prospect. I also felt that playing for a school like Oklahoma would enhance my chances to play pro football. I still believe this to be true for today's players.

In some ways, I was very fortunate. I was heavily recruited, and Oklahoma offered me an opportunity to play in Division I-A. In many other ways, however, I was much like any other high school player who dreams of playing college football with other talented players, all dreaming of making the NFL. I went to OU with a number of expectations that I am sure are held by most high school prospects. As is the case in most real-life situations, not all of those expectations were fulfilled.

Throughout my playing experience at Oklahoma many things happened that I expected, and many things happened that I didn't expect. Playing Division I-A football produced a lot of positive experiences but some negative ones as well. Looking back, I can definitely say the positives far outweighed the negatives. Would I have done anything differently if I had known about the drawbacks up front? I don't think so. In most cases the negatives are inherent to every program, or they led to situations I couldn't do anything about, anyway. At the same time, it would be unfair to describe only the good things that happened without mentioning the bad. So if you are out there thinking how great it would be to play college football for a national power, consider both the pros and the cons that follow in this chapter.

WHAT'S SO GREAT ABOUT PLAYING COLLEGE FOOTBALL?

Nothing can compare to the experience of running out of the tunnel onto Owen Field on a sunny Saturday afternoon. The atmosphere is charged with electricity. Everything and everyone is dressed in crimson red. The pageantry is awesome. It sends shivers up and down your back when you step out onto the field and hear the band play the "Boomer Sooner" fight song. I was able to attend several of my older brother's games when I was recovering from my Achilles tear. Although the games were exciting to watch, the electricity that seventy-five hundred fans can generate just doesn't compare to the explosiveness of a crowd ten times that size.

The OU fans at Owen Field actually get a better show than the players, who miss the entire pre-game build-up. One time my parents videotaped an entire pregame for me, starting with the tail-gating, then the band's march through campus, and finally the cheerleaders' warm-ups. It made me realize that the players miss the best part of the game-day festivities. Of course, it is more than an even trade because the fans don't get to play, and playing is the center of any college football player's dream. It is hard to explain to someone who hasn't played, but during the game you are so intent on your playing that you don't even notice the hard contact with your opponents. You are so focused on the play calls, the audibles, your assignments, and the snap count that you lose track of almost everything else.

It would be impossible to list all of the big moments I experienced at OU because not all of them were knockdown blocks, spectacular plays, touchdowns, or victories. Rather, the greatness was in the entire experience of playing football at this level. The highs and lows, the practices, the travel, the hotels, the pregame warm-ups, the games themselves, the postgame celebrations, even the locations of the games were all special. The Cotton Bowl games against Texas were especially exciting to me, having played there in high school. Nebraska's stadium in Lincoln and Notre Dame's stadium in South Bend, as well as Owen Field in Norman, were impressive in and of themselves. Each of these stadiums seemed to be haunted by the ghosts of the legendary players who had played there in the past. Players like Billy Vessels, Steve Owens, the silvershoed Joe Washington, Jack Mildren, Billy Sims, and many, many others.

If stepping onto Owen Field on a Saturday afternoon is the greatest thrill, there is no greater satisfaction than stepping off the field knowing you played a great game. The rush you get when you beat archrivals like Texas, Texas A&M, and Nebraska is unparalleled. You feel great after a victory not only because of your own satisfaction, but also because you know an untold number of Sooner fans are sharing in the celebration you helped make possible. Going out to a party in Norman to celebrate after winning a game finishes a close second in the thrill category. Euphoria blankets everyone, and you are at the center of attention.

In addition to the excitement and the extraordinary experiences OU football offers, it also gives you the opportunity to attend one of the finest universities in the country. The most important thing I did during recruiting was to pick the school first and the football program second. That way, if anything changes within the football program, you are still going to the best school. Needless to say, many things changed within the football program during my stay, but through all the changes I never lost my love for the University of Oklahoma.

Another positive result of playing at the Division I-A level is that your tuition and fees are covered, and your room and board are taken care of as well as long as you live in university-provided housing. If you opt to live off campus, the athletic department provides a monthly stipend that averaged then $450 per month. This would be a wonderful benefit if it covered all of your expenses. Unfortunately, it doesn't. I know there are a lot of college students out there who would be thrilled to have a free education plus $450 per month. But it is not quite that simple. Suffice it to say that a free education falls on the good side of the equation, but living below the poverty level while people around you—like coaches, administrators, agents, announcers, and vendors—are getting rich falls on the opposite side. More on this later.

Friends, recognition, and preferential treatment are other positives to playing college football at this level. When you play a team sport in college, you develop a great bond of friendship with everyone associated with the program. In team sports you learn to rely on the other players as well as the people who help you prepare. This includes everyone from the coaches, the assistant coaches, and the trainers to the athletic director and the athletic department staff. Throughout your college career those bonds of reliance and trust become stronger and develop into friendships with your teammates that will last a lifetime. I don't mean to say you become lifelong friends with everyone. Some teammates will remain very close and others you may not see again, but there is always a feeling that if you ever needed help, no one on the team would turn you down.

Business schools say that the most important part of your career after college is networking. Through these relationships you can receive support from friends and colleagues who help you advance throughout your life and career, and you can support them in return. The people I met through the football program at Oklahoma have been invaluable to me. This doesn't mean everyone is falling all over themselves to make sure I am successful; I've had to put in the time and effort. But it never hurts to have the opportunities that friends can provide.

In addition to the friendships you make during college, another important benefit of your football career is name recognition. This is particularly true when you play football at a traditional power like OU. You develop great name recognition not only within the State of Oklahoma, but you also carry the positive aura of Sooner football with you wherever you go. Because of the size of the fan base and the intense interest that Oklahomans have in OU football, when you finish your football career a lot of people in the state will know you. Former OU quarterbacks Jack Mildren and J. C. Watts, for example, have both distinguished themselves in politics. Mildren served as lieutenant governor of the state, and Watts serves as a U.S. congressman from Oklahoma. People outside the state also recognize how impressive it is to have played for a school like OU.

Along with name recognition comes the benefit of preferential treatment, although this perk is greatly restricted by the NCAA and mostly overstated by the critics of major-college athletics. As a player I would occasionally get seating ahead of the waiting list at a restaurant. This usually happened at places with long waiting lines of people celebrating on the evenings following home games. For the most part, this kind of preferential treatment was almost necessary since we obviously couldn't leave the game early to beat the postgame traffic. By the time we finished in the locker room and worked our way through traffic, we would never get a table without such treatment. I need to add that rarely was the preferential treatment we received given without some expectation of a benefit in return. A lot of people in Norman like to rub elbows with OU football players. In return for an early table, the restaurant owner generally benefited from the football players' tacit endorsement or through more lasting visual endorsements, such as autographed football memorabilia like footballs, helmets, or jerseys.

I can honestly say that during my stay at OU I never received anything of substance or monetary value from anyone. I received more than my share of recognition and occasionally moved to the front of the line at a restaurant, but other than some temporary fan adoration and the faint taste of celebrity status, there wasn't much in the way of preferential treatment. I was never given a grade that I didn't earn. In fact, in some cases the faculty were harder on the athletes than on the other students. We did get athletic clothing and shoes from the athletic department, but those were limited by strict NCAA guidelines. All in all, with the exception of the few players who are able to establish careers in pro football, playing college football is of limited value from a monetary standpoint. There are many intangibles that are priceless; the money just isn't there for the players. Does that change my feelings toward my career at Oklahoma? Not in the least.

WHAT'S SO HARD ABOUT PLAYING COLLEGE FOOTBALL?

Then there is the dark side of playing college football. Every program has its benefits and its drawbacks, and knowing up front about the drawbacks at OU wouldn't have changed my decision to play college football there. However, there are several things about college football I would change if I could. First let me describe some of the down sides of college football, and then I will offer some ideas for how the problems might be corrected.

Let's start with injuries. They are a part of the game, right? Right. That's fine, and I accepted the fact that I could be injured, possibly seriously, playing football. The thrill and satisfaction of playing and the relatively rare occurrence of serious injuries made that risk acceptable to me. In general, the injuries that happen in football occur when a part of the body is put into an awkward or abnormal position and then undergoes some impact stress that is greater than the strength of that part of the body. Such situations don't occur often during play. Unfortunately, these forces can also be created outside of play.

My dad spent his fiftieth birthday driving from Arlington, Texas, to Oklahoma City to be with me the evening I went into surgery to repair the tear in my Achilles tendon. My mom couldn't get off work, so my dad came up alone. On a day normally set aside for a celebration, it was instead a day of concern and frustration. This was my second surgery for the same injury; I had tried too hard to come back too soon. The coaches and trainers were trying to get me to come back in time for the Texas game when I was reinjured.

The down side was not the reinjury itself. The second tear led to my medical redshirt, which gave me the opportunity to play for Coach Stoops, play against Notre Dame in South Bend, play in the Independence Bowl, and create some other positive memories. The down side was the way I was injured in the first place. The first tear came during a summer, off-season, "voluntary" workout. As I mentioned earlier, summer workouts really are not voluntary. If you don't go through the off-season training, you don't play during the regular season. Second, you are at the mercy of the weight coach, who in my case had assigned a drill that was inherently dangerous. Even if you recognize that the drill might produce a career-ending injury, you can't say anything about it without being labeled a quitter.

I was told that it was a medical first to tear the same Achilles in two different places. But that was a record I would rather not have broken. Often even one Achilles tear is a career-ending injury, so I am proud that I was able to return to my starting position on the offensive line. Prior to the injury, I felt I had a reasonable chance to make it to the NFL. But the injury took away just enough of my athleticism to eliminate that opportunity.

Another negative aspect of college football involves money, or rather the lack of it. Everyone associated with Division I-A college football makes a great deal of money, except for the players. The only athletes who are treated worse than college football players are racehorses, who get paid only in oats. The coaches, administrators, athletic departments, schools, conferences, and the NCAA all get a cut of the action at the expense of the principal attraction: the players. For example, when Oklahoma was invited to the Orange Bowl in January 2001, the payoff per school was around $13 million—for one football game.

Trust me; very few people pay to come out on Saturday to see the coaches work the sidelines. And no one would pay to watch the athletic director do office work. The coaches, athletic directors, and other staff members all work within a capitalistic, free enterprise system. They are free to go wherever they feel the opportunity is best and to negotiate the best possible deal. In essence, there is no limit to the benefits a coach or administrator can obtain. The players, however, are not allowed to participate in that system. The players are the ones putting their bodies at risk, they are the ones bringing in the fans, but they are limited by the NCAA to an extremely small piece of the money pie.

The reason the players get so little money is simple. If the NCAA allowed the players to be paid according to performance, the rich schools would win, and the leaner schools would lose. The NCAA must enforce parity across the Division I-A colleges to continue to reap the huge profits. Nearly every move the NCAA makes is designed to keep the rich schools from eclipsing the less rich. The move from 125 scholarships to 85 per school was made so the richer schools couldn't stockpile players. The richer schools tried to get around parity by building incredible facilities for athletes. But the NCAA countered by outlawing "jock dorms," saying facilities for athletes had to be equal to those for other students.

You are probably asking why is parity so bad? It has, after all, revived competition. It levels the playing field so that dynasties aren't created. A lot of schools have benefited from parity. So what's so bad about it? The answer is that it's not the concept of parity that's problematic. What is bad is the fact that parity is applied only to the players. Coaches don't have restricted salaries, and athletic directors get bonuses for team performance. The schools get a tremendous amount of money for appearances at major bowl games, not to mention the sale of products bearing the school logo. Everybody gets rich except the players who make it all happen on the field.

So what do the players get? Not much. The monetary benefit is based on what the poorest school in Division I-A is able to afford. In addition, most of what the school provides costs the university nothing, at least technically. Giving an athlete free tuition and fees doesn't cost the school a cent because the students who do pay tuition carry the cost of a scholarship. All a university does when it adds a scholarship athlete to its student population is to add an extra body to a classroom seat, a body already paid for by the tuition of the other students. The same is true for the cost of a dorm room or campus apartment. If the university fills a room that would be empty without the scholarship athlete, then the cost to the school of filling that room with an athlete is only the cost of utilities. Believe me, a significant number of apartments at OU's Yorkshire complex would be empty were it not for the scholarship athletes.

This means the actual outlay to the schools for a scholarship is only the cost of food and allowances. In my years the allowance was $450 per month if you live off campus. That's $4,050 per school year for everything, including food, rent, gasoline, and so on. If you stay over the summer for the "voluntary" workouts, you must be enrolled in summer classes to get the monthly stipend of $450. A coach, on the other hand, might have a $1.4 million salary, and the school might get a hefty share of the $13 million for appearing in the national championship game. What would happen if the coaches' salaries at OU were limited to the salaries of the lowest paid coaches in Division I-A?

Off and on, the NCAA has suggested that athletes should be allowed to work to make some extra spending money. Along the way, some coaches have even made jobs available to their star athletes. Some coaches went to the extreme to try to help their players pay their bills. For example, Barry Switzer wrote in his book *Bootlegger's Boy* that he paid Joe Washington one hundred dollars per hour to baby-sit his children.

There is one problem with the work solution, however: most college football players just don't have time to work outside of football. When you consider that when I worked the twenty hours a week maximum time allowed by the NCAA for football, it was at the equivalent rate of five dollars per hour. The other reason the NCAA won't allow Division I-A athletes to work is because it can't maintain control; that is, it can't guarantee parity. Suppose an athlete is working as a waiter in a restaurant. He provides such outstanding service to a table of boosters that they each give him a one hundred dollar tip. Again, the haves would gain an advantage over the have-nots, and the NCAA won't allow that to happen.

Parity not only has an impact on the players, but it also impacts some of the players' parents, particularly the parents who live out of state. At the start of the season at OU, a large table is set up in the entry to Wilkinson Hall, covered with round, four-inch crimson-and-cream colored pins. There is a pin for each parent. My parents' pin read, "My son is No. 71, Jay Smith, OU." There were more than two hundred of these pins on the table at the start of the season. This was a nice way for the team to give recognition to the parents, who would wear the pins at each home game. As the season went on, there were still a fairly large number of pins left on the table. Each pin that remained at the end of the season represented a parent who didn't once get to see his or her son play football during the entire year. I am sure there were a number of reasons why a player's parents couldn't get to a Sooner home game, but more often than not it was because they lived too far away and couldn't afford to attend. What's worse, there is no way anyone could help these parents to attend even if they wanted to. If anyone outside of the family paid for such a trip, it would be a violation of NCAA rules. Most parents sacrifice a great deal to get their sons and daughters to the level where they can compete at Division I-A. It is a shame they can't be provided with some assistance to see them play.

For me the benefits of playing college football far outweighed the problems, mainly because I had sufficient financial support outside of football. The negatives, except for the injury, were either unavoidable or didn't have a direct impact on me. All in all, the trade-off was worth it.

ON BALANCE

So, like most other endeavors that you will face in your life, playing college football is a sometimes-great, sometimes-frustrating experience. In many ways, your expectations of the college football experience are like dreams, and dreams seldom come true as you envision they will. In the end, however, getting a chance to chase your dream, while having fun and making great lifelong friendships, is more than worth the frustrations.

The old saying goes, "When one door closes, another opens." This was certainly true of my Achilles injury. Although the NFL was no longer a possibility, the injury did allow me two more years of college eligibility and an additional year during rehab to enjoy college and college football. The year during rehab was difficult because of the pain and agony it took to come back. But it was also rewarding because I was free to follow my older brother's senior football season at Angelo State University.

My brother Allan played left tackle for Angelo State in San Angelo, Texas. The university has a solid NCAA Division II football program that has ranked consistently in the top fifteen in Division II polls. The year I was hurt, I was able to attend all but one of his games, many of them on crutches. That year Angelo State's record was 10–2, they went two deep into the playoffs, and at year's end they finished at No. 6 in the national Division II rankings. I would have missed all of that had it not been for my injury.

In the middle of the season, Angelo State played Midwestern State University in Wichita Falls, Texas. This was the second of only two games Angelo State had played on artificial turf that season. Since their budgets didn't allow for two sets of game shoes, they had opted for cleats, and so the players didn't have shoes suited for games on turf. The Sooners happened to be on the road that weekend and had already left town. So on Friday afternoon I went through the OU locker room and picked out five pairs of turf shoes corresponding to the shoe sizes of the Angelo State offensive linemen. That Saturday, Angelo State's entire offensive line was dressed from helmets to socks in their traditional blue and gold, but on their feet were crimson shoes. On the sidelines, the middle linebacker found out about the deal and borrowed the shoes I was wearing myself. It didn't matter that my shoes were size fourteen and his feet were size eleven. They worked better than the tennis shoes he had planned to wear that night. When I returned to the OU campus on Sunday, I put all of the shoes back and no one there ever knew they had helped a Division II football team.

The medical redshirt year also gave me the opportunity to play in South Bend against Notre Dame the fall of 1999. The Sooners went into that game undefeated at 3–0, and the game was hyped as the return of the Sooner tradition. We seniors spent a lot of time with the press that week. ESPN spent the entire week filming in Norman, and I had a chance to be on the ESPN pregame show. This was another great experience that I would have missed if I hadn't been injured, so there was a bright side to my injury after all.

My year off also gave me, along with all the seniors on the team, a chance to fulfill our promise to help Coach Stoops restore the Sooner Magic at OU. No one has any doubt now that we set the underclassmen on the right track to reach that goal. Later that season we also handed Texas A&M its worst defeat in ninety-eight years. Again, I wouldn't have those memories had it not been for my injury.

The sixth year also led to my second bowl game at OU. I was the only member of the team at that time who had even been to a bowl— the Copper Bowl after the 1994 season. This second bowl game was different for me. I was able to spend extra time in the stadium to savor the whole experience, watching the postgame fireworks that celebrated the start of the new millennium. At the time I thought it was the end of my football career. Fortunately, there was still one more chance for me to play.

The Gridiron Classic All-Star Game was held the end of January 2000 in Orlando, Florida. I was fortunate enough to be chosen to play for Team USA against Team Florida. Team USA was made up of seniors from across the nation. Team Florida was made up of players from the Florida universities and high school graduates from Florida who played for universities outside the state.

This game was different from any other; it was almost a throwback to playing in junior high school. It was an opportunity for players with great skills to play without the pressure of a national or conference championship at stake. We were all acknowledged already as established players, so we didn't have to fight to keep our positions. The emphasis was on the positive. My coach was the legendary pro coach

Buddy Ryan, who is a great guy, contrary to some public opinion. We didn't need to worry if we messed up an assignment. I even did the long snaps when the center got hurt; I had never before made a long snap in my entire football career. It was a chance to truly enjoy playing football again, and I am thankful I had that chance.

The Gridiron Classic in turn led to an invitation for me to join the NFL Combine, where I had the chance to work out for my dad's former college offensive line coach, Kent Stephenson, now with the Pittsburgh Steelers. Unfortunately, the NFL didn't draft me, but then I was invited to the Combine for the new XFL. When I wasn't drafted by the XFL, I felt I had gone as far as I could go in football. But what a glorious run!

If I had not played football for the Oklahoma Sooners I would have missed out on so much, and if I had not been injured, I would have missed out on so much more. So don't get discouraged if things don't work out just the way you hope they will. Even the setbacks can lead to other opportunities you had not envisioned. The bottom line is this: if you want to play college football and you have the talent and work ethic to do it, my best advice is to go for it.

Just go into it with your eyes wide open.

NOTES

CHAPTER 1

1. See *Oklahoma Sooners: Football '99* (Norman: University of Oklahoma Sports Information Department, 2000), p. 29.

2. Ibid., p. 19.

3. Gary King, *An Autumn Remembered: Reflections of College Football's Greatest Team* (Red Earth Books, 1988), p. 12.

4. For historical views of the Owen and Wilkinson coaching eras, see Harold Keith, *Oklahoma Kickoff: An Informal History of the First Twenty-Five Years of Football at the University of Oklahoma, and of the Amusing Hardships That Attended It* (Norman: University of Oklahoma Press, 1948; reprint 1978); Harold Keith, *Forty-Seven Straight: The Wilkinson Era at Oklahoma* (Norman: University of Oklahoma Press, 1984); and Gary T. King, *An Autumn Remembered: Reflections of College Football's Greatest Team* (Red Earth Books, 1988).

5. For a historical view of the Mackenzie and Fairbanks coaching eras, see *Oklahoma Sooners: Football '99* (Norman: University of Oklahoma Sports Information Department, 2000), p.12.

6. For historical views of the Switzer era, see Barry Switzer and Bud Shrake, *Bootlegger's Boy* (New York: William Morrow & Co., 1990); and Charles Thompson and Allan Sonnenschein, *Down and Dirty: The Life and Crimes of Oklahoma Football* (New York: Carroll and Graf Publishers, 1990).

CHAPTER 2

1. H. G. Bissinger, *Friday Night Lights: A Town, a Dream, and a Team*, tenth anniv. ed. (Cambridge, Mass.: Da Capo Press, 2000), p. 47.

2. High school football rankings by *USA Today*, September 11, 1994.

3. The national recruiting services are usually staffed by talent scouts who poll high school coaches and visit high schools to make up lists ranking the top football players, regionally and nationally. Their rankings are usually based on physical attributes such as height and weight; performance measures like vertical jump, bench press, and forty-yard dash times; and other measures like high school grades, the quality of high school competition, and the number of colleges that have indicated an interest in the player. Coming out of high school I was six feet, four inches tall, weighed 275 pounds, ran a 4.8 forty-yard dash, had a thirty-one-inch vertical jump, and came from a quality program in Texas.

4. Electronic timing provides a much more accurate measure of speed than a coach-held stop watch. In some cases (not mine), high school coaches have been known to have a "quick thumb," resulting in some remarkably lower times.

5. Miami offered me a scholarship, and Coach Williams did an outstanding job of recruiting. He would call and we'd have some honest and candid conversations, which I greatly appreciated. The rapport was very strong, and I did consider Miami based on that factor alone. But Miami's program was in turmoil, and the fact that my father had graduated from FSU was too much for Coach Williams to overcome.

CHAPTER 3

1. For a historical view of the OU-Texas rivalry, see *Oklahoma Sooners: Football '99* (Norman: University of Oklahoma Sports Information Department, 2000).

2. For a report of Coach Gibbs's resignation, see Daily Oklahoman, November 7, 1994, Sports section.

3. For a report of the Oklahoma "Mardi Gras" hotel, see *Daily Oklahoman*, December 27, 1994, Sports section.

CHAPTER 4

1. Bill Sullivan, "The Sooner Show," *Houston Chronicle*, August 21, 1995.

2. Dave Sittler, *Daily Oklahoman*, December 18, 1994.

3. Ibid.

4. Rick Bozich quoted by Dave Sittler, *Daily Oklahoman*, December 18, 1994.

5. David Sittler, *Daily Oklahoman*, December 18, 1994.

6. See Bill Sullivan, "The Sooner Show," *Houston Chronicle*, August 21, 1995.

7. Bob Hersom, "Undercurrents of Concern Lead to OU Grid Coach Change," *Daily Oklahoman*, December 24, 1995.

8. Ibid.

9. Dan O'Kane, "OU Very Thorough," *Tulsa World*, August 2, 2001.

10. Ibid.

11. Ibid.

12. Bob Hersom, "Undercurrents of Concern Lead to OU Grid Coach Change," *Daily Oklahoman*, December 24, 1995.

13. Ray Buck. "Schnellenberger Lost Control, Job." December 23, 1995. Sportsline USA. Online. Available at: http://www.sportsline.com/b/page/pressbox/archive/dec95/buckr122395.htm. Accessed July 20, 2002.

14. Dan O'Kane, "Cold Weather, Defense Dictate OU Scrimmage," *Tulsa World*, April 23, 1995.

15. Dan O'Kane, "Probe Doomed Schnellenberger," *Tulsa World*, December 22, 1995.

16. See Case No. CJ96-1436, filed August 9, 1996 (amended April 25, 1997), in the District Court for Cleveland County, State of Oklahoma, Bryan C. Ailey, Plaintiff, vs. Howard Schnellenberger, Chris Vagotis, Kenneth Pope, Dan Pickett, Gary Nord, Jurt Valkenberg, Merve (sic) Johnson, Clarence James, and Donnie Duncan, Defendants.

17. See Case No. CJ-97-1641, filed August 8, 1997, in the District Court of Cleveland County, State of Oklahoma, Bryan C. Ailey, Plaintiff, vs. State of Oklahoma ex rel. The Board of Regents of the University of Oklahoma, and Howard Schnellenberger, Defendants. On August 25, 1997, this case was transferred to the United States District Court for the Western District of Oklahoma as Civil No. 97-1381 L.

18. For Schnellenberger's defense of the rigidity of his system, see Bob Hersom, *Daily Oklahoman*, September 3, 1995.

19. John James, "Howard Stresses Work at OU," Fort Worth *Star-Telegram*, August 27, 1995.

20. See Dave Sitter, *Daily Oklahoman*, October 1, 1995.

21. Ibid.

22. Dan O'Kane, "Sooners Violated Practice Limit?" *Tulsa World*, December 16, 1995.

23. Ibid.

24. Bob Hersom, "OU's Schnellenberger Calls It Quits," *Daily Oklahoman*, December 19, 1995.

25. Angelique S. Chengelis, *Detroit News*, December 19, 1995.

26. Ray Buck. "Schnellenberger Lost Control, Job." December 23, 1995. Sportsline USA. Online. Available at: http://www.sportsline.com/b/page/pressbox/archive/dec95/buckr122395.htm. Accessed July 20, 2002.

27. Ibid.

28. Pat Forde, *Tulsa World*, December 19, 1995.

29. John Underwood, "The Coach Takes a Beating . . . Howard Schnellenberger Did Something Unforgivable at Oklahoma: He Lost Football Games," *New York Times*, Sports section.

30. President Boren quoted in Berry Tramel's column, *Daily Oklahoman*, June 18, 1996.

31. Ibid.

32. Associated Press article, printed in *Topeka Capital-Journal*, July 13, 1999.

33. Rick Bozich, "Howard Has New Team to Dream Over," Louisville *Courier-Journal*, August 19, 2000.

34. On two occasions in the spring of 2001, the authors attempted to contact Howard Schnellenberger through his public relations representative, Barry Epstein, for reaction to the published stories and allegations against him concerning reports of his drinking, abuse of players, and violation of practice limits set by the NCAA. Mr. Epstein thanked the authors for the opportunity to respond, but by press time, the authors had received no response from either him or Coach Schnellenberger.

CHAPTER 5

1. Dan O'Kane, "Probe Doomed Schnellenberger," *Tulsa World*, December 22, 1995.

2. Armen Keteyian, *Big Red Confidential: Inside Nebraska Football* (Chicago: Contemporary Books, 1984), p. 37.

3. Ibid.

4. James Barnett, "Sports Injuries: Achilles Tendon Injuries," ESPN.Com Web site, September 23, 2000. Online. Available at: <URL>http://espn.go.com/trainingroom/s/1999/0915/59775.html</>. Accessed May 14, 2002.

5. For the AP story about John Blake's pending departure, see CNNSI.Com, posted October 26, 1998.

6. Ibid.

7. Ibid.

8. Ibid.

9. Ibid.

10. For comments by President Boren, Joe Dickinson, and Jason Freeman, see the AP story at CNNSI.Com, November 22, 1998.

11. For John Blake's farewell comments, see the AP story at CNNSI.Com, November 23, 1998.

CHAPTER 7

1. Pete McEntegart, "The 2000 Regular Season," *Sports Illustrated* special commemorative issue (*Perfect!*), December 13, 2000, p. 21.

2. Ibid.

3. George Schroeder, "Works Steals Show as OU Rips UTEP, *Daily Oklahoman*, September 3, 2000.

4. See the special *Daily Oklahoman* publication, *Oh You Sooners!* (Birmingham, AL: Epic Sports Books, 2000).

5. Berry Tramel, "Return of the Sooners," in the special *Daily Oklahoman* publication, Oh You Sooners! (Birmingham, AL: Epic Sports Books, 2000), p. 56.

6. Nebraska Coach Frank Solich made his comments to the *Daily Oklahoman* following the October 28, 2000, game with OU.

7. The Sooners and their win over Nebraska was the cover story of *Sports Illustrated* on November 6, 2000. It would be the first of two times that season they grabbed the cover of the magazine's regular edition. The second time came in the issue immediately following the Sooners' January 3, 2001, Orange Bowl victory over Florida State. The Sooners were also on the cover of the special commemorative *Sports Illustrated* edition about their perfect regular season on December 13, 2000.

8. George Schroeder, "Big Plays Give Sooners Win," *Daily Oklahoman*, November 12, 2000.

9. Texas Tech Coach Mike Leach's comments on the Sooners were made to the *Daily Oklahoman* following the Sooners' win over Tech on November 18, 2000.

10. Jenni Carlson, "Stoops' 22 Tops A&M's 12th Man," *Daily Oklahoman*, November 26, 2000.

11. See George Schroeder, "Orange Bowl Next Stop for the No. 1 Sooners," *Daily Oklahoman*, December 3, 2000.

12. Ibid.

13. Matt Franklin, "Champs Again," in the special edition of the *Oklahoma Daily*, January 4, 2001.

14. Ibid.

INDEX